The Mélusine of Lusignan

in History, Legend and Romance

edited (with translations) by

Gareth Knight

SKYLIGHT
PRESS

© Gareth Knight, 2013

First published in Great Britain in 2013 by Skylight Press,
210 Brooklyn Road, Cheltenham, Glos GL51 8EA

Designed and typeset by Rebsie Fairholm
Photos by Gareth Knight
Publisher: Daniel Staniforth

www.skylightpress.co.uk

Printed and bound in Great Britain by Lightning Source, Milton Keynes.
Typeset in Adobe Caslon Pro. Titles set in Bucanera Antiqued, a font by
Manuel Corradine.

British Library Cataloguing in Publication Data.
A catalogue record for this book is available from the British Library.

ISBN 978-1-908011-67-1

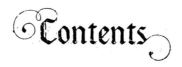

Contents

Introduction

CONSIDERABLE interest in faery tradition has grown up in recent years and not least in the story of Mélusine of Lusignan, the subject of a prose romance by Jean d'Arras at the end of the 14th century, swiftly followed by one in verse by Couldrette. Both versions have been translated from the French by Dr. Matthew W. Morris in two magnificent bi-lingual editions published by the Edwin Mellon Press, although as is often the case with academic publications for a limited audience, their price may be somewhat beyond the pocket of the average reader.

I have in the past done my best to make amends with my own short monograph *Melusine of Lusignan and the Cult of the Faery Woman* (R.J. Stewart Books, 2010) and also by translating an evocative novel by André Lebey, *The Romance of the Faery Melusine* (Skylight Press, 2011). But I think the lady deserves better. Hence this book, which provides a collection of material from various sources to give an all round picture of the remarkable faery, her town, her church, her immediate family, and the great Lusignan dynasty she founded.

In Part 1 I have provided my translation of a short account of her story as told by the Abbé Vergnaud, a former parish priest of Lusignan, who quotes largely from a mid-19th century version of Couldrette. He wrote for the general enquirer and above all for his parishioners, and his pastoral comments have a certain charm although perhaps not completely in tune with some modern secular sentiments.

Part 2 contains a gloss on the complete romance, again from the version by Couldrette, the first known translation into English, at the beginning of the 16th century. The rhymed Middle English is however not likely to be much more comprehensible to the modern reader than if left in the original French. The prose redaction, provided as a marginal crib by the famous Victorian scholar Walter Skeat, is perhaps more terse than my own, but is the version I have provided. At least you can track through the whole story in full detail from here.

Part 3 is my translation of a scholarly analysis by the distinguished French scholar Louis Stouff. It is probably the definitive academic work on Mélusine. Published by the University of Dijon some ninety years ago, it covers all aspects of the romance, including the identity of the original author, Jean d'Arras, who commissioned him and why, along with the cultural, geographical and historical background to the work.

In Part 4 I have collected together and translated some interesting odds and ends about the Castle, Town and Church at Lusignan. The first from a 19th century history of the House of Lusignan by the Canoine Pascal, and the rest from the local church bookstall and tourist bureau when I last visited there.

Part 5 is a result of my own work researching the history of the Lusignan family during the 12th century, when they had a remarkable record in the crusades, two of them becoming kings of Cyprus and Jerusalem. My main interest being to examine the possibility of a familiar spirit guiding a family in its destiny

Part 6 is a somewhat speculative investigation into those rulers of the Crusader Kingdom of Jerusalem who had traditions of having faeries in the family! That is to say, in addition to the Lusignans, those descending from a countess of Lorraine, who married the Knight of the Swan (later known as Lohengrin), and others from an early Count of Anjou who married a water sprite. In the midst are the puzzling activities of Philip Count of Flanders, who provided Chrétien de Troyes with the blueprint for his *Conte del Graal*, and lost his life on the 3rd Crusade.

Lusignan: Legend of the Faery Mélusine

• Abbé Vergnaud •

*I have provided here my translation of a short account of the romance as told by the **Abbé Vergnaud**, a former parish priest of Lusignan, who quotes largely from a mid-19th century version of Couldrette. He wrote for the general enquirer and above all for his parishioners, and his pastoral comments have a certain charm although perhaps not completely in tune with some modern secular sentiments. It serves as a good introduction to the more challenging complete version of the romance that follows in Part 2.*

ΧΙΧΙΧΙΙΧΙΧΙΙΓΙΧΙΙΧΙΙ

Introduction

We think it will be interesting to all Mélusins, sons of Mélusine, to publish a résumé of the marvellous legend about the existence of their venerable ancestor. We are helped in this by a recent edition of the romance of Couldrette, published towards the middle of the last century.[1] This book, written in Old French, reproduced the first edition, published in 1401, of which several manuscripts are conserved in the national archives.

One of these volumes has the title: "Mélusine, according to the true

---

1   *Mellusine, poème relative a cette fée poitevine,* Francisque Michel, (Robin & L. Favre, Niort, 1854)

chronicles, furnished for Jean, Duke of Berry, written in French verse." This work of Couldrette seems only to be putting into verse a more famous work, published a little before, in 1387, by Jean d'Arras at the orders of Duke Jean de Berry, then ruler of Poitou, and consequently of the Barony of Lusignan which he had recaptured from the English.

Our famous legend is one of those fabulous stories much enjoyed in the Middle Ages, a complete fabrication to glorify the famous family of the lords of Lusignan. We sense here the work of those joyful troubadours, singers and travellers, who, to find themselves accommodated and well looked after, went around to entertain ladies in the dark feudal castles, by telling them flattering stories, lengthened as desired. The story of our Mélusine is the application to the Lusignan family of a very old legend, lost in the night of time.

One might also see in this serpent woman a distant memory of original sin, where Eve, the first woman, was tempted by the Devil, dissembling in the form of a serpent, and led by him into evil.

The great Greek historian, Herodotus, 500 years before Jesus Christ, tells a story of the same type, found among the Scythians, very close to where tradition places the cradle of humanity. In different forms, the legend appears again in Germany, Luxembourg, Poland, and with us, in the Dauphiné. Monsieur Canon Jarlit, former curé at Lusignan, and Monsieur Léo Desaivre, have written some interesting articles on the subject.

Through her eldest son, Geoffroy la Grand'Dent, a very famous historical character who lived in 1225, our legend especially concerns Eustache Chabot, a woman of great beauty and nobility, married to Geoffroy I, son of Hugues VIII of Lusignan, a prisoner at the battle of Harenc in 1165.

These accounts by Jean d'Arras and Couldrette are quite dense works of about 200 pages. They are difficult to read and sometimes boring because of their repetitions and ancient expressions. For greater clarity, we have divided this confused story into short chapters containing all the essentials of the legend.

The birth of Mélusine

Elinas, King of Albany, the father of Mélusine, had lost his wife and went hunting to forget his grief. Pressed by thirst, he approached a fountain in the deepest part of the forest. What a surprise! He heard a ravishing voice singing. Forgetting to drink, he looked around and saw a lady of marvellous beauty, called Pressine. He approached to greet and talk with her as a young page led a magnificent horse, richly harnessed, to the faery. Elinas helped her to mount and she rode off. Immediately regretting having let her leave him so quickly, the king followed in her tracks and rejoined her. As night was approaching, he invited her to return to his hunting lodge, which was quite near. She agreed.

In their long conversation he confessed his sorrow at the death of his first wife. Then, regarding Pressine, he added, "I would love, Madame, to console myself for the death of a princess who loved me tenderly, by finding someone like you who could dry my tears."

"Such a person would be very happy to do so," replied Pressine, "for the tenderness you have shown for the first would be a good augury for the second."

They parted for the night, and each had delightful dreams. Next morning very early Elinas invited the beautiful lady to accompany him to Scutari, capital of his kingdom. They met with a magnificent reception. All the people came into the streets to welcome them. They were particularly struck by Pressine's beauty, who was herself ravished by their enthusiasm. Finally that which should come to pass did so, the king proposed marriage to her. She gratefully accepted, but with one very firm condition, that under pain of eternal punishment, *he must promise never to try to see her at the birth of their children.* He swore to this with a solemn oath. The marriage was celebrated with great pomp; however, not realising the secret power of faeries to bend the will of men, some blamed the king for marrying an unknown woman.

While Elinas was at war on the frontier, the princess gave birth to three girl triplets – Mélusine, Mélior and Palatine. On hearing the news he returned to court, but forgetting his promise, rushed into the room where the queen was bathing her daughters.

"Traitor!" she cried, "you have betrayed your word, and you will regret it. I will be avenged by a descendant of my sister, queen of the Lost Island. Farewell, I can no longer stay!"

And she left, taking her children with her, while her unfortunate husband wept and lamented with great cries.

The sin of Mélusine

The unhappy Elinas was so afflicted by the departure of his dear Pressine that he could do no more than cry and sigh, to such an extent that they said he was bewitched. While Pressine, deeply saddened on being forced to leave her beloved husband, affectionately preserved his memory. Each morning she took her daughters to the summit of a high mountain from which they could see Albany, and told them tearfully: "My children, see that beautiful country, it is where you were born. Your father is its king and you also could reign there if he had not betrayed his word."

At the age of fifteen the children had grown and were resentful of the fault committed by their unhappy father that had destroyed their good fortune. Their afflicted mother had told them all about it. (It has always been difficult for women to keep secrets!) Led by Mélusine, the resentful children resolved to be avenged.

All three returned to Albany, kidnapped the poor old man, and without more ado, carried him off and shut him up with his treasure in a high mountain. In their naivety, they thought they had done well, and went back to tell their mother about their easy victory.

"Wicked children!" she cried, "What have you done? I loved your father. It was not up to you to punish him. Now you will be punished yourselves. *You, Mélusine, who led your sisters, will on every Saturday be a serpent from the navel downwards. If you should meet someone who is willing to marry you and to promise never to see you on that day, you may live and die like a normal woman, if not you will suffer your punishment until the end of the world!*"

Driven off by their own mother, Mélusine, Mélior and Palatine left sadly for their cruel fate.

Mélusine's husband, Raymondin

After the terrible cursing by her mother, Mélusine left. Where did she go and how did she travel? Nobody knows. The story does not say, only that she made her way through great forests. At the same time, a nephew of the Duke of Brittany, who had accidentally killed his uncle, tried to hide his crime near Poitiers, in a place covered with woods, which was therefore called Forez. Was this the same forest as

Mélusine's? We do not know. The description of the tale lacks a little precision, given that throughout all France in those days there were great woods. In any case Mélusine's retreat and the place of the murder must have been near each other, for we shall see how our powerful faery met Raymondin, third son of the Breton lord.

Aimery, Count of Poitiers, had taken affectionately to the young Raymondin, noted for his charm and his qualities. He thus asked the Count of Forez, his sister's husband, to entrust this fine child with him. He had him taught all kinds of sciences, and in the way of sport, frequently took him on great hunts where the young man was not slow to distinguish himself.

One day it was said that an enormous boar had been seen in the forest of Coulombiers. The count quickly saddled his horses and gathered his hounds. Raymondin accompanied him and many great lords as well. They found the animal in its lair, where to receive its fine visitors it had planted itself proudly and waited. It was of such a great size that the astonished dogs and the frightened men dare not approach it.

Strength always inspires respect, so they gave up the hunt. "What?" cried the old Count of Poitiers, "will it be said you were all scared of the son of a sow?" At that, Raymondin jumped to the ground, seized his sword and threw himself alone at the monster. Wounded in the shoulder, the animal leaped up and threw itself in turn at the intrepid young man, knocked him over … but Raymondin leaped up, threw himself at the boar again, which was now seized with fright and ran off like a rabbit. Bravo! This young man was not afraid. May we find more like him today!

Excited rather than exhausted by this hard combat, our hero set off in pursuit of the beast, followed by the calls of his concerned uncle. But night overtook them deep in the forest and they had to stop. His uncle caught up with him.

Aimery, greatly skilled in astrology, observed the stars while Raymondin made a fire. "Leave all that, uncle," he said, "it is not right for so great a prince to spend his time on such uncertain things."

"Alas," replied the old man, "if only you knew what I can see. By the conjunction of those two planets up there, I read that if, just now, a subject were to kill his sovereign, he would become the greatest of lords."

"That is crazy! How could heaven reward such a crime with so much good?"

"Ah, my son, God does all for His glory, and His providence is impenetrable. It could happen by accident. The prince might be a great sinner who needed to be punished, for example like Judith and Holoferne."

At that moment they heard a movement in the bushes. Surprised, they looked and saw the terrible boar of the morning, only a few yards away and charging them at great speed, maddened by its wound and the light of the fire.

"Climb a tree, uncle!" cried Raymondin.

"It would not please God if I abandoned you," replied the courageous old man, seizing his spear. ... Raymondin, sword in hand, tried to make a barrier with his body and placed himself to the fore.

The boar turned and threw itself at Aimery. The count met it firmly with the point of his weapon where it impaled itself to the bone. The young man leaped to the rescue and with a violent blow of his sword tried to transfix the beast. But what misfortune! The blade glanced off the bristles on its back and struck the prince full in the chest. Blinded by fury, Raymondin did not realise this, he recovered his weapon, raised it again and with another blow pierced the beast right through.

Triumphantly he turned to his uncle, thinking he had fallen through exhaustion. Oh terror! He found the old man was dead. Overcome with love and remorse, he was tempted to fall on his guilty blade. He covered the frozen corpse of his greatly loved uncle with tears and kisses. Then he fled though the forest, wherever his horse might take him. For hours he galloped without aim or reason, until suddenly his horse stopped at the foot of a high rock from which a clear fountain flowed. Raymondin looked and was surprised to see beside it three fine ladies of ravishing beauty dancing in the moonlight.

The meeting of Mélusine and Raymondin

Preoccupied with the memory of his involuntary crime he at first took no notice of the beautiful ladies at the fountain of "Soif Jolie". (This fountain was not the Fon-de-Cé, but the fountain that still runs at the far end of the promenades, facing the house of the late Monsieur Pin.) Astonished by his indifference, Mélusine, "the most pleasant, the most graceful and the prettiest" said to her companions:

I never saw in my life
Either by night or day
A nobleman pass straight
Before ladies without greeting them;
I shall go and speak to him.

For in those times men owed politeness to ladies, who were offended if they did not receive it, which caused Mélusine to say:

By Heaven, young knight, you do not show yourself very friendly
When you pass before the three of us
Without a word and pass on.
That shows little gentility.

Poor Raymondin! Although insult was added to his sorrow, it was not enough to wake him from his nightmare. Our Mélusine, little impressed by his rank, it must be said, approached closer, seized the reins of his horse and cried to this apparent deaf mute:

Whoever taught you,
To refuse to say a word
To maidens or to ladies when you see them,
Brought you to base ignobility!

This time our unfortunate recovered his senses. Astonished, he did not know if he were dead or alive.

But when he saw the figure
Of the lady who held him
Was of such beauty
He almost forgot his troubles.

Thus the ravishing vision surprised but did not frighten him. On the contrary she produced a most happy effect in him. He found his voice:

......Fair lady
Graced with such beauty
To which none can be compared
Forgive me for the love of God,
My heart is heavy with such grief.

This eulogy to her beauty flattered Mélusine. Without any bitterness for the past misunderstanding she revealed her marvellous wisdom and promised Raymondin the most wonderful future if he would obey her.

Raymondin, I am most sorry to hear your troubles
The beautiful lady then said.
Now listen, my handsome youth,
According to the will of God
And of his glorious Mother
Everything that your lord told you
Will come to pass at my command
If you do just what I say.

Raymondin, surprised to hear himself addressed by name, promised all, but wanted to be sure just who this marvellous lady was. In full response to this and to show he could have confidence in her, she made her profession of faith:

I affirm that I believe
In the holy Catholic faith,
And know and believe each article
Of the holy Catholic faith.
That God was born to save us
Of the Virgin without blemish
And that for us He endured death,
And on the third day He arose,
And afterward, ascended into Heaven
Where He is a true man and true God,
And sits at the right hand of the Father.
Now listen Raymond, my dear brother,
I believe all of this most fervently,
Without doubt in any way.

Thus our Mélusine was a Catholic. It gave her honour and glory and nothing better can be found to prove it.

Mélusine's secret

By her proud profession of the Catholic faith, Mélusine won over Raymondin:

My dear lady, I will do
In good faith and straight away
Whatever you command.

She profited from his good disposition to say now what she had meditated upon for a long time concerning the cruel curse cast upon her by her mother Pressine.

"Raymondin" she said, "That was well said.
Now listen to me carefully,
You must swear to me, before God and his image
That you will take me in marriage
But that never in your life –
Whatever anyone might say –
Will you seek to see me on a Saturday
Or even enquire about
My whereabouts that day –
Neither where I go nor what I do –
And I will swear to you
That I will not be in any dishonourable place."

Usually a proposal of marriage is made by a young man. Here it was the opposite. Our Mélusine did not beat about the bush. She wanted to marry and she said so. Why not? Nor was she much concerned about the funeral of the poor Count of Poitiers that Raymondin had killed by misadventure when trying to save him from the boar. She advised him simply to plead ignorance.

Say that you lost him in the woods
And that you waited a long time for him.

And with a certain audacity, avowing this, she suggested that he ask a reward from the Count's successor, of the land all around the fountain. And for that she taught him a cunning stratagem.

Ask your new lord for a gift of land
Right here at this very spot
Where we are standing now;
As much as the hide of a stag will enclose
Of the woods and country around.

Then:

You will see a man carrying
A stag's hide, very large and wide.
Buy it. This I charge you to do,
However much it costs.
Then have the hide cut up
To form a very thin strip.

Founding Lusignan

Mélusine had promised Raymondin that if he would marry her, and never see her on a Saturday, he would be successful in all his ventures, and become the greatest lord in the land.

Her complaisant fiancé promised all, so once more it came about that "what the woman wants, so does the man." Hence the need to beware of perverse women, for following the sacred word of the Bible: "Better to be alone in the desert than to live with an evil woman."

Thus Raymondin obeyed Mélusine and soon discovered the benefit of her marvellous powers.

Exiled a thousand leagues from beautiful Albany where her father Elinas reigned, Mélusine brought with her only her beauty. Raymondin, the son of a Breton lord, after hiding his crime in the forest of Coulombiers, did not possess more. Both were of noble origin, which was good, but not sufficient to set up a home. Mélusine set out to do that.

We have seen that she suggested a ruse for Raymondin to obtain a domain from the new Count of Poitiers. He obeyed her and went to find the prince.

"Dear lord", said he, "Please give me
Near the Fountain of Soif

Of wood or rock or vale
Be it meadow or arable land
As much as can be enclosed
Within the hide of a stag."

"I will give it you willingly," said the good Count. He was asking for very little. A stag's hide could not cover anything very large. Without delay, Raymondin went to buy one, for a hundred sols. Hides were not expensive in those days. Then, following Mélusine's advice, who had said: "Have it cut in a strip, the finest that you can", he had had it cut into a thread so fine that no one knew for what it could be used.

Then they planted stakes and unwound the thread that extended so far that having made a tour of the rock, there remained still more. They extended it into the meadows all about for a length of two leagues. What a hide! And there where they planted the last stake there rose a wonderful spring, so abundant it soon formed a brook, the modern Fon-de-Cé.

Thus was determined the location of the castle and town of Lusignan.

Building the church

On passing over the viaduct everyone is impressed by the beauty of the countryside around our town, proudly seated on the promontory that dominates the valley of the Vonne and the surrounding hills. At the summit they see rising above all our beautiful church, whose imposing mass rises above the roofs, as proud witness to the age and elevation of our faith. The traveller who can stop always starts his excursion with a visit to our ancient sanctuary, sole remaining witness of the past glories of Lusignan. Whatever is said and done our religion is the one thing that crosses the centuries without changing, and its works are always what is the most durable. History says that the construction of the beautiful edifice was begun in 1024 by Hugues IV of Lusignan, who recruited all the masons round about for its construction. The work was long and difficult and not completed until 1110. The legend of Mélusine simplified things a lot!

His eyes full of tears but his heart full of joy, Raymondin was present at his uncle's funeral, the Count of Poitiers. He then solicited and obtained from his son the fountain of Soy and the surrounding land, as we have told in the last chapter. He came to tell the happy success of his endeavours to Mélusine, his marvellous fiancée. She welcomed it and promised him even greater favours. But great was his surprise when, on approaching, he saw upon the rock a magnificent chapel, completely built, where two days before there had been nothing there. He could not conceal his astonishment.

"Nothing is done in this world without the permission of God," replied Mélusine. "This chapel is the work of my hands, but all you see from now on will be an expression of His will. The chapel will be dedicated to the Virgin, his dear Mother, and it is upon this pious foundation that I wanted to begin the happy establishment of our house."

𝔐élusine's wedding

• By the marvellous enchantment of Mélusine our beautiful church sprang from the Earth in a day. Alone in the midst of the woods that covered the hillside she raised a beautiful steeple of new stone to the sky. Excellent Catholic, as we have seen elsewhere, Mélusine thus began the celebration of her marriage and announced to the docile Raymondin that the hour he desired had arrived. It was she who decided it. Happy bride! She feared no failure in her projects. She enjoined her future spouse, her servant, to go straight away and invite the Count of Poitiers with all the knights and ladies of his court. But where could the wedding be in this wild wood? It seemed that everyone would have to sleep outdoors, eat grass and drink water, which would be very meagre for such a feast! No matter, a faery is not troubled by anything so trivial.

Raymondin, who desired nothing so much as to possess his gracious spouse (at last!) obeyed her and went off to Poitiers. The young Count greatly welcomed his invitation but could not resist asking where it might be. "God works miracles when He pleases," replied the pious Raymondin, "and we must accept all His works with great submission." (It was very easy in this case!) "At least tell me from what great House your Lady comes."

*"I have not asked about her lineage
If she is the daughter of a marquis or a duke.*

I never saw one so fair as she,
She pleases me and I want her."

Decidedly our man was very confident. He is set to marry a girl he does not know. Simply because "she pleases me and I want her." How many reason any further on such occasions? In any case, it was his affair! At Poitiers they thus prepared to go to the wedding with great pomp. No one thought any more of old uncle Aimery, whose funeral they had celebrated with such tears only a few days before. A ray of sunshine is enough to dry the dew; how many tears disappear as quickly?

Barons, knights, princes and princesses in their greatest finery escorted the Count of Poitiers. What a surprise for all when they saw a vast church on the hill, and below, in the meadows, a concourse of magnificent pavilions, expressly designed to serve as lodgings, kitchens, stables, with a multitude of servants for their service. It was an entire town, bustling and magnificent, formed in the valley at the foot of the chapel, in the shadow of the great woods. Each guest was lodged in a special richly decorated tent.

After having rested, the lords went to meet Mélusine. She received them graciously in a sumptuous apartment, draped in cloth of gold and decorated with precious stones. They were dazzled by it all. At the same time the ladies did not fail to remark the beauty of her dress and all her splendid finery.

The tables were laid in a special pavilion, with vessels of gold and silver, ivory and crystal throughout, and above their heads, central lights ornamented with jewels, and chandeliers of gold and silver. Such riches amazed them, but without spoiling their appetite. This first meal lasted into the night. It was still only the eve of the wedding, so what would happen tomorrow?

Very early the Count of Poitiers and his escort went to meet the bride to lead her to the chapel. Raymondin took the Count's high chaplain to celebrate the marriage. The pious prelate was somewhat afraid of so many marvels and feared they might be the work of the Devil. Before anything else he employed the strongest exorcisms of the Church and then blessed the chapel, dedicating it to the Mother of God. During the ceremony, some did not dare to enter the holy place, fearing that the Devil would reclaim his own and carry the whole building off on his shoulders. First, what an idea, to believe that the Devil, the enemy of God, had built a chapel! We admit though that it would have been a famous victory to carry off, alone, such a burden. Some, again, feared that Mélusine herself would be taken off at the consecration. But happily, the Devil did not appear and all passed off for the best, very solemnly.

Great was the beating of drums
The sound of music, high and low,
All the woods resounding.

Then, the ceremony over, as in our day, all went off to the banqueting hall. For a long time eating has been one of the first pleasures of man. They ate, and above all, they drank.

Wines from Aunis and from La Rochelle
Which make the head grow hot.
Wine from Thouars and wine from Beaune,
Which had no taint of yellow hue
Wine from Saint-Jean of Angely
All was greatly esteemed, etc., etc.

Thus for a fortnight, with feasts ceaselessly renewed, tournaments, balls, hunts, etc. The folly of weddings is thus not new. It is rather this that is work of the Devil – who gains more from this than building chapels.

Building the castle

Tents are all very well to celebrate a wedding but not as a place to live. Where to find a lasting living space on this steep rock or in the wild woods? One can only see lairs in the ground and nests in the trees. Mélusine did all to resolve this difficulty. Raymondin was sent to accompany the Count of Poitiers as far as Coulombiers. On his return she told him she wanted to build a formidable fortress at the highest point on the rock which would serve to found their House.

How to gather the materials and find the workmen? Here they are! From the first day they arrived from all directions, with provisions in abundance. So much so that in only a few days the castle was complete, to the great surprise of all who lived round about. Would not anyone be!

The castle completed, Mélusine soon had all the precious furniture from the pavilions installed. Again they had a great feast to celebrate their entry into this palace of "great towers, high walls, strong forts, keep and bastions." We will see later that this was the impregnable fortress of which only the site remains today.

This suddenly transformed place did not yet have a name. Modestly, Mélusine gave it her own, simply transformed. It was be called Lusineem, (Mélusine), which became in time Lusignen and then Lusignan. This name suited very well because it recalled the remarkable benefactor of the place and in the Scottish language meant "well established and miraculous."

One could say that there was nothing so well established as this famous castle, even though it no longer remains today. Men are very wrong to be so proud of their little works. They are all, like themselves, limited and fragile. Time ruins all, and more often than not, one defeat leads to another. So it was with our fortress, demolished by royal decree in 1575. And if such a matchless construction no longer remains with one stone standing on another, what will become of the fragile houses we live in today, and above all of the poor body in which our soul lodges?

The sons of Mélusine

The marriage celebrated and the castle built, Mélusine and Raymondin were happy. God put the cap on their happiness by giving them children, equal in number to the ten years of their marriage. All were strong and well made, but with some extraordinary birthmarks.[2]

Thus the first, Guy, had a face wider than it was long, and very big ears, which could not have looked too well. The second, Odon, had one ear very small and the other very large. The third, Urian, had one eye lower than the other. The fourth, Antoine, bore on his cheek the imprint of a lion's paw. The fifth, Regnault, had only one eye but it could see for twenty leagues all round. The sixth, Geoffroy, had a tooth that jutted out of his mouth, larger than a thumb, hence his nickname of Geoffroy la Grand'Dent (Great-Tooth). They said, all the same, that he was a very beautiful child (but how can that be?). The seventh, Froimond,

---

2 The Abbé's listing of the sons is not in quite the same order as in the original romance. And he neglects to name the three-eyed Horrible. And not all of them "made good marriages" – although most did.

had a little furry patch at the end of his nose. They say nothing of the eighth, Raymond, or of the ninth, Thierry. The name of the last is unknown, we only know that he had three eyes, one in the middle of his forehead, which must have looked very curious.

All the young men were distinguished for their courage and made good marriages.

The vocation of Guy and Urian, young men of 20 and 23, is known from the tale of two knights, come to the Holy Land. They tell how, over there, the Christian princes were persecuted by the Saracens, particularly by the Sultan of Damascus, who laid siege to Famagousta to force the King of Cyprus to give him his daughter, "the most beautiful girl in the world and sole heiress to the crown." Moved by this violence and perhaps a little desirous of seeing the beautiful captive, the young men armed a fleet and sailed to the help of the King of Cyprus. They arrived in time to repulse the enemy and to save the old king, who in reward, gave his daughter's hand to Guy, while Urian became King of Armenia.[3] Thus the expedition was a very happy one for all.

Odon married at Guérat the princess Constance, heiress of the Count of La Marche, despite promises made before to the dauphin of Vienne.

Antoine and Regnault went to the aid of the Duchess of Luxembourg, Cristine, a girl 18 years old, whose capital the King of Metz was besieging to try to force her to marry him. To announce his arrival Antoine sent the young princess a courtly letter which is a model of the genre. "Madam, it was never seen until now that one lays siege to a heart to take it. It is a place that is gained by tenderness and not by force. The strongest battalions are a feeble means to win it. Their constraint negates possession. Happy, Madam, he whom you would find worthy to be yours. Antoine de Lusignan."

Such an approach, allied to bravery, could not fail to be successful. The King of Metz was defeated and driven off. Antoine married Cristine and became Duke of Luxembourg, and Regnault was elected King of Bohemia.

Let us recall the high character of these brave knights whose delicate love was upheld by heroism and piety.

---

3   That is to say, Lesser Armenia, north of Cyprus on the coast of Asia Minor.

Geoffroy Great-Tooth

There really was, in about the year 1200, a lord of Lusignan, grandson of Hugues VIII, called Geoffroy, and nicknamed la Grand'Dent, no doubt because he had a tooth somewhat long. This Geoffroy burnt down the abbey of Maillezais, in Vendée, to avenge the religious about whom he had complained.[4] On this fact legend embroidered the following tale.

The sixth son of Mélusine, Geoffroy, was noted for his violence. When very young he had killed several wet nurses by gripping their nipples too fiercely.[5] He was hardly seven years old when he killed two of his squires. When grown up, he delighted in barbarous duels in which he defeated his adversaries pitilessly. What a monster!

On the other hand, his brother Froimond was pleasant, docile, and virtuous. Despite the difference between their characters the two brothers loved each other very much but evidently did not follow the same career. While Geoffroy fought with his neighbours, Froimond became a monk at the abbey of Maillezais. Hearing of this, Geoffroy was enraged. He did not like monks, whom he thought both lazy and useless. Might this have been because he had suffered their just reproaches? Poor monks, for a long time they have been slandered. It is a way people avenge themselves for the penitence they practise and the virtues they preach, which annoys the depraved. He did all he could to turn his brother away from this awful plan. He acted so even before the most holy Abbot, whom he threatened. All the same the gentle Froimond left the helmet and armour of a knight in favour of the dark robe of a monk.

Mad with rage, Geoffroy brought with him some of his most trusted knights and set fire to the four corners of the monastery. In an instant the whole building was in flames and the monks, surprised at their prayers, could not escape. All were burned alive, including the beloved Froimond.

Sad example of vengeance. Sometimes rage brings about things hardly less insane. Raymondin was then at the castle of Mervent (Vendée) and Mélusine at Niort, where she was building the towers of the keep. At the news they hurried to join each other. The good Raymondin was extremely upset at this violence by his son; Mélusine

---

4   The historical Geoffroy persecuted the abbey, but did not actually burn it down.
5   This in fact was Horrible, not Geoffroy.

indulgent almost to weakness. Like many mothers she at first blamed the crime, then excused it, suggesting that Geoffroy's act was perhaps God's punishment against these too sensual monks. Oh, perversion of the human heart that claims its crimes are virtues, and blames on God what is only the malice of men!

How often things are still like that!

Raymondin's betrayal

The world is always ready to regard anything it does not understand as evil. Thus public malignity did not fail to misinterpret the fact that Mélusine had reserved each Saturday to hide the curse that she suffered on that day, as we have seen. The Count of Forez, jealous of Raymondin's extraordinary prosperity, resolved to avenge himself by revealing to him the horrible suspicions of many. He thus came to visit him one Saturday and asked to see Mélusine. He was told that, according to custom, she was not available. Then, taking Raymondin apart, he asked him maliciously, "Do you really know why your wife is never seen on this day? It is because she dallies with another. Do the right thing, look and you will see."

The good Raymondin had never suspected such a thing.

Distraught, he wanted straight away to see if it were true. Forgetting the solemn promise he had made, he went through the dark corridors of the castle to the hidden chamber where Mélusine retired each Saturday to suffer her distressing punishment. With the point of his sword he made a hole in the door and peeped through... Oh surprise! He saw his wife bathing in a great marble pool, to the waist she was as normal, but the rest of her body was a great serpent's tail, striking the water furiously, making it splash up to the ceiling, for she sensed she was observed, which caused her intolerable pain. Seized with fright and remorse Raymondin fled weeping.

Hate and discord are engendered by jealousy! This is behind most unworthy spitefulness. Nothing seems repugnant to one who seeks to avenge something that is envied. Revenge even takes pleasure in losing it, as happened here!

Mélusine's farewell

Past midnight Mélusine rejoined her guilty spouse. At daybreak she withdrew to a lonely room where she rolled on the floor with such cries of desolation that her ladies in waiting were terrified. It was because she knew the sad moment was at hand when she would have to go and resume her unhappy existence of before.

"Why?" she cried, "must I leave this place I have loved so much?" At first she cursed Raymondin, but then she embraced him once more and made her farewells in the most touching terms:

"Pray for me now, my gentle love,
For I shall remember you.
And all the days of your life
You will have aid and comfort from me..."
Then she leapt on the window sill,
Her feet together, and looked outside
Over the flowering orchard.
But she did not want to depart
Before taking leave of everyone
At which all wept out of pity.
Then she said: "Farewell Raymondin,
Whom I have always loved with a pure heart.
I shall never see you again.
Farewell my sweetheart, farewell my love,
Farewell my gracious friend
Farewell my precious joy.
Farewell good, Farewell my sweet one,
Farewell my husband
Farewell the friend of my heart
May God help and console you."

Raymondin's farewell

Poor Raymondin was no less afflicted than his unhappy wife. In his turn he lamented broken heartedly.

"Alas, what can I do?
Never again have a joyful heart.

Farewell lady of the fine fair hair
Farewell I say, sweet mistress
Farewell my wealth and my joy
Farewell my wife, my beloved spouse
Farewell my gracious lady
Farewell my glory and my joy
Farewell the beauty I have ever loved."

He beat his breast, crying tearfully:

"I have deceived my own true self
Have dug the pit into which I fell.
Now am I unhappy indeed
Now am I am the most tortured
Of whoever felt grief in their lives."

At the moment of her departure they saw Mélusine change shape. Her skin became covered in scales, her arms took the form of wings and her body lengthened into a serpent's tail more than eight feet long. Then she threw herself into the air. Three times before the terrified gaze of her family she made a tour of the fortress, making piercing and appalling cries. Then, she gradually disappeared over the horizon, drawn to her unhappy destiny, which must last until the end of the world.

That is the story of Mélusine, the faery of Lusignan, victim of the curse of her mother Pressine, for having mistreated her father Elinas, King of Albany, and then victim of the betrayal of her husband Raymondin.

The legend tells that on leaving the places she knew Mélusine cursed them. Since when unhappy folk attribute to this curse all that has broken the harmony of the later days of Lusignan.

The Tale of Mélusine

• Walter Skeat •

Here follows a gloss on the complete romance, again from the version by Couldrette, and is taken from the first known translation of the romance into English, at the beginning of the 16ᵗʰ century. The rhymed Middle English is however not likely to be much more comprehensible to the modern reader than if it were left in the original French. To take one stanza as an example:

> *For of ſo fair A ſwete creature*
> *Approcheth non ille, but ay al goodneſſe,*
> *Fro you may noght come but good auenture,*
> *I beleue noght that terrene boody ſothleſſe*
> *Of luſty beute may have ſuch richeſſe,*
> *So moche of ſwetneſſe, for moche of connying*
> *As in your gentil body is berying.*

which we would perhaps rather see rendered as: "Since no ill, but only goodness can come from so sweet a creature, nothing may come from you but good adventure. I cannot believe that an earthly body of lusty beauty could have such richness, so much sweetness, and be so thoughtfully put together!"

The prose redaction provided as a marginal crib by the Victorian scholar **Walter Skeat** *is perhaps more terse than my own, but is the version I have provided. At least you can track through the whole story in full detail from here.*

Like the good Abbé Vergnaud in Part 1, as an aid to the reader I have also divided the work up into subtitled sections as an aid to following the changes of scenario between Raimond and Mélusine on the one hand and the activities of their sons on the other.

Translator's Prologue (starting with the 2nd folio, the 1st folio being missing)

I would gladly, had I the cunning, forge something here to please you; but my soul is barren, and lacks skill. I am not acquainted by birth with the perfection of French, and may mistake one word for another; for rhymed French is difficult to display in English. As nigh as the metre will permit, I will follow my text, in due order; albeit I cannot paint my book as most books are painted.

In ancient times, men invoked deities; thus Velerius Maximus invoked Tiberius, and explained in the proem of his notable book, how the gods were created. Midas, the rich king of Phrygia, besought Bacchus that all he touched might become gold; which the god granted, even with respect to his meat and drink. Some gods owed their origin to poets' fancy; others were malign spirits, giving oracular responses. To call to my aid gods such as these, who are of no value, and were only imagined by poets, would be against our Christian faith. I deny them, and call rather upon Almighty God, to guide my pen as may please the Trinity, that I may translate the French into English. I will do my best, asking pardon for defects, and will now begin to translate the prologue prefixed to the French text.

ⅠⅠⅠⅠⅠⅠⅠⅠⅠⅠⅠⅠⅠⅠⅠⅠ

The philosopher was full wise, who declared in the first page of his "Metaphysics" that the human intellect naturally endeavours to *learn* and *know* things; for all a man's endeavour is to know that which he before knew not, especially in matters that concern him closely. Old things, when rehearsed, are good and fair; as when we speak of Arthur, and of his noble knights and worthy people; or of Lancelot, Percival, or Gawain. Whoever inquires of their marvellous adventures by sea and land will find it an excellent thing to know them. Science is a most worthy thing: and every one should study history, more especially if he be of high degree. Such a man ought to know his pedigree, and cause it to be duly recorded. Thus it was that a great lord of Poitiers and Parthenay commanded me to labour after this manner; and men should always obey great lords.

His bidding was, that I should make a copy of a book of his; which book he gave me, so that men might know who made the castle and town of Lusignan. I promised accordingly to do so. He then told me that this castle was built by a fairy, from whom he was himself lineally descended, and whose name was Mélusine; whose arms, indeed, he still bore; and he bade me rewrite the whole history of it in rhyme, because then people would the sooner recite or hear it.

I replied, I would gladly undertake it, but desired to receive no praise, for that it had been put into rhyme once before already. Still I would try and put it into another shape, which would please him better; and would consult two books that had been found in the tower of Mabregon,[6] originally written in Latin, but which had been afterwards translated into French; the contents of which books had been subsequently confirmed by Anthony, earl of Salz and Barry,[7] in another book, which, they say, was compiled from three others; and I do not doubt it, as I have seen the substance of it. Thereupon, I took my leave, and will now endeavour to write the history of the castle of Lusignan, with God's assistance, without whom one can write nothing, whether in French or in Hebrew. Of Him cometh goodness, wit, and sense. I pray Him, with my whole heart, to aid me; and that his sweet mother will conduct my work to the end. Thus endeth the prologue.

The Romans of Parthenay

The boar hunt

In ancient times, after the time of Octavianus, lived in Poitiers a certain earl named Amery, well-skilled in astrology and other sciences, as well as in canon and civil law. Never was there a better astrologer, or one more learned in the science, excepting only Him, who gave stars their names. He was also great and rich, and very fond of hunting. He had a fair son and a fair daughter, whose names were Bertram and Blanche. Neither Rochelle nor Macon were yet founded; and there was, throughout Poitiers, abundance of trees, and especially a large forest called that of Coulombiers.

Now there was an earl in the forest, who had a huge great number of children, not very rich, but who lived sagely, and spent warily, and was beloved by all. He was cousin to Amery; who, hearing of his great number of children, thought to assist him. He made therefore a great

6 The famous Maubergeon Tower at Poitiers.
7 That is to say, Salisbury.

feast at Poitiers, and invited the earl of the forest and his feudal barons. They came gladly upon the day appointed; and the earl of the forest brought with him three of his sons.

The earl of Poitiers was glad to see them, and regarded the three sons closely, especially the youngest, and said, "My fair sweet cousin. I beg you to give me one of these children; he shall be well taught, and I will make him a rich man."

"My lord," said the earl, "do your pleasure as regards these three: I will not refuse you. Take whichever of them you like best."

"Then give me the youngest," quoth the earl of Poitiers; "and declare to me his name."

"My lord, his name is Raymond."

The third day after the feast, the earl of the forest departed. The three brethren mutually commended each other to God, and Raymond remained behind. Raymond served earl Amery faithfully, and was much beloved in return. But after this did Raymond slay him; cast stone-dead to the earth, to death must Amery incline, through the false gluttonous cruelty of fortune.

The earl Amery went often to hunt in the aforesaid forest, during five or six years; and he went to hunt one day with a large number of knights, with Raymond on a high courser beside him, bearing his sword. The chase began; the beast ran before the hounds, closely followed by them and by the earl, who never returned again home. Raymond followed him as closely as he could; and, as the moon rose, the boar was still slaying the dogs. The earl's people knew not where he was, having ridden away after the boar.

"Come hither, Raymond!" said the earl, "and tell me what you advise."

"Let us find some retreat," said Raymond, "where we may tarry awhile."

"So shall it be," said the earl, "for the moon and stars shine clearly."

Traversing athwart the wood, they found at last an easy path, which the earl thought would lead them to Poitiers. Raymond thought the same, and advised that they should ride on fast, and inquire their way of some one whom they might meet.

The earl, as he rode, began to behold the stars, being (as was told) a skilful astrologer. Thereupon he perceived, by a certain star, that a strange adventure was at hand, and wrung his hands, and cried out, "O Lord God! Why doth fortune make a man prosper by ill-doing? For

I perceive that prosperity will thus happen. Raymond! Behold those stars, and know that if, in this hour, a man were to slay his sovereign lord, he would become himself a great lord, and more puissant than any in the country, and be more beloved than his neighbours."

Raymond answered not, but alighted, and found a little fire kindled in a heap of wood. The earl also alighted to warm himself.

Then heard they a noise. The wood brake, and they beheld a huge boar, in marvellous wrath, and whetting his tusks. Raymond begs his lord to climb wightly into a tree, who boldly refuses to flee from a pig of a foul sow. The earl advances to pierce the boar, when his sword glances; for, as the boar came fast towards him, his sword would not pierce the boar's hide; so that, missing his stroke, he falls from his horse upon the boar's tusks. Raymond runs up to aid him, but his sword also turns aside. A second stroke, however, is successful, and he cleaves open the boar with his steel sword. He finds his lord dead, and his soul commended to God. For he was as valiant a man as any on this side of Rome.

Raymond exclaims against Fortune, saying that a man who trusts her is a greater fool than any mute beast; that she is no godfather nor godmother; that she makes a king of a small man; that she has perdurably condemned him, unless Christ will have pity on him. Hereupon he swoons, and does not come to himself again for an hour.

Again regarding his lord, he invokes death, for that his lord is slain by his misdeed. He would commit suicide but that is against providence. God would not that any should despair; yet it had been better for him to have been born dead. Leaping again into his saddle, he leaves the body, and rides away from the spot, leaving the bridle-reins loose. Thus rode he along lamentably, till he approached suddenly the fountain of Thirsty Gladness, said to be of fairy origin. The horse chooses his path at will, and thus brings him to the fountain. The rider is so distressed that he cannot look about him.

Raymond meets Mélusine

Beside the fountain were three ladies of high degree. He sees none of them; but the most good-looking and "jolliest" exclaims, "I never, all the days of life, saw a gentleman pass ladies without salutation."

She then seizes his rein, and tells him that to go by without a word is not the deed of a gentle heart. Raymond suddenly perceives her, and thinks it is all the effect of his imagination, and knows not whether he is awake or asleep. He returns her no answer.

She asks him why he will not speak, and wishes to know who taught him such behaviour; for that it is a dishonour to him that he thus forces his heart to be unnatural.

Raymond is many times astonished, and, perceiving the human body of this fair lady, his heaviness of heart troubles him yet more. Knowing not whether he is alive or dead, he alights hastily, and says, "Most gracious image, pardon me, sweet thing! My heart is heavy with misfortune; I remembered not what I ought to do. I perceived you not; pray, pardon me."

She addresses him by name: at which he is much astonished; but, reassured by her beauty, he trusts that he will soon recover himself; since only goodness can come from so sweet a creature. He cannot believe that an earthly body can have so much sweetness.

She then recounts to him all he has been doing, explaining that she is well acquainted with all that has happened. She then declares that all the good fortune which his lord predicted for him will be brought about if he will attend to what she says. Yet more assured, he gladly promises to do all her commandments. Yet he wishes to know how she knows his name and circumstances.

"Raymond," she said, "I counsel you not to be astonished. You shall be yet more successful than your dead lord predicted. I am, after God, your best friend; but you must trust to me entirely. Do not doubtingly think that I am not on God's side; for I hold every article of the Catholic faith; viz, that God was born of a spotless virgin, endured death, rose the third day, and ascended into heaven, and is at the right hand of the Father. Trust me entirely, and you shall attain to great honour."

Raymond, much amended of his care and sorrow, promises to do what she commands without gainsaying.

"Swear then to me," she said, "at this time, that you will marry me, and that you will never inquire as to where I go on a Saturday; and I promise, in return, to go to no ill place, but always to labour that day on your behalf."

Raymond swears, but was, in the sequel, foresworn, to his great misfortune. She tells him that if he breaks the compact, he will lose her; and that himself and his heirs will lose their lands. Raymond swears a second time; but alas, this miserable man spake not the truth!

"Raymond," said she, "you must go to Poitiers, and give out that you lost your lord in the wood while hunting, and that you sought for him a long while unsuccessfully. At last he will be found, and brought to Poitiers, when his wife and children will lament in woeful wise. You must counsel them concerning his burial, and wear black as others do; and when at last the time shall come for his heir to receive the earldom, demand of him a gift ere ye go, as payment for your services to the late earl; beg him to give you so much land as may be enclosed by a hart's skin, and cause deeds of the gift to be duly executed; and, when you have the deeds ready, depart; and go on till you see a man carrying a large hart's skin, which buy at his own price. Next cut the skins into small thongs, very narrow, and tie them up into a bundle, and make men deliver you up the land which you can enclose with them around this fair fountain. But if the thongs will enclose more than such a circuit, draw them down along the valley. When assured at Poitiers of all your possessions, return hither, and you shall find me here."

Raymond promised to obey at whatever cost; and, greatly rejoiced, returns to Poitiers, where he gives out that he had lost his lord, and knew not what had become of him. Thus Raymond excused himself, and accused not the soul of the homicide (himself); and none ever thought of accusing him.

Many now return from hunting, both high and low. There were none but were sorely annoyed at not knowing the truth, as to where the earl was that night abiding. At last his sorrowing wife and children saw two men approach, bearing the body, which they had found in the woods, with the dead boar lying beside him.

All bewailed his death. His Countess wrung her hands, and tore her hair. Raymond joins in the general mourning. Everyone bewailed his death, throughout the town; and buried him with all solemnity, distributing alms, and burning great store of wax. The cursed boar was cast into a fire and burnt up. Raymond hears many remarking his excessive grief, which was indeed real.

After the burial, the barons busily went to do homage to the new earl; and Raymond approached to prefer his request. He asks for as much land, lying near the fountain, as a hart's skin would enclose; and requires no other payment. The young earl accedes, if it will content his barons. The barons think Raymond well deserves it, and the earl commands the deeds of gift to be duly executed and sealed. It was sealed both by the earl and the barons, and the day fixed for its becoming of force.

In the morning, a courteous man brings him the skin, and the earl bids men to deliver him up his possession. As soon as they come to the fountain, Raymond produced the skin, to their great wonder, when they see how narrowly it is cut. Two men then approach, who make the thongs up into a bundle, and bind one end to a stake; and enclose the whole rock with a part of the skin. They again bind an end to a stake, and carry it down the valley. A stream suddenly wells up, which had never been seen before. All wondered when they saw the immense tract enclosed. Raymond receives all the neighbouring country, and news of it is carried to the earl, that the circuit enclosed is two miles about. He also hears of the two men, and of the new stream. The earl is aware of the marvels connected with the fountain, and rejoices at Raymond's luck. Raymond thanks the earl, declaring that he hardly knows what is coming to him.

Raymond rides away to the fountain, and finds there the lady, who welcomes him. They enter a chapel, and find there knights, ladies, clerks, prelates, and squires, all nobly apparelled. He cannot refrain from asking her about them. She replies that he need not marvel, for they are all his. They humbly do him reverence. Raymond muses within himself, and hopes the end may be as good as the beginning. The lady tells him he must take her in marriage. Raymond declares himself ready at once; but she tells him that all is not yet ready. He must bring a number of witnesses to the marriage with him, and come again on the Monday.

The marriage of Raymond and Mélusine

Raymond returns to Poitiers, and comes into the presence of the earl. He salutes the earl, and says he feels that he ought not to hide anything from him, but to declare to him all things. He therefore confesses that he is to be married on Monday to a great lady, and beseeches him to come to the wedding. He also hopes the earl's mother will be present. The earl is willing to come, but wishes to know the lady's name, and warns him against marrying one of whom he knows nothing. Raymond asks him not to inquire further, for that it will suffice to see her. The earl marvels greatly at such conduct; but Raymond says she is like a king's daughter; and that a fairer lady was never seen. The earl promises to come, with his mother and all his barons.

On the Monday, the earl and his mother, with many attendants, set out, wondering where they will be lodged and entertained, though they need not have wondered, as all was ready. Riding on, they at last approach the rock. There they found pavilions pitched beside a valley, where flowed the new stream. They heard sweet songs of birds; and saw a wild wood with many people; also several kitchens, with much smoke. Next they saw coming about 60 knights, well horsed and armed, who asked for the earl, whom many pointed out to them. The knights ride up to the earl, and salute him humbly. The earl returns their salute, yielding to every man the respect due to him, according to the place whence each came. The knights say to him that the fair Mélusine thanks him heartily, and that due lodging was provided for his retinue.

The coursers were well lodged, and provided with rack and manger. The Countess was received in a golden chamber, where many ladies welcomed her. All marvelled at so rich a sight. The chapel was well apparelled, high and low, and stuffed with rich jewels. The earl and countess demand the bride. Mélusine enters the chapel, freshly attired, and looking not human, but angelic. The earl and countess duly receive her. Minstrelsy is heard, both of high and bass instruments. Never was so noble a feast. The woods rang merrily, and all agreed that human eye had never seen the like of it.

The mass done, the earl led forth the bride, and a prince conducted her to the chief hall. The earl sat beside the bride, and the countess next to him. The courses were brought in by squires, including great plenty of dainties. There was wine of Anjou, and of Rochelle; of Touraine and Beaune; also Clarre Romain and Ypocras. Wine, moreover, of Tours and Dijon, of Auxerre and Saint Jougon; of St Jean d'Angely, and others. Every one had abundance, as much as he asked for, whether of wine or meat.

After this began the jousting, where Raymond jousted mightily. Next they went to vespers, and then to supper. After supper came the dancing. At last the bride retired into a costly pavilion, portrayed with painted birds. Then laid they the bed, and made it ready. A bishop gave his benediction, *"in nomine dei."* The earl and his mother also retired to their tents. All went to their allotted chambers, but some spent the whole night in singing and dancing.

Mélusine addresses Raymond, reminding him of his good fortune, and of his oath lately made to her. She tells him how she is aware how the earl inquired concerning her lineage; she proceeds to tell him that his good fortune will last as long as he holds to his covenant: but that if he breaks it, he will suffer huge harmful pains, and be disinherited of all. He again swears to be faithful, giving her his hand in pledge of his sincerity. Mélusine cautions him yet once more, declaring that she will never fail in her part of the covenant. Their eldest son was named Uriens, whose famous deeds will be told of hereafter.

The feast concluded, Mélusine gives very rich presents to all, who wonder at her wealth and liberality. She opens an ivory casket, and draws from it a clasp garnished with precious stones, which she gives to the countess. The earl and his people depart, Mélusine taking her leave of them. Leaping up to their saddles, they ride away. Raymond accompanies them to the edge of the forest. At leave-taking, the earl would fain have asked Raymond who Mélusine is, but durst not. Raymond, seated on a courser, takes his leave of the earl, and returns to Mélusine, who receives him joyously.

At the end of eight days, all the trees in the wood were uprooted by labourers of an unknown nation. They made hideously deep ditches, and were diligent, finding themselves well paid. They made deep foundations, building a castle upon the live rock according to Mélusine's plan. There were two strong towers with a huge dungeon; insomuch that all the country marvelled. Mélusine baptized the castle after the latter part of her own name, calling it Lusignan. The meaning of Mélusine is, "no marvels are lacking," she being a woman *a-per-se*. When this castle was built, high walls and all, people wondered how it had been finished so soon.

The sons of Raymond and Mélusine

Mélusine bare a son, named Uriens, whose visage was very short and broad, and who had one eye red, the other grey; also a huge mouth and great nostrils; yet well made as regarded his legs, arms, and feet. After that she made a city, with high walls and towers, well provided with loop-holes. The ditches were of great breadth, and the gates large and long. Between the town and the fort was made a strong tower, called "Trompe"; for it was garrisoned with Saracen trumpeters.

The second year Mélusine bare a son named Oede, who had a face as shining fire, resplendent with redness. That year she made the castle and town named Mel, and some others, including Parthenay. She also made the castle of Parthenay with good lime and stone, towers, turrets, pinnacles, and wall.

Her third son was named Guy, who was of great beauty, saving that he had one eye a little lower than the other. The same year was founded Rochelle; and soon after she built a great bridge, for which she received great praise.

Her fourth son was Anthony, who had on his jaw a mark like a hurt made by a lion. All these things are true.

And when it pleased our Sovereign Lord, this lady had the fifth son, whose baptismal name was Raynold. He had but one eye, but his sight was clearer than that of a person who has two eyes, for all their plenty.

The next was Geoffrey with the great tooth, which issued from his mouth, great and square. It was he who slew the black monks of Maillezais abbey; which event caused his father to be angry with Mélusine, and was the cause of all his misfortunes.

The seventh son was Fromont, who had a blemish on his nose. It was rough as a wolf's skin, so that his nose was a strange sight.

The eighth son was Horrible; he had three eyes, and was of a very wicked disposition.

The adventures of Uriens and Guy in Cyprus and Armenia

We now return to Uriens, who was grown big, mighty, strong, and light; and was fond of war. He took ship at Rochelle in a barge, with Guy and much people; intending to go and acquire lands. They took with them much silver and gold, and went to sea. Soon came they to Cyprus. The king of Cyprus was then being besieged in Famagousta, which the Sultan had nearly taken. Uriens lands, and, calling his men together, displays his banner. Both Saracens and citizens see them coming. Soon they arrayed against the Sultan. The Sultan meditated flight; which the king perceived, and was at once armed by Ermynee his daughter, and mounted his horse. Trumps and clarions sound. A hard conflict ensues, and many Christians and Saracens are slain. The king is shot with a poisoned dart, and the surgeons fear that they cannot heal him. The Cyprians thereupon retreat, closely followed by the Saracens. Great clamour in the city. Ermynee bemoans her father, and tears her goldish hair, perceiving that he had arrived at death's door.

Meanwhile Uriens and Guy had displayed their banners and attacked the Saracens. The men of Poitou, owing to their good victual and plentiful wine, were stronger than their foes. Uriens and Guy are dreaded by the Saracens; and, at last, the Sultan presses forward at full speed, smiting down a Poitevin with his furbished sword, so that both wooden hilt and iron blade pierced his body. Uriens grips his sword in both hands, and cleaves the Sultan to the teeth, at which the Paynims are distressed, so that Paynims, Turks, and Syrians flee fast to their ships, hard pressed by Uriens.

Uriens determines to rest awhile in the tents of the conquered foes; but before long come a troop of Cyprians, who beseech him to visit the king, as the king cannot visit him, being so sorely wounded. He answers that he will come gladly. Uriens and his brother dight themselves freshly in noble array, and set off. Many a Cyprian, seeing Uriens' face, said that he would conquer all lands by his appearance, for that none would dare to stand against him.

On arriving, they ascend the palace steps, and find the king's nose and mouth swollen, and the king replete with venom. Uriens salutes him humbly, who returns his salutation, and great thanks also. The king further demands Uriens' name, who answers that he is Uriens of Lusignan. The king is glad to see him, but tells him that he feels he is incurably wounded, being stuffed full of venom; wherefore he besought him to please to condescend to accept his gift, which Uriens does.

The king thanks him for his assent, and sends for his barons and his daughter Ermynee. He tells his barons he expects not to live longer, and that he wills to leave his kingdom to his daughter, she being the true heir. The barons thereupon do homage to his daughter; and the king adds, that his subjects cannot be defended by a simple woman against such cruel neighbours as the Saracens; that Uriens is puissant and mighty, and has discomfited the Sultan, as they all saw for themselves; and that he therefore asks them to beseech Uriens to grant him all his request; which the barons at once accede to. The king is glad thereof, and tells Uriens that he wishes to ask nothing of him, but to confer on him something of his own, namely, his kingdom and his daughter. The barons are of the same mind.

Uriens thanks the king, and says he would not take the gift if he saw in the king any respite from death. The marriage is performed; and, as the priest was raising the host at the mass, the king yielded up his soul. Their great joy is thus turned into woe. The bride's heart is "locked up" with heaviness. The king is buried royally; and there were therefore no plays or tournaments at the wedding, which was, nevertheless, honestly done. No blame attached to those who were busy about that matter;

for many nobles, knights, ladies, damsels, and squires, honoured the marriage feast, and danced thereat. Thus joyed the people on account of the good rule of those two, viz. of the bride and Uriens.

Their firstborn was named Greffon, who conquered many countries, including Colchis, where was an isle in which the golden fleece was gained by Jason, with the aid of Medea. It would take up too much time to tell all that story. I should then be going aside from the matter in hand. Greffon was quick and ready in war, and conquered many places. At last he came to Tripoli, which he assailed and took. Thus he acquired land, honour, and praise.

Uriens is crowned king of Cyprus. His wife's uncle is king of Armenia. This king of Armenia dies, to the great sorrow of his subjects, many of whom died of grief. His daughter was his only heir; wherefore the Armenians send to Cyprus, requesting Uriens to send them his brother Guy, who should have the damsel, Flourie, to wife. The messengers come to Cyprus. Uriens takes counsel with his barons, and they agree that Guy should be sent at once. Guy agrees to the proposal, takes ship, and arrives at Armenia. Disembarking, he soon meets some lords, who receive him gladly; and marries Flourie, and is king of the country; so that two brothers are once more kings of Armenia and Cyprus. The two kings aided those who were descended from them, and the people of Rhodes too. They had many children, and ruled well, trampling under foot those who annoyed them. I will now turn to Raymond and Mélusine.

When these heard of the success of their two sons, they said the 7 Psalms to the King of Glory, because each of them was called a king. Moreover Mélusine, for her soul's health, built a minster to Our Lady, and founded also many other churches. Next she married her son Oede to the earl's fair daughter.

The adventures of Raynold and Anthony in Luxembourg and Bohemia (Brehayne)

Raynold and Anthony set out from Lusignan. They soon came to Luxembourg, which was then being besieged by the king of Alsace, who had nearly taken the town. They asked the cause of the war, and find that it was for the duke's daughter, an orphan, whom the king of Alsace wished to marry forcibly. The brethren defy the king by a herald, whereof the king is glad, as he is fierce and cruel. From afar the brethren perceived the host, armed with knives and halberds. The Lusignans attack the foes boldly, so that the earth trembles at their encounter. The men of Alsace assail the Poitevins, who hammer at them in return. The Lusignans bid their foes abide the taste of their swords. The two brothers, each by himself, behave in so warlike a manner, that their men are the victors. In Anthony's hands the king "seemed nothing". Anthony receives his sword in token of submission. The Poitevins pursue the men of Alsace till they are all taken and slain.

Anthony and Raynold take their ease in their tents, and send six knights, with the captive king, to the fair maiden. The fair creature inquires who are the two noble lords who have thus come to her assistance. An aged knight tells her they are the "sons of Lusignan"; and that their names are Anthony and Raynold. She is very grateful for their services, and expresses a wish to counsel with them ere they go.

She tells her council she shall invite the brethren and their host into the town. The messengers find the brethren in the king's pavilion, where they had found much treasure and had distributed it among the soldiers. When the messengers from Luxembourg had arrived at the pavilion, they delivered their message to the two brethren, who received them humbly. The messengers receive their answer, and at once 500 knights set out to lodge within the town. The brethren leave their 'marshals' with the main army, and send their foragers on before them. Every place and crossway are filled with people. The nobles of the city convey the brethren to the castle.

The maiden arrives thither; her name is Christian. She is accompanied by many ladies, both married and maiden, who receive the brethren nobly. A feast is provided; they wash their hands, and sit in order; the king of Alsace highest, Anthony next, and Raymond and three barons next. A more 'honest' feast was never seen. After dinner they washed their hands; and grace being said, the king said to the two brethren, "I am your prisoner, and ask to be put to ransom." Anthony replies that they have been as courteous as he has been villainous, and that they now put his body in the lady's power, because he had annoyed her wickedly. But the fair lady at once, without any prompting, returns thanks to the two lords, and says in return that she leaves the king at their disposal, as she could not 'guerdon' them if she had heaps of gold. The king's life and death are therefore in their power.

They answer, "If so, he shall have a quit-claim of us, provided he kneel down here debonairly, and cry you mercy, and swear he will never do you annoyance, disturbance, or damage". The fair maiden sweetly consents. The king is full glad, and cries mercy at once. She accordingly consents to his freedom. The king next cries with a loud voice, that he should be glad to have such chivalrous men for neighbours, and he bids Anthony look on the pleasant Christian, this duchess, with fair rents, and consider that it is reasonable that he should be repaid for his kindness. He thinks that Christian might be given to Anthony, as he is so worthy a bachelor. The barons and lords of Luxembourg applaud him; and the marriage feast is held, and lasted for eight days.

The feast ended, every man is about to take leave, when a messenger arrives from the king of Brehayne, with a letter to the king of Alsace. Having read the letter, he begins to sigh and weep tenderly; and, being asked the reason says he has had hard news; that the Saracens have besieged a town in Brehayne, and that he pities the king his brother.

Anthony listens to his appeal, and bids him not to be discomforted; for that he will send his brother's aid; and that Raynold should go and slay the Saracens. The king hereupon pledges his life that Raynold shall marry his niece; and, after his brother's death, succeed as king of Brehayne; as his brother had no heir but this one daughter. Anthony bids the king go and assemble his army, and return again to Luxembourg within a fortnight; for there should Raynold meet him. He himself (Anthony) would appear there.

The king hastily departs, and soon returns to Luxembourg with all his people. He next sends a messenger to Anthony to say that he was all ready to go to Brehayne, and that his hosts were beneath the town in the fields. Duke Anthony says he is welcome; and tells Raynold that the king of Alsace is come, and he must find his army good lodging, and make them take their ease. Raymond obeys, and all is well provided. The king departs to Luxembourg to see the duke. A great feast is made, the particulars of which I need not rehearse.

Anthony makes all ready to go to the aid of the king of Brehayne. The number of the two hosts was, in all, 30,000. The duke had as many men as the king. Ere the duke departs, the fair Christian calls him, and beseeches him to wear the coat of arms of Luxembourg, and no other blazon. Anthony says he will not exactly do that, but proposes always to bear on his shield a lion, because that, when he was born into the world, he had on his jaw a mark like that made by a lion's claw; with this exception, he will do her pleasure. She thanks him, and says that, excepting the azure, he can bear both his own arms and hers, which were the old arms of Luxembourg. He accordingly assorts them, and takes his journey to Brehayne at full speed.

Bavaria is passed, and Almaigne; and Brehayne is soon reached. I must now speak of the evil Paynims. The king of Cracow was mighty and strong, and with his men made great war against the Brehaignons. One day the king of Brehayne, whose name was Fedris, armed himself for a sally, and bade the gates be thrown open; but the Saracens beat these free knights, overwhelming them with the number of their men. These men drove back the Brehaignons, and chased them into the town. But the duke of Luxembourg came up, while the king of Brehayne was fighting for his life, like a wild boar at bay, smiting and casting down his foes. But by a javelin this noble knight was smitten through the body and his soul was commended to God. The Brehaignons wept sore, and fled; but the Saracens pursued, reaching soon the flying troop, and slaying them fiercely.

The few who escaped came spurring to the town, and told the sad news; to the great grief of the slain king's fair daughter, Eglentine. The people ran fast back into the city for fear of the Saracens, when they saw their king dead. But the Saracens are overjoyed; and, making a great fire with bushes and wood, burnt the king's body before the gate. Those within cry and grind their teeth.

But soon came Anthony, Raynold, and the king of Alsace towards Brehayne, their basnets glittering like the bright sun. The Brehaignons had great need of succour, and were sore astonished, and defended themselves feebly. Eglentine would rather have been dead. She laments her father, and knows not what she, an orphan, will now do; for now she sees the destruction of all her realm. The country would be robbed, pillaged, and worse, by evil Saracens. She would have to deny our Lord, and believe in Saracen customs.

Meanwhile they assailed the town furiously, and thought to take it. But soon came a messenger secretly into the town unto the Brehaignons, and bade them make another rally, and look out and see the king of Alsace approaching, with Anthony and Raynold; and not to talk of death, for the Poitevins were at hand, so well nourished with meat and wine as to astonish the Paynims. When the barons of Brehayne heard this, they praise God. Every man takes good heart, and the Saracens begin to quake, wondering what news they had received. But soon comes a messenger to them, saying, "Lords, leave off your skirmishing and retreat, for behold the Christians fast approaching, by whom all the fields are covered over."

The Paynims thereupon retreat, returning to their tents. Preparations are made for battle on both sides, and the Saracens are struck with terror. Then were many shields pierced and broken; there might be seen a mighty battle. Anthony smites Paynim, whom neither helm nor harness guarded from the blow; for the sword clove his head to the teeth. Then went the Lusignans, crying out "Lords and barons, fight well!" The king of Cracow, in great wrath, comes to the rescue, and smites down a Christian to the grass; then he cries aloud, "O ye Christians, you shall all die!" But Raynold strained his brand of steel fiercely, and smote the king with such force that he rent his head to the teeth. To death fell the king; and the Saracens stayed no longer, but turned their horses round and fled openly. In the swift pursuit, all the Saracens are cut to pieces like flesh cut upon the stalls. Anthony rent and tare all he could attain to, and at last all the Paynims were slain.

The king of Alsace bids that all the dead bodies should be laid upon a heap, and burnt; and thus was it done. It was in revenge for the way in which the king of Cracow had burnt his brother's body. The Poitevins lodge well in the enemy's tents. The king of Alsace and 100 knights ride off to the town. Eglantine comes to meet them, and salutes her uncle. He assures his niece that her father's death is well avenged; and she should now comfort herself, since her enemies were fully repaid all their wages, and had failed utterly in their design; so that no shame or reproach now attached to her. She replies that her heart is sorrowful when she thinks upon her father's death. "Was not he my brother?" replies her uncle; "we will perform the funeral rites tomorrow and pray for his soul." A thousand pounds of wax were made for the occasion.

Then began the Brehaignons to behold these two worthy brethren; and none were ever weary of looking at them. Many were astonished at the mark upon Anthony's face, as it was very plain to the sight and large. They also thought Raynold was well shapen for conquering kingdoms, and commended him for everything but his lack of one eye.

The king of Brehayne being honourably buried, the king of Alsace holds a council, and advises them to choose a new king. They reply that it is his business entirely, as he is the next heir, if Eglentine should die. It is therefore for him to choose whom she shall marry. The king inquires whom they wish her to marry. They reply that they leave it entirely to him. He replies that in that case they shall have for a lord one who is a worthy and famous knight. He reminds them that two brothers, both noble knights, and one of them a duke, have saved their city. He therefore calls Raynold, and tells him he will perform the promise he made him, that he would make him a king. Raynold is to have his niece and all the kingdom. Sir Anthony thanks the king heartily, and promises that Raynold shall defend the country well. The barons praise Our Lord and Our Lady when they perceive how strong and large a man Raynold is.

Raynold and Eglentine, being finely arrayed, are married; and the marriage feast lasted 15 days. Never were fairer presents given than were then given by Eglentine. There were 100 men there from the country, besides the 'townish' people. Raynold gained great honour in the tournaments, and is greeted with loud acclaim on all sides.

Duke Anthony takes his leave, and returns home to Luxembourg. Raynold acquires great honour as king of Brehayne, and carries on a great war in Friesland, and also conquers Denmark. We leave him now, and return to Duke Anthony.

Anthony and the king of Alsace arrive at Luxembourg, where they part; and the king of Alsace returns home. Anthony remains awhile with his wife, whom he loved heartily. They had two children, one named Bertran, and the other Lochier; who freed the passes of Ardennes, built Givet, and made the bridge of Mezieres over the Meuse. Anthony conquers the Earl of Friburg, and passes through Austria, where he conquers many a region. Bertran, Anthony's eldest son, marries the king of Alsace's daughter, and succeeds to his kingdom. Thus he and his brother put underfoot all that troubled and annoyed them. We shall speak of them no more.

Fromont seeks to become a monk

We return to Mélusine. Raymond reigned excellently, and all did him homage. Geoffrey with the great tooth became a full great man; and conquered and discomfited the giant Guedon, for fear of whom all men were taking refuge in Rochelle. When Geoffrey heard of his, he swore he would go against him and discomfit him. But his father Raymond was woeful and sorry, and in fear for Geoffrey's safety. Geoffrey arms, and departs with nine others.

I shall return now to Mélusine, who had yet two more sons, one called Fromont, the other Thierry. Fromont was a great clerk, and loved religion, so that he wished to become a monk in the abbey of Maillezais; and therefore ran to his father, and besought him to consent to his wearing the monk's habit. Raymond marvels greatly, and bids him regard Anthony and his other brethren, who are all noble knights. He ought not to wish for the order of monkhood, but of knighthood. But Fromont says he would never take on himself this order, and covets nothing so much as to remain in the abbey for ever, and spend all his life there. Raymond sees it is hard to refuse, and therefore sends a message about it to Mélusine, to the end that she should make Fromont a claustral monk in the abbey of Maillezais. Mélusine sends back an answer that she always submits to her lord's command, and will obey gladly.

The messenger, arriving next morning, finds Raymond ready dressed, and delivers Mélusine's message. Raymond tells Fromont that Mélusine has left the whole matter at his own disposal, and he will therefore permit him either to go to the abbey of Maillezais, or to "Merk" minster, or to "Broughdieu"; or, that if he wished to be a canon, of Poitiers and also of Tours in Touraine, and of Saint Martin's, and of Chartres also. Or he might go to Paris if he pleased. Afterwards he should have a bishopric, or, if he liked, two, whether of Paris, Beauvais, or Arras. But Fromont chooses to be simple a monk of Maillezais, and nothing else.

Raymond at last accedes, and Fromont promises to pray for him. He therefore takes the habit, and is richly clothed, and gladly welcomed by the whole convent. This was the source of the evils that afterwards befell the family. For Geoffrey, in his wrath, set the abbey on fire, and burnt there 100 monks on a certain Tuesday, the day of Mars the god of battle.

Meanwhile Mélusine was at Vouvant city, whither Raymond came to visit her. They see two messengers come, who bring letters from Anthony and Raynold. Raymond reads them, and laughs for joy, and calls Mélusine, who thanks him, and rejoices with him, and praises the King of kings, who had raised her sons to so high an honour. She rejoices to think that one of her sons is in an abbey, and prays God daily to be mindful of them. Four of her sons are yet at home; but they will want nothing, if God and our Lady Mary aid them. The glad news soon spread throughout every city and a fifteen days' feast is held in celebration of it.

Raymond betrays his trust

It befell on the Saturday, that Raymond lost Mélusine, as he had often done before on that day of the week. But that day, his brother, the Earl of Forest, arrived at Vouvant, the day being without wind and clear. Raymond received him brotherly; and many barons and ladies came to the feast which was then being held. Then said the Earl to Raymond, "Bid your wife appear." But Raymond says she shall appear the next day.

After the feast is over for that day, the Earl draws Raymond aside, and tells him that the people say he is bewitched, and that he is never so hardy as to ask his wife *where she goes to* on the Saturday; also that it is said she is unfaithful to him on that day. He therefore advises him to know the truth, because she ought to hide nothing from him.

Raymond blushes for anger, and sweats for sorrow. He seizes his sword, and hurries on till he sees before him a door of iron. Drawing his sword from the scabbard, he drove the point against the iron door till he at last pierced it. Looking through the hole thus made, he perceived Mélusine bathing, her upper part white as snow, and her fashion most fair, but beneath she had a serpent's tail! It was great and horrible, barred with blue and silver. Raymond, perceiving this, cried to God, though he could scarcely utter a word.

In order to stop the hole, he cut a little piece of cloth, and fastened it with wax. He returns to his brother, who, seeing him sad, asks him what he has discovered, and where he had found her. Raymond tells him he lies in his throat and in his teeth, and bids him depart; for that his lady is pure. He tells him that, unless he departs, he will slay him; and that he advises him to go at once. He curses the hour in which his brother came, and seems all witless. The Earl, sore amazed, departs home, cursing the hour in which he thus spoke out. He laments bitterly that he has made Raymond so wroth. Afterwards Geoffrey came, and slew the Earl, and gave away the country he thus gained to one of his brothers.

But to return to Raymond. He wept and wailed, and waxed pale, having no end of his grief. "Alas!" he cried, "there is no poorer man on earth than I am! Alas! Mélusine! I have lost you! Now shall I lose my joyous thoughts, and cast myself into some pit. Never shall I laugh again!" Concluding his lament, he undresses and goes to bed; but cannot sleep. He sighs, and cries, "Ha! Mélusine, if I lose thee, I shall go to some desert place. Ha! Mélusine! That I should thus lose you!" He tears the hair off his head, smites his breast, and wails. He turns from side to side on the bed.

Mélusine then returns, undresses, and lies beside him. She embraces him, and finds his neck cold, so he was all uncovered. Softly she whispers to him, "Are you feeling anguish? Tell me the truth, I pray. Am I not your love? Tell me all. Confess if you feel any ill, and I will cure you."

Hearing this, he rejoices, thinking she knows nothing. Yet she knew all, but would not speak of it, seeing his repentance.

Raymond says, "I have felt great heat; and now the fever has changed to a shivering." She embraces and kisses him, and he feels at ease. I must now leave them.

Geoffrey fights the giant Guedon

Geoffrey goes to Guerrand to seek the giant, and at last sees the rock whereon his castle is built. Geoffrey alights, arms himself, and again mounts, making fast to his saddle-bow a steel mace. He takes also his shield and his iron spear, and leaves his men, commending them to God on high. He bids them farewell, and departs alone, ascending the mount to reach the castle. He waits at the drawbridge, and in a shrill voice defies the giant. The giant, hearing him, rises and puts out his head, showing his visage and his chin. The giant thinks himself sorely disgraced that a single man should wish to fight him, and at once arms himself, taking a falchion of steel, three flails of iron, and three great sledgehammers. He lowers the drawbridge, and issues out. He is fifteen feet long; yet Geoffrey fears him not, but defies him boldly.

"Who art thou?" asks Guedon.

"I am Geoffrey with the long tooth."

"Wretch," says Guedon, "I will slay thee with one sole stroke."

"I pity you," says Guedon, "and advise you, as a friend, to depart."

But Geoffrey bids him rather pity his own life, which should soon end, as he cannot possibly escape.

Geoffrey advances to the encounter, and overthrows the giant. The giant, astonished, rises up, and tells him his stroke shall be repaid. Being wrath at having been thus struck down by a single blow, he seizes his steel falchion, and cuts the legs off Geoffrey's horse. The horse falls, Geoffrey leaps off, and at a blow nearly severs the giant's left arm. But Guedon, to end the fight, deals Geoffrey a blow on the helm with his flail, which almost fells him. Geoffrey runs and fetches his steel mace, and with it strikes the giant so that he stumbles and drops the flail. Guedon seizes a sledgehammer, and with it knocks Geoffrey's mace out of his hand, and then picks it up. Geoffrey draws his sword, and shears Guedon's arm completely off. Down fall all his weapons. The giant strikes at Geoffrey with his sword, but he slips aside, and with a marvellous stroke cuts his foe's thigh right in two. The giant falls. Geoffrey cleaves his head to the teeth, and, seizing his Saracen horn, blows it loudly.

Geoffrey's men come up, and find the giant slain. They marvel at his length and breadth. The lords compliment Geoffrey highly, and tell him he has done "an inly good deed". Geoffrey says he has but done his duty. They enter the castle, which is well built and fair. Huge joy is made both by small and great, because the giant was discomfited and stone dead. Geoffrey is made lord of that country.

A messenger tells the news to Raymond, who laughs; and Mélusine gives the messenger a rich gift. He next takes paper and wax to his secretary, and dictates a letter, which he seals and sends to Geoffrey in Guerrand, telling him how Fromont had become a monk in the abbey of Maillezais, where he would spend his life in prayer for his friends. Alas, this letter was written in an evil hour, for thereby did Raymond lose Mélusine!

I shall have to leave the life of Raymond and Mélusine and speak of Geoffrey, who was now in Guerrand country, where he was royally feasted for killing the giant. While he was there, came a messenger from Norbeland[8] to him, and having found him and presented his letters, he proceeds to tell of a giant who had come to Norbeland, savage, cruel, and dangerous, and had brought war on all the country. He begs Geoffrey to help them speedily, as the nobles of the land have great trust in his might. Urging him he adds that all the country will be given up to him, as he may see from the letters. The people trust wholly to him to destroy the giant.

On reading the letters, Geoffrey swears that he will go, but it is not for lands or possessions, but for the sake of helping the people, on whom he has pity, because he has great zeal for Christianity. Also he would win honour; therefore he prepares at once.

Geoffrey burns down the abbey of Maillezais

Meanwhile a messenger from his father brings him letters to tell him that his brother has become a monk, at which he is angry and sad. He

---

8   Northumberland

was pleased to have good news of his father and mother, but he lost his wits at the disgrace of Fromont being a monk, and he grew as red as vermilion. Fuming like a swine with rage, he made all afraid who came near him. Then in his passion he exclaims, "These vile monks have surely enchanted my brother to make him turn monk and have a shaven crown. But they shall suffer for it. The errand into Northumberland must be put off a while. I will go at once and burn up all these monks together."

He bids the messengers from Northumberland await his return, when he will go with them as promised. They promise to guard his house in his absence, and to wait till his return. He sends them away without further parley, and summoning his people, rides with all speed till he reaches Maillezais Abbey on a Tuesday.

He finds the monks in the chapter-house. They are delighted at his coming. But roughly and angrily he demands of the Lord Abbot why they have so foolishly made his brother leave chivalry and turn monk. He threatens them all with death, and grinding his teeth savagely, puts them into great dread.

They weep and sigh for fear, and the Lord Abbot declares it has all been done of Fromont's own free will. He may see Fromont, who coming to his brother, bears out the Abbot's account, and adds that he will be nothing but a monk. His father and mother, he says, had consented, and were glad that he should enter on this life, that they all might benefit by his prayers.

Geoffrey, almost mad with rage, replied to him sadly. Then departing, shut the doors, and savagely orders fuel to be collected, which he has piled about the Abbey, and then sets it all on fire. The Abbey, the Abbot, and a hundred monks, are consumed. Most of the building is destroyed, and not one soul escaped.

Geoffrey, on coming to himself, laments what he has done, the burning of the minster, and his brother unburied, and the Abbot. For there was no getting them back again. Leaving Maillezais, he rode hard, thinking much of his good religious brother; and then upbraids himself, that he is more worthy of damnation than any man, even than Judas Iscariot, and shall be shut out of God's sight. He prays for death.

In this frame he reaches Guerrand, and finds the messenger waiting for him. Geoffrey is pleased to see him, and goes at once, taking but ten retainers. He was feasted by the people before he went on board. With a fair wind he sets out at once on his voyage. The people bless them as they start, and with a fair wind and good ship they go on their way. I shall now leave Geoffrey and speak of Raymond.

Raymond curses Mélusine

He was living merrily at Vouvant with his wife, Mélusine. At dinner one day a great piece of ill news is brought them. Afar off they saw a messenger who humbly saluted them; but in doubt about how to give his message, he changes colour. Raymond bids him welcome. They inquire his news.

(Alas, I must utter strange news, for which I am sad, for the message is right naught, owing to which Raymond shall lose his wife's company).

Then he tells them that one of their children, Fromont, is dead, and Raymond asks if he is interred in our Lady's Abbey at Maillezais. But the messenger replies that Fromont had not been buried, but burnt by Geoffrey in the Abbey. The abbot and monks were all scorched and burnt to ashes; Geoffrey shut them in and burnt them, out of spite against Fromont. Raymond, at the news, bathes his heart in sorrow, but sternly commands the messenger to be sure he is not lying. He replies that he saw it with his two eyes.

Raymond, in great dolour, leaps upon horseback, and rides at once to Maillezais. There he hears men complaining, and sees the abbey reduced to a ruin. Much enraged, he swears that Geoffrey shall die in a cruel manner, if he can but get hold of him. Again he mounts his horse, having no wish to stay there, and rides fast homeward. He reaches the fort of Vouvant, and alights from his horse. He enters his chamber, and shuts the door.

Then he begins to lament and wail, saying, "Ah Fortune! Thy dealings are too manifest, thou art not secret enough. When I put Earl Amery to death by moonlight, thou wert the cause. Alas, he was a peerless man! And next, thou madest me marry this infamous serpent; and one of my ten children by her, a holy monk, is dead, and his brother slew him. Her children will do no good. I could not have believed it, had I not seen her in the bath. I saw through the hole in the door that she was a woman from her head to her middle, but beneath a serpent, with a tail striped with blue and gold. No man could have beheld her as I did, and not have fled for fear. God keep me from diabolic works!"

Mélusine unlocks the door, and brings with her into the chamber a company of squires and maidens. Raymond is much vexed at the sight of her, and begins to lament anew. The moment of their parting was now nigh at hand.

Mélusine says to him, "Be not vexed. Even though Geoffrey has thus sinned, and has destroyed the abbey, he may yet, perchance, make his peace with God by repentance, and suffer pain in the body; for God's mercy is at all times ready. For God willeth not the death of a sinner, but that he should live to repent and to do good."

But Raymond was spiteful and angry, and his reason awhile departed. Soon shall he say a word which he shall never retrieve. With fierce look, proudly wroth, he spake plainly his foolish thought, uttering aloud the fatal word. "Ha! SERPENT! Behold and see what Geoffrey thy son hath done! He hath scorched and burnt a hundred monks, of whom Fromont thy son was one. But they died not all *cold*, but every one was *hot* enough. Geoffrey, thy mad son, *burnt* them!"

Mélusine's farewell

Alas, the sorrow caused by that fatal word, which lost him Mélusine! When Mélusine heard that word, she swooned away, and lay in that swoon a whole half-hour, prostrate and astonied. The barons raised her up, and a knight moistened her face with cold water.

She revives, and exclaims, "Alas, Raymond! Ill for me that ever I saw thee! Woe is me that ever I saw thy beauty, thy array, thy virtuous conduct. Alas that ever I saw thy precious body, that ever I loved thee! Evil was the hour and season wherein I first saw thy treason and falseness! Thine unmeasurable language has condemned me to eternal pain. Never shall you see my face again. O false, perjured traitor, murmurer, liar, betrayer, and false knight. Thus hast thou caused us huge loss. Yet I could forgive your seeing me in the bath, because you told it to no one. Your revealing it has brought misfortune. Had you kept your covenant truly, I should have been a woman at all hours, and, at death, the King of glory would have borne away my soul, and I should have been buried with great honour. Alas, I must now suffer pain till doomsday! Thou too shalt suffer pain, thy great deeds shall decline, and thy land, at thy death, shall be divided. Some of your posterity shall lose both land and ground, and never return again home. Remember thy sons, for I shall be with thee no more!"

Then she draws three barons aside, speaking to all sensibly in an undertone. "Raymond, it behoves thee to beware of Horrible. If he live, war shall never cease, nor bread nor wine increase, for he shall lay waste all the country. He will destroy all I have made, and bring his brethren to poverty. Thy sorrow for Geoffrey's deed is needless; it was a punishment upon the monks for their misdeeds. It is for that reason they are scorched, exiled, and destroyed. They have harmed themselves with lechery. If your son be dead with them, pity him not. A hundred men perish for one sinner's sake. So here 100 died, beside the abbot. If Geoffrey have destroyed them, he may easily rebuild a fairer minster, and place in it more monks than before. There shall they pray for our lineage, and the place shall be fairer and better than before. But, ere I go, I tell you one thing more. In order that men may remember me, they shall see me in the air. I shall be seen whenever the castle is about to change its master; if not in the air, on the earth, or by this fountain. For, as the castle was baptized after my name, it may be considered as my goddaughter. Three days before the castle changed its lord, I shall appear. Raymond, when first we loved, we had all joy and solace; but now is our solace turned into vexation. Now is our good fortune turned to mischance, and our surety is in doubt. Our freedom is turned to service by perverse fortune, and all owing to the jangling of your blabbing tongue. Now must I go. God pardon you for being the cause of my suffering torment."

Such grief had Mélusine that none that heard her could withhold from weeping. Raymond was so grieved at her words that he could say no word himself. The two kiss each other sadly. They both swoon away, and the barons trow they are both dead and cold. Recovering from the swoon, they sighed and wrung their hands. All the whole rout who see them, weep. Raymond entreats Mélusine to pardon him, but she says that this cannot be.

She bids him especially to think of his son Raynold, for that he should be Earl of Forest. The Earl of Forest would soon die. He is also to provide for Thierry, who would afterwards rule the land from Parthenay to Rochelle. Also Thierry's lineage should be good knights, and long endure. She asks Raymond to pray for her, for that she would aid him in all his needs. He must bear his adversity well. She now must go.

She then leaps upon the window, but will not yet depart before she has bidden all farewell.

"Adieu, Sir Raymond, my heart, my sovereign joy, my gentle jewel! Adieu, my sweet nurse, my grace, and noblest debonair youngling!

Adieu, my sugar-sweet sovereign lord! To God I commend you, to keep your sweet life. Adieu Lusignan! And adieu, sweet sounds of instruments!"

Thus having said, she leapt out of the window, and so passed away. She was at once changed wholly into a serpent, striped with argent and azure. Three times she went round the castle, uplifting a loud cry at every turn. This that I write is truth; I lie not.

Raymond's lament

Raymond tears his hair and curses his hour of birth. "Adieu!" he cries, "my fair mistress, my joy, my goods, and my surety! Adieu, my jewel, my sweet flower! Adieu, fair rose, fair violet! What shall I now do? Never had man such sorrow! I myself made the ditch wherein I now fall; now am I sadder than any 'ghost' alive."

His barons comfort him, and bid him bear his burden softly. A baron advises him to slay Horrible, as Mélusine suggested. Raymond commands them to do so, and they depart to find him. Raymond retreats into a chamber alone, and there renews his lamentations.

The barons shut Horrible up in a cave, fill the entrance with moist hay, and set fire to it, so that he was soon stifled. Then they put him into a fair bier, and buried him nobly. They then commend him to God, depart, and return to Raymond.

Raymond again laments, saying, "It was all through my cousin that I became a foresworn man. I was unfortunate at first, when I slew my sovereign lord; and secondly, when I was false to my lady. False fortune's cruel envy has brought me to this, whereby I have lost all my riches, and eternal joy. Mélusine always loved me; my heart trembles with pity. I had rather die for evermore than suffer so grievous pain. My sorrow will never end till I die. For so Mélusine told me."

Raymond is sore tormented. But Mélusine came often by night into Thierry's chamber, and often dressed and fed him. She was often seen by the nurses, who told Raymond of it, to his great joy. Thierry grew more in one month than other babes in four, but it was due to his mother's nursing. She was often, too, in his father's chamber. I must now leave speaking of Raymond, and tell you about Geoffrey. Remember that I am not lying.

Geoffrey fights the giant Grimold of Northumberland

Geoffrey sailed swiftly on, and reached Northumberland, where the giant made war. The barons come to greet him, both great and small. A baron tells him how their country was enthralled by that fierce, huge, troublesome, and proud giant. In one day he slew a hundred knights, and could as soon slay a thousand as one.

Geoffrey answered, "Then is he a fiend, but nevertheless I will soon destroy him. I must find this soldier. He shall fare ill ere seven weeks pass. Provide me a guide, that I may see him to discomfit him."

Geoffrey takes a debonair guide, and commends himself to God. He and his guide at last spy the giant under a tree, sitting on a marble stone. The guide is frightened. Geoffrey laughs at him, and says he has not been misled. The guide wishes to be off, as he has shown him Grimold the giant; and he assures Geoffrey that remaining there is no jape. Geoffrey laughs, and asks him to remain and see the battle, which will be soon decided. The guide says he does not care to see it. Geoffrey laughs sweetly, and again begs him to wait till he sees who gets the best of it. He can then return and tell the others. The guide consents, but declares he is in great dread, and that if Geoffrey knew the giant as well as he did, he would think twice about it. But Geoffrey promises that the giant shall die. Now our Lord aid him. Grimold has, singly, slain a thousand or more men. Never was there a worse man seen.

Geoffrey mounts, leaves the valley, and rides up the mountain, leaving the guide below. Grimold, perceiving Geoffrey, wonders how one sole man dare come to assail him, but he thinks he must be coming to propose a peace. Grimold says he shall soon go down again. Then he takes in his hands a huge lever, which he uses as a staff, or as a little child would a stick. Without gainsaying, the staff was huge, and could not easily be bent.

Seeing Geoffrey coming, he cries aloud, "How comest thou here? Thou shalt have no warrant from death."

Geoffrey answers, "Ribald, look that thou save thyself; I shall smite off thy head."

Grimold, hearing this, began to laugh, and ironically asks Geoffrey to spare his life. But Geoffrey sternly replies, that he trusts to rend his head to the teeth. Geoffrey braces on his shield, and shakes his spear, being no coward. Riding straight at the giant, he deals him such a blow that only his steel hauberk saved him.

Grimold fell on the ground, throwing up his legs. But soon he got up again, while Geoffrey alights that his horse may not be killed under him. Grimold looks at Geoffrey, and in wonder asks his name. He says he never threw his limbs up like that before, yet he is ashamed to revenge himself, and again asks his name.

Geoffrey answered this bachelor, "I am Geoffrey of Lusignan, Mélusine's son."

The giant says that he knows him now, for that he had slain Guedon his cousin, for which he will now pay him off. The giant thought he was speaking truth, but he was nearer lying. Geoffrey tells him that desire of revenge will increase his hurt.

The giant strikes at Geoffrey with his lever, but Geoffrey blenches, and the lever makes a great hole in the rock. It tears the rock a foot deep. Geoffrey lends the giant a stroke on the elbow. The grass round about becomes red. The giant again raises his lever. Geoffrey again blenches, and the stroke tears the ground three feet deep, so that the giant finds his arm stunned and his lever broken.

Then Geoffrey shows his strength, and smites the giant a grievous stroke on the skull. Next the giant smites Geoffrey on the head, but Geoffrey returns him a marvellous stroke on the shoulder, which rends both hauberk and mail. The giant, severely wounded, curses his gods and abjures them, both Magot, Apolin and Ternagant. But his great wailing was useless. Geoffrey will conquer at last, but will have much trouble first.

The giant leaps at Geoffrey, and grips him fast by the reins, and they wrestle together. They hurtle, beat, and pull each other till they at last separate, and then Geoffrey smites him on the haunch with a knife which he held in his sleeve, piercing through his coat of mail. The giant flees for his life.

The giant enters a chine of the rock, being greatly afraid. Geoffrey mourns that he has lost him, but returns to his guide, and tells him all the story. The guide marvels strongly, beholding how Geoffrey's helm was broken, and how full his hauberk was of holes. He compliments Geoffrey.

Many nobles approach, and ask Geoffrey his name, and whence he came. One of the barons addresses him, and tells him the giant will not return to fight him for any worldly wealth, for that he knows he is predestined to die by Geoffrey's hand. Geoffrey declares he will never depart till he finds him.

One of the barons tells him that the mountain is enchanted, and that the noble Helmas, king of Albany, was enclosed therein with his three daughters, because he had wilfully beheld their mother in child-bed, after distinctly promising he would not do so. She had at that time three fair daughters. This fair lady's name was Pressine, and Helmas had made her the above promise; but he failed to keep it, and he and his three daughters were enclosed in the mountain. Ever since then a huge giant had been their warden, and (till Geoffrey's coming) there had never been a man whom the giant had not slain when they fought together. All of them had been forced to yield to Grimold the giant. Grimold was the fifth, the sixth, or perhaps the seventh of these wardens who had made war abound to all men.

Geoffrey discovers his grandfather's tomb

When Geoffrey heard the news, he took an oath that he would die as a recreant or else discomfit the giant. Next day Geoffrey leapt on his courser, and went up the mountain spurring him nimbly. Perceiving the hole in the rock where the giant entered, he descended and looked in; but saw no more than he would in an oven.

"I wonder," says he, "how he got in, seeing he is so wondrously 'corporal', so much more than I am. See here the cave. This is the great rock wherein the cave is hewn, and it is big enough inside. Whatever happens, I will seek him inside." So he enters the cave.

Letting down his spear, he pushes the spear head before him, and follows it, clenching his teeth. Thus came he to the bottom. His spear being of a hard wood, such as could not be broken, he seizes it near the head, and goes on, pushing it always before him, testing the way.

At last he arrives at a fair chamber. It was carved in the rock, with no place of egress, and was full of all kinds of riches. It was adorned with pure gold and rich jewels. In the midst was a tomb, supported on six pillars of fine gold. Above it was a king, well formed of chalcedony, and beside him a fair lady of alabaster. Geoffrey marvels at this, but observes a tablet which the lady bare in her hands, on which was written the following:

"Here lieth Sir Helmas the king, who promised me ere we were wedded that, whilst I lay in child-bed, he would never inquire about me, nor see me, till I was recovered. Then it befell that I had three fair daughters at once, and Helmas contrived to see me; whereupon I vanished and took my daughters with me, and brought them up. When they were fifteen years old, I told them how I had lost their father. The eldest, Mélusine, was very vexed about it. With her two sisters, as was right, they talked over every circumstance, and told me, who was their mother, they wished to avenge me on their father. The three daughters agreed to bring a fate upon their father, to avenge me of the great misdeed that he had foolishly done against me. To this they all assented, and enclosed within the mountain Helmas, who was their father, and who had broken his promise. When he died, I buried him beneath this tomb, and enclosed him there, and caused this tomb to be thus made, thus sculptured and painted. Thereon I caused my likeness to be put that there might be remembrance of it in him who should read the tablet. For never should man enter here except he were of the lineage (in Avalon and the fairy country) of my three daughters, of whom you may hear tell when you will. I bade the giants to watch, from the hour I set them there, that none should enter by this passage except he were sprung of our line.

I provided gifts for my daughters, who were beautiful and fair: to Mélusine, the eldest, who was very wise and prudent, I give her a gift for life (according to the order of the fairies), that, as long as her life lasted, she should be a serpent every Saturday; and, whoever would marry her, must not approach her on that day, but take good heed, wherever he was, and in every thing. He must not see what she then was, nor tell anybody of it. And whoever followed this rule, to him would Mélusine always come just like a mortal woman, as women naturally do. Then should she die naturally, and as others usually do.

To Mélior, the second daughter, who was so fair a creature, I give a fairy gift, and 'tis well that I should tell you what. In a castle strong and massive, which is situate in Armenia, (in great Armenia, verily,) I bade her that, during her life, she should keep a sparrow-hawk there. Whoever wishes to ask a boon of her must watch there three nights and he shall have it; but he must not ask for herself. But if he yield to somnolency, he shall be her prisoner for ever. Such is the gift I give her.

Palestine, the youngest, shall have this destiny: she shall dwell in a very high mountain, where men's hearts fail them, and shall there guard her father's treasure, till a knight of our lineage comes and takes it by force, and afterwards conquers Palestine, the land of promise. This mountain is situated in Arragon.

Thus Pressine avenged herself on her three daughters, because they shut up their father Helmas in the mountain in Avalon. For I (Pressine) loved him heartily though he sinned against me."

59

Such was the writing on the tablet. After reading it Geoffrey greatly wondered whether he was of Pressine's lineage or not. Passing thence he searches for Grimold everywhere, and at last sees a fair field with a tower in it. The gate being open he enters and sees a number of prisoners behind a great lattice; they warn him off, lest the giant should destroy him. But he laughs, and asks where the giant can be found, for he is come to fight him. One of the prisoners again warns him to go, but Geoffrey tells him not to fear, as he can fight the giant alone.

Geoffrey kills the giant Grimold

Just then the giant came up, and, perceiving Geoffrey, fled in to a chamber hastily, and drew the door after him. But Geoffrey follows, and bursts the door open with a kick, and enters. The giant smites Geoffrey with a mallet, and would have slain him but for his helmet. Geoffrey falls, but rises again, and says, "I received then a fair stroke, and now I will repay it." Drawing back he lunges at him, driving the sword through him up to the hilt.

Then fell the giant who had so often made men thralls. He cast up a marvellous cry, and all the tower sounded. Then Geoffrey drew his sword out of Grimold, and put it in the scabbard. Then he went to the prisoners, and asked if they came from Northumberland, and why they were in prison. They said it was because they had not paid the giant the tribute they owed him.

"Rejoice then," said Geoffrey, "for ye are struck out of his papers, and I have acquitted you of your tribute by killing him."

Then they were glad and asked Geoffrey to let them out. So Geoffrey searched till he found the keys, and coming to the 200 prisoners, undid the lattice, and gave them leave to go. Geoffrey leads them to the chamber where lies the giant.

All wonder how Geoffrey could kill this monster, of so 'unfitting' a stature. They all said they had never seen such a man in all their days. Geoffrey tells them they now owe the giant nothing, but that they may carry away all the treasures they can find, for he would have nothing for himself. They thank him greatly, and ask him how he came there, where no one dared come for the giant. Geoffrey tells them, and they all say that no man so bold ever issued from that rock, except the giant and his antecessors, who had slain 400 knights. They said too that they would accompany him till he found his own people.

Then they set the giant's body up upon a cart, to which it was fast bound and attached. Wherever they went all men marvelled at the monster, and blessed the hour when Geoffrey came there. They would gladly have made Geoffrey their king, but he would in no wise longer sojourn there. Then he leapt upon his courser, and bade the barons adieu. Then he and his people galloped fast till they came to the sea. There he took ship, desiring to see his father and Mélusine. The wind was good and he soon came to port. Then he disembarked and arrived at Lusignan that same night.

All the world came to meet him, and Raymond with the rest. Geoffrey salutes him humbly, embraces and kisses him. Then they entered a chamber and talked together. Geoffrey told his father many tales, and next he is told how he had caused the loss of his mother. He knew it was for his sin in burning the abbey of Maillezais. Then he remembers the tablet he saw in the mountain of Avalon, upon the tomb of King Helmas. Then he knew that Mélusine must be Helmas' daughter.

Geoffrey kills his uncle

When he knew that Raymond had been tempted by the Earl of Forest, he swore an oath that he would go and kill him. Away he goes with ten chosen knights, who were worth twenty others, and the result was this: they rode till they came to the castle where the earl was; then Geoffrey entered that fort suddenly and unperceived. Moved with wrath he neither saluted any nor spake, but ascended the steps of the great hall, and found his uncle Fromont there amongst his people.

Drawing his sword, he declares him a traitor, and terrified his uncle, who fled away in great trouble. Never had he been so frightened; he entered the tower and ascended the steps. But Geoffrey hastened after him, pursuing him so fast that the earl had to flee alone, for all ran down the steps as if they were mad, being greatly afraid of being caught. Thus the earl ran up into the tower and got to the top as soon as he could. Geoffrey swore that he would not spare him. In extreme terror the earl leapt up to a window and, missing his footing, fell on his head upon the rock.

Thus this Earl of Forest died by his own folly, and Geoffrey caused his body to be buried, and proclaimed his own brother Raymond the lord of Forest. This done, he returned to Lusignan, and soon came to his father who was sore lamenting the earl's death.

Raymond turns to the religious life

Raymond exclaims, "All is due to my sin and vice: I will quit the world and its fame, and make a pilgrimage to the holy apostle at Rome, whom men call Leo. I will then become a recluse in a strange country and spend my life in prayer."

Geoffrey, alighting from horseback, tarried not at the dismounting stone, but sought his father and craved his pardon, bitterly repenting his wickedness.

"It needs not," said Raymond, "to mourn longer; you cannot bring your mother back again, nor can I restore the dead to life. You must rebuild the abbey which you burnt in your folly."

Geoffrey promises to do so.

Raymond says, "It should be built up so as to be fairer than before; but I must leave you now, for I go on a pilgrimage. You shall guard the country and take care of your youngest brother. Give him Parthenay, Vouvant, Aiglon, and all the country as far as Rochelle; for so Mélusine gave direction."

Geoffrey promises to do so, and tells his father he need not fear its not being done.

Raymond, all being made ready for his journey, sets off. He takes leave of his people and goes to Rome. Geoffrey and Thierry go with their father; and, on the road, Geoffrey relates how he found good King Helmas within the rock, and how he had seen Helmas' tomb, and Pressine's image in alabaster, and the tablet which her hand held. Raymond rejoiced to hear Mélusine was of such high descent, and seemed in his joy a foot taller. Afterwards Geoffrey tells about Pressine's gifts to Mélior, Mélusine, and Palatine, and how Pressine loved Helmas dearly. Raymond again rejoices.

Thus his two sons brought him on his way, and bring him at night to his lodging. Next morn they take their leave, and there was great weeping on both sides. Then Geoffrey and Thierry went back; and Raymond went on to Rome. Geoffrey went to Lusignan, and Thierry to Parthenay.

The good qualities of Thierry are here enumerated. Thierry married a lady of high degree who came from Britain, and who was very wealthy. From Thierry descended the line of Parthenay, a line which is still distinguished for virtue, according to Mélusine's prediction. It were tedious to relate all their deeds.

Geoffrey sent everywhere for masons, who rebuilt the abbey of

Maillezais which he had burnt. It was rebuilt so as to be fairer than before: so that men marvelled, and said that Geoffrey had become a monk after all!

I return to Raymond, who confessed all his sins in full to the pope, who wondered at the strange things he told him, and appointed Raymond a penance, which he promised to perform before returning to Poitiers. He undertakes to live a hermit's life for Mélusine's sake, saying that he would never forget her, nor return to the place where he lost her. He craves the pope's pardon; and Pope Leo, accordingly, asks him where he thinks of going to.

Raymond answers, "To Montserrat in Arragon, where there is fair sojourning."

Leo bids him go; and Raymond sets off, soon coming to Toulouse, where he bids adieu to his men, sending them all home except a yeoman and a chaplain. Next he has hermit's robes made, and goes to Arragon, and so becomes a hermit at Montserrat. His yeoman and chaplain lived with him there, and thus Raymond forsook the world, and lived there devoutly till his death.

Three days before his death, the serpent was seen going round Lusignan; so that more than 20, who had well heard Mélusine say that she would appear, know that they are soon to have a new lord.

Geoffrey as Lord of Lusignan

Geoffrey was then lord of the castle, and held it in peace. Then came to him the barons whom Raymond had dismissed, and told him how his father was now a hermit and had sent them home. Geoffrey sends for his brother, and leaving Lusignan in his charge, departs for Rome, to accomplish all he had to do.

It were long to tell all. He confessed to the pope, and was very penitent for the wickedness he had done in his youth. The pope assoiled him, and charged him to rebuild the abbey of Maillezais, and fill it with monks to the number of 120, and so to endow the abbey that they should never lack bread or wine. Geoffrey promises to do this, and says it is begun already. The pope again charges him, and he promises to obey. The pope tells him he is in danger for his brother's soul, because he burnt him; and that he would find his father at Montserrat.

Geoffrey sets off for Montserrat, and soon finds the way to it. He then ascends the mountain, and finds Raymond. Raymond is glad to see him, but bids him to go home again. Geoffrey refuses to return, and insists on staying four or five days; but at last consents to return, and takes leave of his father. Returning to Lusignan he calls his barons together, who humbly do him homage as their lord. He then rebuilds the abbey he destroyed, and establishes there 120 monks, endowing the abbey richly, and making rich grants to it.

In course of time he visited Raymond; for, when the time of Raymond's death drew near, Geoffrey remained at home no longer, but came to the abbey of Montserrat to provide for his father's burial, and made grants to that abbey also. Geoffrey did his duty at Montserrat, and then returned to Lusignan.

Thierry reigned at Parthenay long and justly, and did fair deeds. None durst break his hests, but obeyed him. Oede (Eudes) reigned sagely in the marches. Uriens reigned in Cyprus, and warred against the Saracens his neighbours. Guy was king of Armenia. His heirs warred against the Saracens, who sorely dreaded them. Raynold was king of Brehayne (Bohemia). His heirs reigned after him. Anthony was duke of Luxembourg, and his heirs did fair deeds. Raymond was earl of Forest, and was much beloved. Thus all these brethren bare them well, and prospered; all except Horrible, who had been smothered, and Fromont who had been burnt. All these were descended from Raymond, and bear his arms. To this day the Cyprians use "Lusignan" as a war cry. The earl of Pembroke in England was also of this line; as also the lords of Cambron in Arragon. But Fromont was buried at Maillezais, where also lies Geoffrey under a stone tomb. Here ends this part of the romance.

Mélior and the Sparrow-hawk

Here begins the romance of the Sparrow-hawk Castle in Great Armenia; where knights had to keep awake three nights, and whoever did so might ask a boon of the lady Mélior, provided that he did not ask for her love. If the watcher went to sleep, he became her prisoner there for ever. Mélior was the lady's name, daughter of Pressine.

There was then a mighty king in Armenia, a fair knight, who undertook to watch three nights at Sparrow-hawk Castle, intending afterwards to demand a boon. So he did, but afterwards repented of his rashness. He therefore departed, declaring that if he found the lady Mélior fair, he would ask for nothing but *herself*. Such was his foolish resolve.

Thus came he thither on St. John's day, and having remembered to bring his tent, pitched it there in the meadow. Then came he to the castle gate, holding a piece of flesh to feed the sparrow-hawk. There saw he an old man, clothed in white, who asked him what he sought, and next offered to show him the way. Then they mounted the steps and entered the hall. The king marvelled much at the wealth he saw there, and perceived the sparrow-hawk on his perch.

Then said the old man, "King, you must here watch this sparrow-hawk for three days and nights. If you succeed you may ask a boon, demanding any earthly thing save lady Mélior's body."

The king said he would watch, but he took ill counsel with himself. Then the old man departed.

The king watched all that day and that night, feeding the sparrow-hawk. Seeing also plenty of food and wine, he took a repast of what pleased him. Next day, he again watched all day and all night; and the third morning again fed the bird.

Seeing a door open, he entered another chamber, which was full of birds, painted in vermilion. The portraits were there of many knights, and under each was written the name of each, with the date of his undertaking the adventure, and how he failed, and had to remain there till the Day of Judgement. There were also three places where were seen three coats-of-arms, and beneath each was written the date when each of the knights undertook the adventure and *succeeded*. The walls of the chamber were painted from top to bottom. These three knights were valiant, and did not go to sleep.

The king mused on these things till he almost slept; then fearing lest he should do so, retreated. The third night he also watched; and on the fourth morn came the lady, clothed all in green.

The king salutes the lady, who praises him and asks him what he will have, for she will only refuse him *one* thing, which she will not pay. The king thanks her, and asks her love. She, greatly angered, denies him flatly, and bids him ask something else. But he reiterates his request, and will have nothing else. She is very angry, and tells him that, if he persists, he will find that great mischief will befall him, for that he shall lose his kingdom, and his heirs shall be disinherited. He again says he will have nothing else.

"Fool," says she, "thou hast lost all; thy trickery deceives thee, and moves thee to folly. Thine ancestor, by his folly, lost his spouse. His name was Raymond, and he espoused Mélusine. King Guy, from whom thou art descended, was my nephew. We were three sisters, and enclosed our father Helmas within a rock, because he broke his oath made to our mother Pressine. And when we had done this, our mother was angry with us, and made me watch this sparrow-hawk here, without ever departing hence. To Mélusine she gave the property of becoming a serpent every Saturday, as a punishment. Her husband was never to see her that day, but he broke his oath. Palestine, my youngest sister, is in a mountain in Arragon. There she keeps watch over King Helmas' treasure, which none but one of our lineage may win. You ought not then to wish to have me to wife. Owing to this, you shall suffer great misfortune, and your successors shall lose their kingdom. The last of them shall bear the name of the king of beasts. Thus shall it be. But for your folly you might have had a blessing; but now shall you receive a curse."

Then Mélior vanished away; and great mischance happened to this king. He was beaten on the haunches, sides, legs, arms, and head, so that he came to a 'hard fast,' and felt the stroke on his chine. He cried for mercy, and fled, being well anointed, and having no sleeve or rag whole on him. His people asked how he had sped, and if he had kept good watch. He replied that he had fared ill.

Then rode they to the sea, and took ship, where the king took off his armour. Then rowed he strongly so that he soon arrived at a haven of Armenia. From that day his fortunes declined. He was well aware it was all his own fault. After him reigned another unfortunate king, and after him nine others. They at last lost all. One of them came to France, died at Paris, and was buried in the Celestin convent. His men wore white at the funeral; not black as men do in France. This is no jape, but true. People wondered, not being used to it; why they did it I know not.

Palestine in Arragon

I now speak of Palestine. She was shut up in a place in Arragon, where she wards her father's treasure; which none shall win except he be of her lineage. The chronicle treats this story briefly. I only put down what it says, inventing nothing.

Now I return to Palestine, who is in the high mountain. Many men, both stern and meek, went thither, but none returned; all were foully destroyed. There were many men who sought to win that treasure, but could get nothing. None returned.

There was in England a mighty knight, who did deeds of arms in plate and mail; who was brought up in Arthur's court, and was of the lineage of Tristram. This knight heard of this treasure, and said he would win it, and the Land of Promise afterwards. He departed thence on a Tuesday, riding merrily to Arragon. He had only one page with him.

Within the mountain dwelt a serpent, a hideous monster, whose paunch was as big as a wine tun. It had but one ear, and no nostrils, and only one eye, which was a yard long. Its breath came out at its ears. It always slept; and when it snored everything near it was disturbed. Here dwelt Palestine. The monster guarded the cave's door, where the treasure was shut in. None but one of Helmas' line could enter.

Here many men perished. The ditches round about were full of serpents, very dangerous. No man went there but he soon came back again. The path up the mountain was very narrow and three miles long. Men had to go up without resting; for there was no place to sit down except one sat upon serpents.

This knight came riding thither, attended only by a page. When he drew near the place, he met a man, who led him to within a mile of the place, and then left him to go on alone, showing him the path whence none returned. His guide departed, and the knight rode on. At the mountain he dismounted and gave his page the rein, and bade him wait; though he only had to wait in vain. The knight commends himself to God, and enters the path, being well armed.

He soon sees a serpent coming, running at him to devour him, and advancing with yawning throat. The knight brandishes his dagger, and cuts its neck in two at a stroke. The serpent fell down dead. It was 10 feet long.

Upward again he mounted, but soon sees a huge bear coming apace, which , however, he encounters boldly, drawing his sword like a mighty man. The bear gripped his shield, and clutched at his shoulder, tearing his hauberk; but he smote the bear in the groin, giving him a wound a foot long, and cutting off his snout, so that he could not bite. The bear was very chapfallen at this, yet raised his paw against him again; but the knight leaps lightly aside. With a back stroke of his sword he cuts off the bear's paw. But it reared up, and clutched him with the other paw. Both fell together. Then the knight with his dagger cut the bear's throat, so that it quitted its hold. Then the knight cut off its other paw. At last the knight smites it through the belly up to the cross-hilt of his sword.

On went he slaying many serpents. At last he reached the top, and drew near the iron door of the cave, which the monster guarded. But he entered the cave in an evil hour; for he soon perceived the monster with its eye a yard broad, which at once attacked him.

The knight saw it come, but would not retreat, but determined to face it at all risks. Drawing his sword he smote it, but his strokes failed to harm it. Neither iron, steel, nor wood could wound it. It bit his sword in half, though it was all of steel. Then with a yawning throat it swallowed the knight down whole. The knight seemed no more in its mouth than a pasty in an oven. Thus died he, and it was a great pity. Thus was this good English knight devoured by this monster, and it was a great pity.

No one ever got so high up the mountain as he did. His daring should be remembered, not lost to oblivion. No man ever went higher. His page waited for him two days, and then returned to England, there relating this adventure to many. A certain divine, who had been clerk to Merlin, dwelt there (in Arragon), to whom many went to hear the story. He was a scholar of Toulouse, and during twenty years gave true replies to any questions he was asked. The page, therefore, went to him, and learnt from him all the truth just as I have now told it you.

There was also a man of noble birth in Hungary, who came to this mountain; but he was not there long, being very soon devoured by serpents; but he went not up so high as that other. Pity the English knight was not of the right lineage. He was descended from Tristram, and had assuredly won the treasure, had he been of the right lineage.

The death of Geoffrey

Then came a messenger to Lusignan, where Geoffrey was enjoying himself with all honesty. With him were ladies and damsels in a fair arbour. Geoffrey tells the messenger he is welcome, and asks him the news. Then the messenger relates the adventure I have just told you, and tells where the monster was who guarded the treasure of Helmas. At this Geoffrey greatly marvels, and says he will go and destroy the monster.

He made ready, and sent to his brother Thierry to come and govern his realm. This Geoffrey was of a fierce courage and would never marry. Then he made over his land to Thierry, saying he should depart. But he was prevented by sickness and age. Alas, had he lived, he would have had the treasure, and the Land of Promise, that Holy Land. But death, who spares none, made war on Geoffrey; and against death hath no man any power.

Death smote Geoffrey sorely with his cruel dart, piercing his heart. What good deeds he would have done in Poitiers, had he lived! But alas, these things were left undone. His death will cause great heaviness. He can take no food. His confessor came and said mass. Then he made his will touching both spiritual and lay matters. Then was he buried at Maillezais abbey, which he had rebuilt after destroying it. There lieth he, and the author of the French Romance there saw his tomb. Thus he made his will, and yielded his soul to God. Had he lived longer, he would have done more.

Thierry was Geoffrey's heir, and governed both Poitiers and Parthenay, being at first powerful, but afterwards he alienated much of his property. Yet the descendants of Thierry reign at Parthenay still, as Mélusine foretold; and may they long do so! The line endureth to this day, and contains many noble knights, of whom we shall speak a little, and then end.

The Lords of Parthenay

Especially should be mentioned that worthy knight, who caused this book to be begun. When it was partly done, this knight died; for who can escape death? All must pass along death's path. Alas, it cometh unexpectedly, man sees not when nor how. Death is swifter than an arrow. When I think on it, my heart sigheth. Every man should fear its cruel hand. Whoever thinks on death, must leave all pastime, and muse on his soul's safety. Whoever thinks on it well, will depart from sin.

One William was then Archbishop, and he well knew how good a man this lord of Parthenay was. He died on the Tuesday before Pentecost, May 17, A.D. 1407,[9] and was buried at Parthenay. He lies in the church of the Holy Cross. He was very solemnly and honourably interred, be ye sure. The day of his death was the very day on which the head of the blessed Saint Louis, king of France, was translated to Paris. I do not mean that my lord died in that same *year;* for the translation of St. Louis' head took place long before that. But I mean that he died on the anniversary of that event, following his master as a servant should. Thus I make an end here of my good lord.

---

9   This date is wrong; it should be 1401. W.W.S.

His noble son, John of Parthenay, performed the funeral obsequies well, using many wax lights. But it is not wise to sorrow overmuch, when the matter cannot be mended. Those who do so are not wise.

I return to his heir, John, lord of Parthenay and seigneur of Matefelon, who is no cruel man but very courteous. He is sweeter than any maid; this he inherits from his mother. For she was very sweet and charitable, and did much good to the poor; and especially to those in great need. Many she raised to riches, of her great liberality.

Hence my lord had a fair beginning, and, moreover, he is of royal lineage, being cousin to the King of France, the mightiest king in the world. There is no king so noble as the King of France. He is cousin to the king on his mother's side; and, through his father, allied to the King of Cyprus, and also to the King of Norway. For knights of Mélusine's line still live in Norway, and it is well known that they belong to the Lusignan family.

No family was ever equal to this; nor can any man hear such marvels elsewhere as are told of Mélusine's sons. Think not I dream; or, at least, it is a true dream. Whoso hath not seen this history, will scarcely believe the fact.

The seigneur of Matefelon, who is also lord of Parthenay, shows himself to be a sweet creature, for he will not leave unfinished the book his good father began. I believe that no man hates him, and, indeed, any one who sought to harm him would be a great sinner. He never refuses any deserving man. He should be named Alexander, I would say much more, only men would say I flatter; because he is still living and we ought rather to praise the dead; yet men will praise my lord in time to come. I hear many speak of his gentleness, countenance, and demeanour; for he is descended from kings, dukes and marquesses. He is found, on inquiry, to be of high parentage.

His wife also is humble, courteous, and intent on good; so that they are well met. This lady is of Perigord, daughter of the late earl. His marriage is no disgrace to his kindred; for she too is of a noble line. For when Charlemagne had conquered all Guienne and the country round it, he gave it to one of his nigh kinsmen, one of his cousins-german, who resided there till he died. His inheritance went to his heirs male. There is a place called Perigord whence this lady comes. She lacks nothing that is lady-like, but is gentle and sage. A very fair marriage was made between them. I pray they may have good issue; some heir to maintain the noble line of Mélusine.

I speak no more of her nor of Parthenay, for I found no more recorded. I would have said more, could I have found more. There's no more than I have already told, so that I must now perforce take rest. Now must my ship rest. Thank God, I have arrived at port, and the dangers of the sea are past. I thank God, by whom the book has been brought to an end. If any one wants to know the name of this romance, it is *"The Romans of Parthenay"*, or, *"The Romans of Lusignan"*; choose which you like. Here shall Couldrette hold his peace, saving that he will here make his orison, putting it into the form of a litany; and when this litany is done, the book shall end, and Couldrette shall hold his peace.

Couldrette's litany

O Glorious Trinity, Three Persons in One, One Essence, Sovereign Majesty, that has made summer, winter, and all things, Thou knowest all our thoughts, and the consciences of men. Man oweth Thee due obedience, and diligence in Thy service. Here humbly I pray thee to have mercy and pity on this lord and lady; and to succour them in adversity.

Glorious Virgin, mother, daughter, and hand-maiden of God, that didst nourish Thy divine Son, and didst also comfort Theophilus; comfort this line of Parthenay.

Saint Michael, archangel, protect them from the fiends of hell; and let them have linen and woollen vesture.

Saint John the Baptist, that didst show men the Lamb, and all ye glorious patriarchs, forget them not.

St Peter, St Paul, St Andrew, and all apostles, let not this noble line be forgotten that hath spread so far.

St Stephen, St Vincent, St Lawrence, St Clement, St Dionysius, and all ye holy martyrs, grant that we may dwell for ever in heaven, where reign the Father, the Son, and the Holy Ghost.

St Silvester, St Augustine, St Martin, St Maurice, St Severinus, and all confessors, let not this line be forgotten, but guard them from the fiends that come at the third hour or at mid-day: grant us the solace of the celestial sphere.

St Mary Magdalen, I pray to thee. St Agnes, St Edith, St Catharine, be pleased to beseech our Lord to save us.

All ye friends of God, put away our sins that we feel not hell-pain, but dwell with the saints in heaven.

Lord Jesu, grant that nothing may turn to their harm. Guard them from our adversary, and save us all.

Sweet Lord God, our Father, guard us from the fiend; grant that we offend Thee not, but may gain everlasting bliss.

Jesu, that shalt judge all, teach us the way of salvation, that we may praise Thee hereafter for ever.

The translator's epilogue

I yield thanks, after this prayer, to God, the Virgin, saints, martyrs, and confessors, that I have now translated this. I have done it in order, as closely as I could, almost line by line, saving that I have often had to change the order of words, as when men write Latin verse. Whoever translates in metre must do this, whether in ballad, verse, rime, or metrical prose. Yet have I preserved, I trust, the matter unhurt, without excess or diminution, making it intelligible in our mother tongue. Perchance I may have made an oversight, but it is no great one, not such as to violate the sense. Also the French lines have fewer syllables than the English, so that two lines may be put into one; and I have sometimes done so. I would that both books could be seen at once, that if any man wants to count the lines, he might see how closely they are alike.

Here I make an end; and beseech you, in whom is all nobleness, to excuse all faults, since it was at your request I made the translation, and wrote it out from end to end in black lines. Now all ye that read this, remember my simpleness; though this book is not painted (for I cannot flourish), yet excuse all faults that you may see.

Essay on Mélusine

• Louis Stouff •

*This is my translation of a scholarly analysis by the distinguished French medieval scholar **Louis Stouff**, probably the definitive academic work on Mélusine. Published by the University of Dijon some ninety years ago, it covers all aspects of the romance, including the identity of the original author, Jean d'Arras, who commissioned him and why, along with a detailed cultural, geographical and historical background to the work.*

I I I I I I I I I I I I I I I I

1: The Romance Of Mélusine

The romance of Mélusine saw light of day at the court of France in the time of Charles VI in the middle of the Hundred Years War. It appeared under the patronage of the royal house of France and the imperial house of Luxembourg-Bohemia, closely united for almost half a century in memory of Jean l'Aveugle, King of Bohemia, Count of Luxembourg, former governor of Aquitaine and Gascony for King Philippe de Valois, and his ally in the war against the English, who fell at Crécy at the head of the French army.

Both the sister and the daughter of the King of Bohemia became queens of France. Marie married Charles le Bel. Bonne, Countess of Luxembourg, married Jean le Bon.

From Bonne's marriage to Jean le Bon, Jean, Duke of Berry, was born and Marie of Valois (wife of the Lorraine prince, Robert, Duke of Bar). These two were the godfather and godmother, so to speak, of Mélusine. The Duchess of Bar begged her brother "to have a noble history made" of the faery of Lusignan. Two grandsons of Jean l'Aveugle were interested in the work of Jean d'Arras. For Josse of Luxembourg (Marquis of Moravia, later king of the Romans) asked his cousin, the Duke of Berry, to send him the story.

Through the patronage of these powerful protectors, Jean d'Arras then had access to the Count of Salisbury, Guillaume de Montagu, and with the King of Aragon, Jean I, son in law of Robert and Marie of Bar. The author thus wrote for the high aristocracy of Europe – but over the centuries, his book came to charm great lords, gentlemen, burghers and the common folk.

Daughters of the faery Pressine and Elinas, King of Scotland, Mélusine and her sisters Mélior and Palestine were themselves faeries. Elinas had thoughtlessly betrayed his wife, and his daughters imprisoned him in a magic mountain in Northumberland from which he could never escape. His wife, deprived of *"he from whom she had received all her pleasure in the world of mortals…repaid her daughters as their evil action deserved."*

Mélior was sent off to a castle in Greater Armenia to guard a hawk until the end of the world. *"Any knight of noble blood"* could attempt to watch over the hawk on the eve of the 25th of June (St. John's Day) for three days and nights without sleeping. *"If fortune favours them enough that they can perform the task, you will appear to them on the fourth day. They may ask a gift from you of anything on earth, whatever they wish, apart from for your love, whether in marriage or any other way. And any who are mad enough to try to insist on that will be sent away, and their line cursed until the ninth generation."*

"And you, Palestine, will be shut up in the Canigou mountain in Aragon, with your father's treasure, until a knight of our lineage comes who can release you and take the treasure to help conquer the Promised Land."

Mélusine was the most guilty. She had been the evil counsellor. *"As for you Mélusine, it is through you that your father was inflicted with his harsh imprisonment. For that you will have the greatest punishment. I proclaim that every Saturday you will become a serpent from the navel downwards. But if you can find a man who is willing to take you as his wife, promising never to see you on a Saturday, nor tell your secret to anyone, you may live the rest of your life as a normal woman and die a natural death. But if, by chance he discovers you, you will return to the torment you were in before, and remain like that until the Last Judgement. You will also reappear three days before the fortress that you build, and is named after you, is about to change its lord, or when a lord of your line is about to die. For despite your punishment there will spring from you a most noble line of great prowess and high renown."*

Mélusine becomes the wife of Raimondin, son of the Count of Forez and nephew of the Count of Poitiers. Their love began in the great forest of Colombiers in Poitou that is full of strange adventures. There, at about midnight, under a great rock by a faery fountain, Mélusine awaits Raimondin. The Count of Poitiers has perished in a far off clearing, that Mélusine knew by her faery arts, and now by her faery power she draws Raimondin, the involuntary killer, towards her as he flees through the forest. She approaches him with a piquant and wholly engaging grace, rallies him, gains his confidence and tells him the past and future, gives him two magic rings to preserve him from ill fortune and asks him to marry her.

Raimondin and Mélusine have several sons, valorous and of fine appearance but who each bear on their face some sign of the reprobation with which their mother has been afflicted. Antoine, at his birth, bears the mark of a lion's paw on his left cheek. Renaud has only one eye, although he could see for twenty-one leagues. Geoffroy is born with a tooth that juts from his mouth like a large thumb. Fromond is marked on the nose with a little furry patch like a mole or ferret.

However, the years pass in extraordinary happiness. Only a wise, good and powerful faery, loving only her husband and children, thinking only of how to advance their affairs, could procure such great and constant prosperity. She founds, by a series of marvels, the formidable castle of Lusignan in Poitou, "the most beautiful example of an ancient fortress" according to Brantôme,[10] "and the most noble decoration to be seen in all France." She extends the domains of Raimondin across Poitou, Guyenne, Gascony and Brittany. Several of her sons reign in countries they have gained through marriage, in reward for their zeal in helping royal maidens in distress. Urian becomes King of Cyprus; Guion King of Armenia; Renaud King of Bohemia; Antoine Duke of Luxembourg.

Mélusine appears to Raimondin as a miracle of beauty and good will; for him, she has been his saviour. When she teaches her children she draws for them a model of wisdom, greatness of soul and piety. In everything she shows herself to be magnificent, in marriage festivities,

---

10 French historian and biographer, c.1540-1614.

provision for the journeys of her sons leaving for their conquests, in her generosity to churches and to the poor, in the buildings with which she covers her immense domains in which tradition confounds her with the works of the Romans.

Victim of a surprising betrayal of his oath by Raimondin, who punishes himself by spending the rest of his life in exile and austerity, Mélusine is torn, with hopeless farewells, from the most noble joys that the world can give and is struck back into her obscure punishment. She flies off in the form of a winged serpent and Raimondin retires to a hermitage at Montserrat in Spain.

The Mélusine story is truly beautiful and touching. We sympathise with the poor faery condemned by her own mother, for an error in filial piety, to become half reptile for a day each week until the Last Judgement. We admire the lady of Lusignan, great builder of towns and castles, tender and devoted wife, mother of brave sons, generous and beautiful, also through her good deeds mother to her many subjects. We are moved when the furious jealousy of her curious and impertinent husband puts a brutal end to this sweet and beautiful life, banishing for ever she who was its creator. This whole legend of shining faery and religious sadness appealed to any simple soul, to lovers of mystery and ancestry. But this was not the only reason for the favour it enjoyed.

The legend required that Mélusine be the branch of the Lusignan family whose history is, so to speak, that of Europe and the Crusades. In all the countries where the Lusignans took root, and in all those where certain families could attach themselves to this illustrious house, throughout Poitou, Saintonge, Marche, Agenois, Forez, Dauphiné, Languedoc, the county of Burgundy, Alsace, Luxembourg, Bohemia, England, Cyprus, Armenia, the descendants, true or claimed, of Mélusine were proud of their supernatural origin, and the frightening privilege of seeing their great and tragic ancestor return to this world to announce their next death by her cries.

At the time when Jean d'Arras wrote *Mélusine* a large part of western France was under English domination, and new misfortunes extended the English conquest. Almost all France was divided into a French party and an English party. The war with England was less a foreign than a civil war, although pursued and led by the English who played the greater part in it for their own benefit.

We need to distinguish between the English of the French nation and the English of England. It often came about that a man divided his life between the two warring nations. The French might "turn English" and then return to being French. The chronicler Froissart, after having served the Queen of England, Philippa of Hainault, having delivered an English version of his first book, passed into the service of princes loyal to France, and revised his work. Nothing was stable, everything was confused. At Poitiers "three quarters" of the inhabitants wanted to be French, but the majority in a single quarter of the community claimed to be English. In Poitou fortified houses and castles were intermingled with each other, some English, others French. This was true of many provinces.

It was the "translation" of a rhymed version of Jean d'Arras' romance, appearing in the first years of the 15th century by a Poitevin named Couldrette, which becoming known to English subjects and partisans, doubled the number of readers at a stroke.

One could say that the book by Jean d'Arras is on the French side. It was Jean de Berry who had commissioned it, one of the fiercest enemies of England, and companion in arms of Du Guesclin, the conqueror of Poitou and Lusignan.

Couldrette's poem is for the English. We owe the rather bad verse of the Poitevin to Guillaume VII, of the Larcheveque family, lords of Parthenay. Charged by the Prince of Wales to defend Poitiers and form "a frontier against the French", and going with him to the siege of Limoges, the taking of which was followed by frightful cruelties. Raiding across Berry and Touraine in the company of Charles d'Andelée, "tormenting" the country and "harrying the poor". Holding the country with the Count of Pembroke and Chandos. Taking part in the siege of the castle of Roche-sur-Yon. Summoned to help Sainte-Sévère in Limousin when besieged by Du Guesclin. Fighting at Leusac. Defender of Thouars, he was a great servant of England.

Perhaps he was still thinking of his English masters when he commissioned Couldrette to write his book in verse so it would be disseminated more. *"Write the history in verse for me. I want it rhymed so it will be more widely heard."*[11]

Indeed, the Poitevin poem is close to the political views of the Lord of Parthenay. Jean d'Arras, whom Couldrette follows step by step, is not even acknowledged – which could be explained by another motive – but neither are the Duke de Berry or the French partisans, the Rochefoucaulds, the Sassenages, the King of Cyprus.

---

11 Froissart – in *Histoire et Chronique memorable.* Vol 1.

On the other hand, the Salisburys and the Pembrokes could not be omitted, and the story of Palestine at Canigou is added to the tale, glorifying a "good English knight" who overcomes a thousand frightful obstacles when attempting to win the treasure destined for the Promised Land.

Written at the end of the 14th century, the story of Mélusine was known in the following century throughout all France, Germany and England.

Jean d'Arras tells a legend of Poitou. He exalts the Lusignans. He celebrates the great deeds of the warriors of Poitou to the point that one would have believed him a native of that country. However the name of Jean d'Arras seems to have been unknown in the region of which he speaks so enthusiastically, and if the book itself had never existed, it would matter little. No edition of Jean d'Arras' romance or Couldrette's poem appeared either in Poitiers or any town in the west. The craze for it was great everywhere except in the Mélusine country.

Countries far from Poitou and from each other claimed to have been witnesses of the wonders of the faery and of her penitence and to have given her asylum. The legends grew. They attributed to Jean d'Arras things he had never said, and took all his fictions seriously.

In the 16th and 17th centuries, otherwise commendable scholars, who no doubt spoke truly when not under the influence of Mélusine, believed or pretended to believe in these imaginings. In the time of Francis I it was Jean Bouchet, the annalist of Aquitaine, author of the *Promptuaire des Medailles,* contemporary of Henri II. And throughout the following century André du Chesne, researcher of antiquities in the towns of France; Chorier and Guy Allard, historians of the Dauphiné; Denis, Lord of Salvaing and of Boissieu, first president of accounts of the Dauphiné, feudal expert, Latin poet and historian. Also de la Mure, historian of the Dukes of Bourbon and Counts of Forez. All confirmed it, citing it one after the other, repeating the same tales, using the same arguments and holding to the conclusions that pleased them.

The Lusignans of the Agenois, the Sassenages of the Dauphiné, the Counts of Forez, the Luxembourgs, the Lutzelbourgs of Lorraine, all wanted to be in the lineage of Mélusine. Jean d'Arras became an authority for all these great houses anxious to acquire a new lustre, and for the historians interested in their glory.

The cause of the Sassenages was pleaded by the obliging Chorier and by Salvaing, the ally of their family. So as to create titles to this illustrious ancestor, they laid claim to similarity of arms, or transformed coats of arms, seized on a vague resemblance of names, they overwrote charters and genealogies, or changed peoples' names.

In the 16th century, a daughter of the first family of Outre-mer, of the family of the Counts of Tripoli in Syria, of the line of the Lords of Nores, was baptised with the name of the good and beautiful faery.

At the court of the dukes of Burgundy and princes of Luxembourg, Mélusine had her place at banquets and in feasts. As in the library of Philippe le Bon, the books of Mélusine were bound with gold, illuminated in gold and blue, covered with gilded and silvered copper, with gilded clasps.

Side dishes of Mélusine brought ingenious surprises. On 17th February 1454, at Lille, the Duke of Burgundy gave a banquet. The second course on the second table was a castle in the style of Lusignan. And high in the lady's tower was Mélusine in the form of a serpent, and from two of the lesser towers when one wanted, gushed orange water which fell into the castle moats.

On 17th March, Louis of Luxembourg, Count of Saint-Pol celebrated at Cambrai the Feast of the Unicorn. The dinner was so great and so noble, as they then said, that one could believe one was at Mélusine's wedding feast. *"They were served,"* says the chronicler, expressing himself in almost the same words as Jean d'Arras, *"good and delicious wines of many kinds in great abundance, and as for hypocras, it was laid on as if it cost nothing."* The side dishes closely represented the story of Mélusine and her children as great personages, leaving in no doubt the Duke's intention to reproduce the magnificence of his faery ancestor.

Among the courtiers of Philippe le Bon was a rich lord of Souabia, the margrave Rodolphe de Hochberg, Lord of Roeteln and of Suzemburg, Count of Neuenbourg on the Rhine. He was one of the confidential advisors of Charles le Téméraire. After the Treaty of Arras that annexed to Burgundy the sovereignty of the Habsbourgs in Alsace, and in the upper valley of the Rhine, as well as the numerous mortgaged lordships of which they consisted, he was one of the commissioners appointed by Charles le Téméraire to take possession of his new domains. He possessed himself many of these mortgaged lordships and the most important.

The margrave had found *Mélusine* at the court of the Dukes of Burgundy and it was he who made her known in Switzerland

and Germany. On his orders, the recorder of Berne, Thuring of Renggeltingen, translated *Mélusine*. Two years after the banquets at Lille and Cambrai the translation appeared, but Thuring had given preference to the *Mélusine* of Couldrette, shorter, less erudite and less packed with episodes.

Another translation was produced at Augsbourg in 1474. The translation of 1456 was printed in about 1477, perhaps at Strasbourg, in 1491 at Heidelberg, the same year that a Flemish translation was published at Anvers. And again at Augsbourg without a date, but with the letterpress of Antoine de Sorg, a circumstance which places this edition in the last quarter of the 15th century. The first French edition, probably the oldest, dates only from 1478. Again it was printed outside France, in an Imperial town, Geneva, and by a German, Steinschaber of Schweinfurth. All these editions, and more, were decorated with woodcuts, and made the story of Mélusine popular in countries of the German empire in the second half of the 15th century.

People in eastern Europe were particularly excited by the Poitevin faery. They had their reason to be pleased with the marvellous tale that had "come from so far away". They provided Jean d'Arras with fresh enthusiasts of his work as they discovered their own legends there. A young mother sacrificed by her husband returning at night to cradle and sing to her little children. Sprites at the end of the day completing the work of artisans. A poor shoemaker discovering in the morning, sewn with such care that there was not a single fault, all the shoes he had cut out in the previous evening. Helpful spirits, but also malicious, who could snatch a baby from its cradle and replace it with a horrible dwarf. Then carry off the dwarf and return the child.

Water nymphs, creatures without souls, could obtain one by attracting the love of a man and marrying him. In the 16th century the Swiss alchemist Théophrast Bombast of Hohenheim, known as Paracelsus, brought the memory of Mélusine to the legends they told of water sprites, summing up the traditions:

"Mélusines are the daughters of kings, in despair because of their sins. Satan raised them and transformed them into spectres, evil spirits, horrible revenants and frightful monsters. It is thought they live without a rational soul in a fantastic body, that they feed on the elements and at the Last Judgement will pass away with them, unless they have married a man. Then, by the virtue of this union, they can die a natural death, just as they can live naturally in the marriage. It is believed there are many of these spectres in deserts, forests, ruins and tombs, open vaults and at the edge of the sea."

However, two charming tales come from these terrifying stories, the Ondine of la Motte-Fouqué and Andersen's little siren.

The happiness of Ondine is even shorter than that of Mélusine. Like Mélusine, grateful to be loved and joyous at having escaped her hard condition, she has showered her husband with riches and the blessings of faery. But Huldebrand is another Raimondin. The husband of the Lusignan faery harshly accused her of being a phantom. Huldebrand, sailing with his wife on the "beautiful blue Danube", seeing the apparitions that surge up from the depths of the river, reproaches her with her connection to the abominable race of water spirits. Ondine bursts into tears, and in a weak voice bids farewell to her husband. Invisible from now on, she still loves him, and forgives him, even when he marries Bertalda. Divine justice decrees that she shall kill her lover with the tears she sheds over him, but the couple are not separated for long. They have immortal souls.

The little siren saves the life of a king's son. He mistakes another woman for her and marries her. The little siren preserves the happiness of the one she loves, she does not undeceive him. By her love, she sacrifices her hope of gaining a soul, for on the marriage day she must change into sea foam. But her devotion preserves her. Gathered up by the daughters of the air, she feels that she has a body similar to theirs, which releases her bit by bit from the foam. She does not yet have an immortal soul, but her good actions will bring her one, one day.

The story of Mélusine seems to date from the book of Jean d'Arras. No previous story is known. Even the name of Mélusine is not found anywhere. However we can recognise traces of ancient beliefs. The Gauls regarded trees, forests, rocks and springs as sacred. They were religious objects or sanctuaries. Each one belonged to a deity. The women that the Romans called *matres, mairae, nymphae, fata,* served these cults of the countryside.

The medieval faery corresponds to this religion. The priestesses became faeries. *Fée* comes from *fata.* Jean d'Arras, among the faeries, names the mothers and nymphs. Pressine, Mélusine, the unknown faery who cleared Forez for cultivation, are water spirits. They play about fountains, with faery voices they sing faery songs. There are also faery places. They would have been called in Roman times places of divine law, the Fountain of Thirst, also called the Faery Fountain, the Forest of Colombiers, and the Isle of Avalon or Lost Island "that none can find again except by chance."

With the ancients there were three Parques. They were seen crowned with flowers, each carrying a wand, and confused with the *fata*. Like the Parques, faeries arranged adventures with mortals, which were attributes of the Parques. Faeries appear in threes in popular tales in the middle ages. Such are the daughters of Pressine. Three ladies, with Mélusine *"the greater lady than the others"* stop the flight of Raimondin by the Fountain of Thirst.

Jean d'Arras has joined to legend several imaginary new adventures to form the story of Mélusine. He has changed it into a romance. But the subject of the book makes it in fact an isolated work, about a particular character. Nonetheless, in its details, his work has many connections with the old epic poems, adventure songs, and Round Table romances then put into prose.

- Breton romances several times name the Isle of Avalon, Northumberland, Britain, Ireland, Senaudon or Signaudon (Snowdon) capital of Wales, the Sion of *Mélusine*, the Forest of Brédigand in Northumberland whose leaves cover the tomb of the magician Merlin, and the fountain from which water flows while remaining colder than marble.
- A golden bowl attached to a long iron chain in the middle of a forest of *"high straight trees"* in which Elinas meets Pressine, takes the bowl that hangs from the fountain, drinks and salutes the lady with the greatest respect he can.
- The Mountain of Brumblorenlio in Northumberland containing a sumptuous underground hall, like a faery palace, that is the tomb of Elinas.
- The Isle of Avalon where Pressine hides is an orchard of delicious golden apples. The Garden of the Hespérides. Morgan, sister of Oberon and of Arthur, takes Arthur there to heal him of his wounds. She keeps Ogier the Dane there. Pressine's sister rules this paradise. She must therefore be Morgan.
- A grandson of Mélusine, Oliphart, renewed the exploits of Arthur, conquered Denmark, Norway and other countries of the North. The chatelain giants, Gardon, the tyrant of the district of Guérande and Bas Poitou, Grimault, the guardian of the tomb of Elinas and

tormenter of Northumberland, the giant of the Turning Castle in the romance of Chrétien de Troyes, are equal in wickedness.

 ◆ Urian will become the father of Yvain, the Knight of the Lion. The magic rings of which Mélusine is prodigal towards her own, have the virtue of the talismans of Morgan and the cups offered by the Elves of Northumberland.

Other episodes bring Mélusine close to the heroic adventure songs. The itinerary of Raimondin towards Rome is that of Charlemagne in the *Chevalerie Ogier.*

Geoffroy á la Grand Dent, burning down the abbey of Maillezais, is another Raoul of Cambrai. The scenario is the same. The knights who accompany their masters recoil before the sacrilege and censure them. Under the walls of the abbey of Origny in flames Raoul of Cambrai prepared a feast but then gave up the meal having forgotten it was Lent. In view of the "damage he had done" Geoffroy expressed remorse with the same violence that he had, just previously, assailed the monks in their chapterhouse.

2: The Author and the Text

We know very little about Jean d'Arras. In 1361 someone of this name paid homage to Philippe de Rouvre, Duke of Burgundy, for a fief in the suburb of Aire in the town of Marcq-en-Baroeul. He held this fief from the duke's wife, Marguerite, Countess of Flanders, Artois and Burgundy. His father, Thiébaud of Arras, possessed it before him. A Jean d'Arras, in 1382, was proprietor of three houses in Arras, paying rent to the Knights of Rhodes.

Jean d'Arras lived at a time when the Kings of France and the greatest lords of the kingdom liked to form rich libraries, where everything could be found to please a bibliophile, the beauty of the calligraphy, the delicacy and brilliance of the illuminations, the splendour of bindings. Now, in 1380, at Saint-Mihiel, a Jean d'Arras, with his varlets and other persons, made a case, probably a book chest, for Robert of Bar. In 1392 a Jean d'Arras, bookseller in Paris, rebound three books from the king's chapel, a missal, and a breviary that he covered with deerskin, and a life of Saint Louis. In 1394 a Paris bookbinder re-gilded, cleaned, re-whitened and covered with green damask silk a book called *Le Pontifical de la chapelle du roi notre seigneur.* In 1398 a Jean d'Arras, Paris bookseller, delivered to the Duchess of Orleans a book called *Guiron le Courtois* "having restored the greater part of the leaves that had fallen, re-covered it with good red leather and provided four clasps, two before and two others beside, so that they hold together."

This case maker, bookseller, re-binder, could also well be the author. Jean de Berry would have ordered the story of Mélusine from whoever was employed to bind his books. The first manuscript of miniatures in the Arsenal shows a person in a chair dictating to a scribe seated on a stool. He has by him a press, the screw of which crosses a sort of little arch mounted on four feet. Three books rest on the press and the principle person's left hand holds one of them open.

Jean d'Arras, if he is the one we think, was no common merchant. The sun shone upon him, and among his customers were the most magnificent and leading connoisseurs: Marie of Valois, the Duke of Bar, Jean de Berry, King Charles VI. He was also a scholar, although also one of his times, happily scattering contradictions, incoherences, careless mistakes and absurdities. He gets muddled with the ten sons he gives to Mélusine: Urian, Eudes, Guion, Antoine, Renaud, Geoffroy, Fromont, Horrible, Raimonnet, Thierry.

In one place he calls Horrible Eudes. He forgets that Fromont is the seventh, Horrible the eighth, and that after the birth of Fromont, Mélusine rested two years before having another child. He makes Thierry the eighth and has him born the year following the birth of Fromont. Here we see that Fromont is born in the ninth year of Mélusine's marriage and that he came into the world after Urian's war in Cyprus, after Guion's marriage in Armenia, and after Antoine's expedition to Luxembourg and Renaud's into Bohemia. Yet Urian was seventeen years old when he went to war.

At the moment that Mélusine leaves her husband and children for ever, Raimonnet is only three years old and Thierry no more than two – Mélusine says so herself. Fromont was thus about six years old when he became a monk at the abbey of Maillezais, and a few days before Mélusine's departure he begged his brother Geoffroy not to burn down the abbey.

The day after this heinous crime Geoffroy leaves for Northumberland.

He stays there a very short time, taking only two days to come face to face with the giant Grimault. He returns immediately after his victory and to find Raimonnet waiting for him, who tells him they no longer have a mother. Geoffroy hurries to Forez to seek vengeance by murdering his uncle. He has only to go and return. Told of his return, his father has him immediately summoned by Thierry.

Mélusine is lucky to have *"such very fine nurses to take care of her children."* They have grown well and profited so well that everyone is amazed, but the faery has her limits and cannot dispense so generously with the number of years.

The King of Armenia writes to Urian to ask him if Guion would marry his daughter Florie. The letter is sent to Urian by the barons of Armenia after the king's death. Urian and Guion have given their consent. The barons have returned to le Cruq bringing this response and have prepared a reception for Guion. They wait, with Florie's ladies and maidens, for their new master, to give him the honours of his future kingdom. It is incredible that at the same moment Florie, waiting on the main tower of the castle at le Cruq, is afflicted with the thought that Urian would not grant his brother to her.

Geoffroy wants to take Fribourg-en-Brisgau by surprise. To have the gates open he disguises himself, along with ten knights, as travelling merchants. Ten great full sacks on the bow of their saddles contain, they claim, their merchandise. The sacks are full of hay but a few lines further on this hay has changed to old cloth.

Telling the adventure of the phantom knight of the Poitevin Tower, Jean d'Arras at first forgets that Raimondin holds Lusignan in fief from Bertrand, Count of Poitiers. *"You others,"* says Geoffroy to his accountants, *"have seen the letters about how the good Count Aimery of Poitiers gave it to my father."* Then the author, who has enclosed Raimondin for ever at Montserrat a little after Mélusine's departure, shows him a few years later at Lusignan, learning how to put an end to the damage inflicted by the mysterious hand on the Poitevin Tower.

For Jean d'Arras, the Saracens are pagans. They swear by the gods Mahon and Apollin; that is to say, Mahomet and Apollo. But sometimes they forget and swear like Christians, by their faith.

Any man who is not a Christian is called a Saracen. The Saracens are not only Turks, but by this word he understands the infidels of Turkey, Syria and Barbary; and Zelodus, the King of Cracow, and his subjects are also Saracens. Grimault, who guards the tomb of Elinas, a

Christian king and father of the pious Mélusine, swears by Mahomet, by his law, by the Koran, like the Sultans of Barbary and Damascus and their intermediaries. And in Brittany, at the castle of Montjouet in Guérande, the giant Gardon, Grimault's cousin, is also a Saracen.

Trying to be moving, Jean d'Arras is false and heavy handed and lacks good taste. Elinas is not a traitor, he has not broken his word to his wife. He is only guilty of an excess of enthusiasm inspired by conjugal tenderness and paternal love. The reproaches of Pressine and her daughters are unjust.

The Lusignan brothers fight the King of Alsace under the walls of Luxembourg. The noise is great with the clash of arms, the cries of the wounded, the blare of trumpets. The young lady of Luxembourg, in the ladies' tower with her maidens, has by her side a gentleman who has come to announce the rescue that the sons of Mélusine were bringing her. He puts his head out of the window, sees the battle and recognises Antoine and Renaud.

"My lady, come and see honour in his royal seat and high majesty. Come and see the god of war in his face."

"Friend," says the lady, *"what are you telling me?"*

"Listen," says the gentleman, *"I am telling you to look on the two children of Lusignan, the flower of all nobility and courtliness, who from a far country have come to venture their honour and their lives to defend you."*

This is piling up sentences as insipid as they are portentous at a time when brief talk is called for.

The demoiselle comes to the window and sees the ground covered with the dead and the horrible mêlée.

"Oh God," she says, *"why do that for this sad orphan? It would have been better if I had been drowned or died some other cruel death rather than that these noble creatures should perish for my sin."*

How can she at the same time invoke God and regret not being done to death? Is it likely that she would accuse herself of her sin when she knows, like all her subjects, that the originator of the war was the King of Alsace?

The King of Arras has lost the war. His power is so greatly reduced that he cannot help his brother besieged in Prague by the Saracens. Later, Raimondin, for having been indiscreet, will be threatened with the loss of his wife. Both sinners curse Fortune, and in much the same terms.

"Ah! Ah! Fortune, lame, blind, sure and bitter as you are perverse, envious and treacherous. A great fool is anyone who trusts your gifts. You

hate, you love, you make, you destroy, there is no more stability in you than a weathercock in the wind. From the top of your wheel you have cast me to the bottom. I am here in the dirtiest and most sordid place in the house where Jupiter throws the weak, unhappy and unfortunate."

Would it not be better to take responsibility for things on themselves rather than indulge in such extravagance?

Jean d'Arras is also pedantic. His remarks about the god of war and of Fortune show this. He is concerned with universality and justice, application and scholasticism. He likes to quote Aristotle but does not always understand him. He loves to write obscure digressions on the invisible world, on the belief which is due to *"faery things"*, and on the singular and unchangeable nature of the seven liberal arts that constitute the sum of knowledge in the Middle Ages.

Whether John of Arras comes from this fraternity we do not know. The proverbs that he cites throughout the work are appropriate. His style, it is true, is often poor and gauche, his transitions are maladroit and hardly vary. *"Why dwell upon this? Why then dwell upon this subject? Why dwell upon this meeting?"* Too often his characters *"do not know what to think."* The praises he puts into the mouths of his good characters expressing a view on the children of Mélusine are the same in all circumstances. *"These men are fit to conquer the whole world!" "This man will cause the whole world to obey him!"* One could say that their admirers in Asia and Europe were given due notice! The stories of battle are full of repetitions. *"There was great killing." "There was great mortality." "There were many men killed and wounded." "There were many dead and wounded there."*

But in general his language is sober, firm, clear and eloquent and touching in Urian's speech to his men before the battle of Famagousta, in Mélusine's advice to her children, in her farewells to her husband and his entourage. The author knew, in detail, things concerning the times in which he lived. He gave names to characters appropriate to the country where they lived. Raimondin's father is a Breton, and is called Hervé. Raimondin's grandson marries the heiress of the Lord of Cabrières in Aragon, and is called Bernardon.

The language of theology, law, heraldry, war, shipping, hunting, are familiar to the author. He uses precisely the terms of the process of drawing up charters, *"the best that can be devised."* Raimondin obtains one from the Count of Poitiers, the gift of land that will later carry the name of Lusignan. He requires a charter of the gift. *"He soon gave him the strongest there could be, sealed with the great seal of the Count in relation to his consent, and the peers of the realm added their twelve seals to affirm that the gift was correct."* The challenge that the six Lusignan brothers send to the Germans before the attack on Fribourg-en-Brisgau, and which is sealed with their seals, is according to all the rules. It conforms to the documents that have come down to us from this epoch.

The descriptions by Jean d'Arras are lively, whether they help us with military scenes, or show wealthy burgesses, proud and jealous of their liberties, secure in their strongly fortified towns. He allows us to see the streets hung with bunting for some triumphant parade of warriors, the notable townsmen, splendidly dressed at their windows, and the trumpeters, fiddlers, players of horns and cymbals filling the crossroads with their *"very great"* melodies.

3: The Geography of Jean d'Arras

Itineraries, descriptions, memoirs

The author of *Mélusine* is exact, even meticulous, in his descriptions.

He represents France as covered with immense uninhabited forests. Mélusine, banished by her mother, goes off into the great forests and heaths. Hervé, fleeing from Brittany *"comes to the high mountains adjoining the sources of the Rhône and several other great rivers"*, the Loire, the Allier, no doubt. The country was deserted and full of heath land, and because of that Hervé and the lady of the fountain he meets call it Forez. Hervé was the first count. The fortress of Marcilly-le-Château, then called Jalensi, dominating the Roman road across the Auvergne from the crest of an imposing rock, was the lordly manor of the masters of this new domain conquered from the wilderness.

Raimondin, returning from Brittany, enters the Poitou country. He finds many great forests there and in some places an abundance of wild fowl, stags, hinds, bucks, roebucks, boar and other beasts, as well as beautiful plains, grasslands and rivers, and many beautiful places by the sea, and it appears to him that they would be very profitable if they were populated. *"It is a great pity,"* he says, *"that this country has no people, for the land is very fruitful."*

It is in the midst of these ancient woods that the first scenes of the romance occur. The forest of Colombiers, of which the modern wood of Coulombiers is the little that remains, is witness to the murder of the Count of Poitiers, the meeting of Mélusine and Raimondin, their courtship and marriage.

Two forests of Brittany then follow, that of Guérande where the traitor chatelaine of Derval lies in wait for Raimondin to assassinate him, and the royal park of Sucinio that, extending southward to the sea, and to the north as far as Saint-Armel on the Morbihan, to the west as far as Tour du Parc on the river Pernef, and covering all the eastern part of the Rhuis peninsula.

The way from Poitiers, an old Roman road, crosses the forest of Colombiers in passing over the mountain. On the way, between Poitiers and the mountain, beneath it is a hamlet called la Villette de Colombiers. From the high road one goes down to the meadows where the Fountain of Thirst rises, known today as the Font de Cé at the lower end of the town of Lusignan; the other fountain springing from the ground at the command of Mélusine *"from which several mills have worked and still do today"* says John of Arras.

Deep in the heart of the forest of Colombiers, among the rocks and ravines, Mélusine built the castle, then the town or bourg of Lusignan.

> *"She set the walls on the living rock. The castle is not just one, but there are two of them surrounded by strong machicolated towers, the vaults of the towers turned in ogives, the walls high and well crenelated, and there are three pairs of "braies" or advanced walls, high, solid, garnished with many towers. The posterns are very strong. And at one side, towards the great forest, over the meadows, the rock is so high and bare that no creature could live there. And everywhere they put good "braies" cut from the same rock. It is thus true that the place is marvellously strong."*

In the courtyard of the castle, as in the castle of Huldebrand, there is a well. It is also a well of apparitions. Mélusine returns there like the phantom in the romance of Ondine, and Death follows them.

> *"The walls of the town were thick with strong machicolated towers and terraces. These too were themselves machicolated and in the wall were covered alleyways to protect the archers from without and within. The moats were deep and made of*

cut stone. Mélusine had good "braies" made; and built between the town and the castle a great tower of Saracen tiles bound with strong cement. The walls of the tower were easily of sixteen to twenty feet thick. The lady made it so high that it overlooked the town by more than a lance height and the watchmen inside could see on all sides whoever came toward the fortress and the town. She stationed guards who blew a horn when they saw anyone approach, and called this tower the Horn Tower."

The castle and town together formed the fortress of Lusignan and there was a tower there called the Poitevin Tower. The romance does not say if this was within the castle or the town. It was, so to speak, Mélusine's tower, perhaps the one that later bore her name.

When Mélusine flew from the window of the castle *"she landed so suddenly on the Poitevin Tower, in so furious a storm, that the fortress seemed about to fall into an abyss and all the stones of the masonry moved one against the other. And in an hour she was lost to view."*

Raimondin was very ill. He had no more than three days to live. Mélusine, in the form of a serpent, made three turns round the fortress tower, and set down on the Poitevin Tower where she sat a long time, sighing and weeping. *"They said with the voice of a lady, and also that it was good."* His sons Geoffroy and Thierry felt great pity, as they knew it was their mother. When she saw them weep she showed even greater distress, leaned over and gave a cry to terrible that it seemed that the fortress was collapsing. Then it seemed to all who were there that she wept very tenderly. Then she took flight, went straight towards Aragon, and that same day appeared at Montserrat.

Raimondin had neglected the penance that the Pope had imposed on him for breaking the oath he had made to his wife. Five or six years after Mélusine had departed, there began to appear, on the last day of August, a great hand that removed the pommel from the Poitevin Tower and pulled at it so strongly that it broke a great part of the roof. Every year after that it did the same, and each time it was necessary to spend twenty or thirty pounds to replace it.

On the advice of an unknown stranger, each year when the hand came, they took a deerskin purse containing thirty silver pieces, each worth four deniers, up to the last stage of the tower, and placed it on a piece of wood supporting the roof on which the pommel sat. Since then the pommel had not shifted. But Geoffroy did not intend to submit to any part of his inheritance to be in bondage, as the Count of Poitiers had given it freely so that he owed nothing to any man. On two occasions he fought the phantom knight who came to claim this tribute. The first time was at the top of the tower and the whole roof trembled at the coming of the apparition.

The fortress of Lusignan contained a chapel and a church. One marvel Mélusine accomplished while Raimondin attended the funeral of the Count of Poitiers was to raise from the earth, above the Fountain of Thirst, *"a stone house in the form of a chapel, beautiful, graceful and well appointed."* This was the chapel of Notre Dame, a monument for the engagement of Raimondin and Mélusine. The church of Notre Dame of Lusignan was witness to Mélusine's recognition of the happy establishment of her sons in Cyprus and Armenia. Later when they made obsequies for Raimondin his heart would be buried there.

Under the walls of Lusignan is a great parkland. The stream that runs from the Poitiers side crosses it. There feasts were held and the warriors assembled. There the pavilions for Mélusine's marriage were erected. There they celebrated the marriage of her son Eudes to the daughter of the Count of la Marche. Here they jousted for the chivalry of Urian and Guion, and in honour of Antoine and Renaud departing to liberate Luxembourg. It was also here that Geoffroy fought his last combat with the spectre of the Poitevin Tower.

The romance mentions many other monuments of Poitou and Aunis.

In the great hall at Poitiers the widow of Count Aimery, who did not yet know the worst, waited anxiously for the return of her husband, and saw the foresters and hunters carrying the body of the deceased *"with many tears and great cries."*

In the church of Notre Dame, Raimondin, the unknown and grieving murderer, was present at his uncle's funeral, while in the square before the church the good people *"in great anger"* at having lost their lord, burnt the boar that they blamed for his death.

In the church of St Hilaire, the barons of the Count of Poitou met with the young Count, who received them in canonical habit like their abbot, to pay homage for their fiefs, and Raimondin, before them all, received the charter which would make him a very powerful lord, by according to him around the Fountain of Thirst as much land as a deer hide would cover.

The next day his vassals went to hear mass at the abbey of Moustier Neuf. Raimondin prayed to God here to help him finish what he had undertaken. It was at Moustier that his son Horrible was buried, who would have destroyed all that Mélusine had built if he had lived, and have done such evil that the death of twenty thousand men would not have been so great harm. They had prevented this destiny by suffocating him with the smoke of damp hay. It was on coming out of Moustier Neuf that Raimondin met the man who carried the marvellous deer skin, that cut in strips and satisfactorily aligned, would trace the limits of the vast lordship of Lusignan.

Leaving Poitiers and travelling towards the sea, after having passed Lusignan we come to Niort. The twin towers here are beautiful to see, says Jean d'Arras. They are great square towers they call the Keep.

We find after that the road to the abbey of Maillezais, *"old, very large and massive, with one hundred monks apart from the lay brothers"*.

At La Rochelle, the main port of the West, the two towers by the sea guard the port. Today one is the Chain Tower, the other the St. Nicholas Tower. The Guienne Gate is surmounted with a gruesome trophy, witness to the victory of Geoffroy á la Grand Dent over the giant of Guérande. We see there, spiked on a lance, the head of the *"dissolute"* who caused the suffering of the country from Brittany to La Rochelle. Mélusine, *"very joyous"* to have received it in homage from her son, had it brought here to the tower to assure their subjects that from now on they were delivered from the great misery they had suffered.

At the edge of the ocean, three leagues from La Rochelle, is a great tower built by Julius Caesar, the old *Castrum Julii* of the Romans. It is called the Eagle Tower, says Jean d'Arras, because Caesar bore the eagle on his banner like an emperor. It was Castle Aiglon, the great legendary town of Aunis, in the time of Charles Martel, and is the modern Châtelaillon.

٭٭٭٭٭٭٭٭٭٭٭٭٭

On the occasion of Raimondin's journey through Brittany, Jean d'Arras says that there are two Brittanies – Brute or Bretonnante, the country where they speak Celtic, and Gallesse, where they speak French. The King of the Bretons reigns over two countries. He lives at Vannes, at Nantes or in the castle of Sucinio, his hunting lodge.

Going in search of his uncle Alain and the king of the Bretons, Raimondin arrives in Brute Brittany at Guéménéguingant, now

Guémené-sur-Scorff, that was called after the name of its founder, Guégant. He finds the king at Nantes, and after that goes on to Pont-le-Léon (which could be Saint-Pol-de-Léon) and through the forest of Guérande to take the road from Poitou once more.

After his departure Alain's sons go to ask the king for a place to build the priory of the Trinity that Raimondin has urged them to found. From Guéménéguingant they come to Vannes, where it appears that the king has gone to Sucinio. They mount their horses and arrive at Port, that is to say on the shores of the Morbihan, cross it, enter the forest and ride as far as the castle. They are told that the king is in the park. They find him under a great oak tree beside a lake, where he is following a stag that his hounds are hunting.

The brothers retire so as not to interrupt the king's pleasure. The king sees this and is grateful for it. The stag tries to leap into the lake but is taken by the pack of hounds and pulled from the water. Parts of the stag are given to the hounds according to custom. The brothers then present themselves to the king and tell him that their cousin has asked them to do so.

"*By my faith,*" says the king, "*the request is reasonable and straightaway I will lead you to the place where I would like the priory to be.*" They leave the deer park and go the length of the wall to the end of the enclosure. "*Good sirs,*" says the king, "*build the priory here and take all the room you need. Use the forest to take the timber and when the monks are established they may take wood to burn for themselves and their followers. I will grant them fishing grounds in the sea extending for a quarter of a league, and allow them to stretch nets in the forest for birds and any wildfowl for their food. Also all the arable land for half a league around.*" And the king granted them the necessary charters.

The brothers thank the king. They bring in workmen and in a short time build the church and the priory, and install eight white monks who wear a blue cross on their robes, to whom they grant good rents so they can live comfortably. We can recognise in this foundation the Trinitarian Priory at Sarzeau.

<hr>

The evil doings of the King of Alsace in Luxembourg, the Saracens at Cracow in Bohemia, and the Austrians in Alsace twice lead some of Mélusine's sons into Germany. Ten days' ride brings them to Champagne. They cross it, staying one night on the Aisne, and after several stages come in the evening to establish their camp in a fine meadow on the banks of the Meuse, under a fortress called Dun-le-chastel or Chastel-de-Dunes, because it is situated on a cliff top above the river. It is today called Dun-sur-Meuse. From there it is only two stages, or twelve leagues, to Luxembourg. The final stage before they arrive there is beyond Virton.

To enter Luxembourg is to enter Germany. *"In the German lands between Lorraine and the Ardennes,"* says Jean d'Arras, *"is the county of Luxembourg."* Austria, Bavaria and Bohemia are on the frontiers of Germany. *"I am going to see my brothers in Germany,"* says Geoffroy á la Grand Dent. *"King Renaud of Bohemia and Duke Antoine of Luxembourg."*

Germany does not have a good reputation. *"I will not enter Germany without men at arms,"* adds Geoffroy. They meet bandits a plenty. They infest the Leffe and all the country up to the Great March of Holland. "The Linfards," says Froissart, are the biggest robbers in the world." These highwaymen of the main roads are the lords of castles between which they pass. Terrible for travellers and stragglers of armies, they do not fear the great lords.

The expedition to Bohemia is agreed. The King of Alsace will take part with Antoine and Renaud of Lusignan. *"When you call up your men,"* declares Duke Antoine to the king, *"I will summon my own, who are at war with a knight of mine in the Leffe who has been badly treated."* It is in actual fact Lothaire, the second son of Antoine, who has sufficient force to take the Linfars' country by easy stages, and prevent its return to brigandage. He founded Ivois, the abbey of St Vitus, the bridge at Mezières over the Meuse and several fortresses, thus opening access to the country. Opposed to these redoubtable robbers are the Church, the townsmen and other chatelains who are the Prince of Luxembourg's men.

When penetrating this dangerous country Antoine is charged to provide the advance guard. He has a warning passed from castle to castle: *"If you are so bold as to take anything from me or my men, I will render such justice on you as will be an example to others."* In this way he peacefully crosses the whole of the Leffe, through promising misfortune to any who would dare rob the army of anything, even if only worth a penny.

One night the army stops before Aix-la-Chapelle. At Cologne it crosses a bridge over the Rhine which is *"a marvellously great river"* not least because full of salmon. The Rhine salmon are one of the fine gifts that the citizens of Cologne offer the Lusignan brothers.

Jean d'Arras does not list the stages after Cologne. *"They travelled thus for some days,"* he says, *"till they came to Bavaria near a great city called Munich,"* and they finally lodge on *"a great river"* the Elbe, half a league from Prague.

✦✦✦✦✦✦✦✦✦✦✦✦✦

The way Raimondin travels to Rome crosses the mountains of Mont Jeu, which are the Great St. Bernard, and Lombardy. They arrive one evening at Rome at Pré Noiron, the original site of the Vatican. The next day he is at St. Peter's, before the Pope, and spends eight days visiting the holy places *"which he had to do."*

He then begins his long ride toward Montserrat. He comes to Toulouse and from there to Narbonne. Geoffroy, who tries to follow his father step by step, says once he has arrived at Toulouse, *"This is not the shortest way to Aragon, but as my father went by there, we will take it too."*

From Narbonne, Raimondin follows the Domitian way. He enters the *"district of the lake of Salces"*. It is a dry place between the lake of Leucate and the mountain. He passes under the castle and sleeps at Perpignan. The next day, by Boulon and Perthus, he comes to Figuières where he dines; and lodges at Gerona then at Barcelona. He takes three days to cross the town, which seems to him very beautiful. He arrives at Montserrat on the fourth day.

At the foot of the mountain is the abbey with the lodge for pilgrims and the village of Colbato that Jean d'Arras, spelling it in the way the French treat foreign names, calls Quillebaston. They stable the horses and give Raimondin a fine room for him and his men.

Raimondin visits the church. Becoming a hermit, he will have his sepulchre in the hall of lamps before the high altar. He climbs to the hermitages. There are seven of them, right against the mountain, one above the other. He looks at the great rocks rearing straight up, and marvels that anyone should dare choose such a place to live. He climbs the steps. When he has ascended about twenty, it is necessary for him to climb as many again on the other side, and thus in turn every twenty steps. In this way he comes to the third hermitage, which is eighty steps higher.

He saw that there was no one in this hermitage for the hermit had a little while earlier passed away. It was the custom that if a hermitage became empty, the hermit next below could come to live there, and thus the place nearest the ground stayed without a hermit if there was no good person moved by devotion to live there. The cause of this permutation was that the first raised up the food for the seven, from which he took his refection for the day, and then he who was the next above pulled up the food, and so on in the same way.

Raimondin was only up as far as the fifth hermitage, which was the St Michael chapel. He looked down and it seemed to him that the church and abbey were like no more than little cells. Raising his eyes, he saw the two other hermitages, but the rock was so steep that he did not attempt the climb.

<hr>

To go off to Cyprus the sons of Mélusine embarked at La Rochelle. Geoffroy disembarked there on his return from Syria. All communications of the Lusignans with the East went via la Rochelle. The Mediterranean ports where crusaders took to the sea, Aigues-Mortes, Marseilles and Venice, were convenient for the speed and security of the voyage, but la Rochelle belonged to the Lusignans; it was their port.

Urian and Guion *"went to replenish themselves"* on the island of Rhodes, where the grandmaster of the Knights of St. John had invited them to call. They stopped for a moment on the way at the island of Colos, which is probably the little island situated before Gorighos in Cilecia, called le Cruq in *Mélusine*. They arrive at Cap Saint-André which is the northwest point of the island of Cyprus and land in a little port under a mount called the Black Mountain. On the mountain is an abbey and a fort.

From Cap Saint-André the Poitevins go, some by land, others by sea, to Limassol, or Limaçon to the French. The port is secure. A harbour precedes it. An enclosure surrounds it, and the entrance is flanked with two towers and enclosed by a chain. From there, the Christians, following the land route, come to Famagousta, the capital of the kingdom, where the king has his castle and the archbishop his see.

The wind blows Guion's fleet toward the coast of the kingdom of

Lesser Armenia. The capital town of the kingdom is le Cruq, with a port defended by a fort and a "baillet", that is to say, a line of palisades fixed to the ground. To land, the Poitevins enter in small vessels. Arriving on land, they mount on horseback and proceed to the town and the fort where the king awaits them, and from where his daughter Florie, from the windows of a high tower, follows them with her eyes as they come from the sea. And when they depart *"in full sail and while she can see them, she does not leave there."* Jean d'Arras only gives le Cruq a rapid glance but it accords with the description of Guillaume de Machaut in *La Prise d'Alexandrie.*

The Lusignan brothers and the Knights of Rhodes attack the Saracens in Syria. Urian, then Geoffroy, enter the port of Limassol by sea. And four days have hardly passed before Urian is in view of the port of Jaffa where the Saracens have gathered their fleet.

After the destruction of their ships, the Saracens retire to the fields before Damascus. Here they invite the Christians to come and fight. Such an invitation cannot be refused. On the way Geoffroy takes Beyrouth, the Saracens flee, some to the port of Tripoli, the others toward Damascus. Geoffroy admires his conquest, the strong town is a marvel, the castle that sits by the sea, the good port and beautiful enclosure garnished with great towers to keep the fleet.

Truce for a hundred years and a day is concluded with the Saracens, and the Christians go to Jerusalem which has not yet been rebuilt after the destruction inflicted by the Roman emperor, Vespasian, when he came to avenge the death of Jesus Christ after the crucifixion, and sold 30 Jews for a denier in memory of the 30 pieces of silver they had paid for the precious body of Jesus Christ. Geoffroy, his brothers, the grandmaster of Rhodes and many Christians stay in devotion at the Holy Sepulchre for three days.

4: Sources for Jean d'Arras

Jean d'Arras describes the sources upon which he has drawn. He has read. He has *"heard tell"*. He has seen, but what he has been able to see is very little in regard to the vast and far countries where the episodes of his romance take place. He has not been very far, he declares. However, there are places that he describes with such great abundance of detail and much conviction – Lusignan, Poitiers, the Meuse region, the journey of Raimondin to Montserrat, Montserrat itself – that it is difficult to believe that he has relied only on books or travellers' reports. He must have seen them with his own eyes.

He must have followed his patrons, Robert de Bar, Jean de Berry, on a few journeys. Perhaps he repeated those of Raimondin in Brittany and in Aragon. He has surely visited the Mélusine country, after the Duke de Berry had taken Niort from the English, along with Maillezais and places named by Rabelais' *Pantagruel* in regard to Mélusine: "Visit Lusignan, Parthenay, Vouvant, Mervant and Pouzanges in Poitou." At the castle of Mervant they showed him the imprint of Mélusine's foot on the stone of the window from which she made her farewell. At Maillezais he stopped before the sculpture of Geoffrey á la Grand Dent.

Books

Jean d'Arras says that he *"has had"* from Jean de Berry and from the Count of Salisbury *"true chronicles"* that they have found for him in *"several other books"* and that he knows old books, grammarians and philosophers. As an author employed by a prince who is brother to the King of France and who loves books, he was able to consult the two finest libraries of the time, that of Charles V and Charles VI at the Louvre, and that of Jean de Berry at the castle of Meun-sur-Yèvre.

The oldest inventory of the library of Jean de Berry is that of 1402, nine years after Jean d'Arras' book. No inventory can tell us certainly the composition (in any case quite variable) of this library at the time Jean d'Arras was writing. But we can discern in the collection of inventories the type of book that the duke preferred, the books that we know gave him pleasure, and that, following the custom of those times, were offered to him as gifts. We find in these inventories all the types of book whose influence can be seen in Jean d'Arras' work – bibles and books of piety, Greek and Latin authors translated into French, Aristotle in the version of Nicolas Oresme, who died in 1382. Titus Livy, Caesar, a treatise on grammar or the seven arts given to the duke by Pope Clement VII in 1387, books on astronomy astrology, divination or magic, authors or travellers telling *"strange and seemingly incredible things, various marvels in different countries"*. Gervaise of Tilbury and Vincent of Beauvais in the French translations of Jean du Vigny, books of chivalry, overseas journeys, Marco Polo, Mandeville, chronicles of France and England in prose and verse, Guillaume de Machaut, Froissart, finally perhaps *"the history, the true history"* that Jean d'Arras cites on every page – *"in this part the history says"* – *"the history tells us"*.

We have not yet discovered this unfailing source. One suspects that Jean d'Arras may have used a quite common device of Middle Age romances. One of the authors of *Maitre Renart* had found "the history" in a secret cupboard. Froissart in his *Méliador* refers to "the book" or "the writing". All the same, it could be that Jean d'Arras has spoken truly and that a lost manuscript will appear one day.

There are several puzzling things about him. He says that he has put his story into prose. This may simply mean that he has not written it in verse, or else that he has turned into prose a primitive version that was in verse.

As for Couldrette, he turns away any praise that his own version might attract to him. He sees no merit in it and says another might have done it differently. But he also adds *"as they relate"*. Yet if there had really been an old poem that was the model for the compositions of Jean d'Arras and Couldrette, it is strange that there remains no record of it – or of its author.

Moreover, it would have had to have been quite widespread, with Jean d'Arras in Paris and Couldrette in the depths of Poitou. And the book that Jean d'Arras mentions would not have been forgotten about a few years after its appearance. Couldrette makes no mention of it.

The story by Jean d'Arras contains a number of precise dates such as are found in annals but which seem misplaced in a work of fantasy. Raimondin's marriage takes place on a Monday. Raimondin and his cousins leave Guéménéguingant on the Tuesday before Pentecost to go to Nantes where the King of the Bretons awaits them. Urian makes a review of troops in Cyprus on Thursday. It is a Thursday when the Lusignan brothers camp before Prague. The deerskin purse containing 30 pieces of silver must be placed under the pommel of the Poitevin Tower on the last day of August.

On the other hand where has Jean d'Arras been able to find that Saintes was formerly known as Linges, and Mareilly-le-Château as Jalensi?

Finally, several of his expressions have a Latin construction *"reigning in great audition, relenqui, escripsi, escrisi, rescripsi, abscondit, spacier, depriant."* These would be the remains of a Latin redaction. It is unlikely that Jean d'Arras would have been its author. The expressions one could cite prove the contrary. It is not admissible that Jean d'Arras was unable to translate into French what he could have written himself in Latin. The story of Lusignan would therefore be the work of another.

The inventory of Jean de Berry mentions two manuscripts which carry this title. They were in Latin and might have been plundered booty. The Duke de Berry could have taken them from the Maubergeon Tower in Poitiers, feudal centre of the country. They would not be other than the two Latin books that Couldrette says had been *"found"* in this tower, translated into French, and from which he could have himself drawn for part of his poem.

Nor do we know what these manuscripts that the Duke de Berry possessed contained or if they said a word about Mélusine.

Suppose that these manuscripts referred to the faery of Lusignan. If we take their title in the strict sense, Jean d'Arras could have borrowed the essential part of his romance, that is to say the adventures of the faery and perhaps those of Geoffroy á la Grand Dent, who was almost as popular as his mother.

But when we examine the reference of Jean d'Arras to the *"history"* we see that it has almost the same extent as the romance. It is cited for the first time at the beginning of the chapter on King Elinas and for the last time at the adventure of the castle of the Hawk. The author invokes its witness not only on the matter of Mélusine and Geoffroy but on the subject of Raimondin in Brittany, his retreat to Spain, and all the adventures of the sons of Lusignan in Luxembourg, Bohemia, Germany, Ireland, Cyprus and Syria. What is more, the expression *"History of Lusignan"* could have had the widest possible sense.

Couldrette, who tells the same adventures as Jean d'Arras, then adds that of Palestine, calls his poem *The Book of Lusignan,* and when the manuscripts of the *Mélusine* of Jean d'Arras have an original title and not one added to, the title is *The Noble History of Lusignan.* Which is the same title as the Latin manuscripts in the library of the Duke de Berry.

The libraries we have mentioned are no doubt not the only ones to furnish books for Jean d'Arras. Among those he used are several not mentioned in the inventories of Charles V or Jean de Berry. The sources that Jean d'Arras derives from the libraries are three kinds:

i)   holy scripture and works of antiquity in Greek and Latin;

ii) books of marvels;

iii) historical chronicles; among which would be romances of chivalry such as the *Histoire du noble et vaillant roi Florimont, fils du noble Mataquas, duc d'Albany* and probably the *Livre de la chevalerie errante*.

i. Ancient books

The Middle Ages included its veneration for sacred books with several books of the ancient world. Plato, Aristotle, Virgil, Seneca were almost regarded as Christians, and cited alongside Solomon and St. Paul. They taught the same truths. At the beginning of the book of Jean d'Arras, David, Aristotle and St. Paul are used to attest the mysteries of the invisible world and are unexpected witnesses of the truth of a tale of faeries.

Many of Mélusine's proverbs are the maxims of Aristotle. Jean d'Arras has given them the vigour and verve of the fine French of his time. "If you start nothing, you get nothing." "You need a beginning and a middle before an end." "A thing well begun and followed through is half done." "Who does not learn his trade in his youth will not make a good workman."

There was in Jean de Berry's library a little book in French "on the rule of kings and princes, called *The Secret of Secrets* written by Aristotle." This was really the work of Pierre de Vernon, who claimed they were taken from the letters of Aristotle to his pupil Alexander the Great. Mélusine must have read it when she gave her children her own instructions to be pious, debonair, humble, to avoid the wicked, to be generous toward a beaten adversary, to render justice without regard to person, to guide their subjects and be loved by them.

Would the ancients also have inspired their battle field speeches by Mélusine's children? *"Victory,"* says Urian, leading his tiny army against 100,000 Saracens, *"does not come to a great mass of people but to good organisation. Alexander, who conquered so many countries, wanted no more than 10,000 soldiers against the world on the battle field. A grain of pepper is better than a ton of wheat."*

Urian exaggerated. Titus Livy, Justin, Arrien, Plutarch, in the only place where they give the number of Alexander's soldiers, speak of rather more than 30,000 foot soldiers and 4000 to 5000 knights. But then Urian was not proposing to conquer Asia!

Caesar marching against Arioviste knew there was fear in his army. He only wanted to keep the brave, and invited the weak and cowardly not to expose themselves to danger. Urian, before the battle against the

Saracens, and Antoine and Renaud at the moment of surprising the camp of the King of Alsace, repeated his words with a Christian nuance and a military severity. *"If there is anyone here without the will to go into battle, without the strength of heart to meet the adventure it pleases God to bring, let him withdraw, because through a single coward a fight can sometimes be lost."* But the "noble hearts" who heard them did not respond like the effeminate captains who had only followed Caesar to enrich themselves.

ii. Books of marvels

The oldest book that Jean d'Arras appears to have known is a bestiary, the *Livre des monstres et des bêtes féroces*, a manuscript of which exists from the 10th century. It is also found in *Mélusine*, a comparison too singular to be seen as the independent thought of two authors. Urian had the biggest ears ever seen on a child. When he was grown they were as big as basket handles.

At the end of the 12th century, Gervaise of Tilbury, and Vincent of Beauvais in the following century, tell a similar story to that of *Mélusine*.

The story of Vincent of Beauvais is very short and takes place in the province of Langres. In the depths of a forest a nobleman meets a beautiful lady dressed in fine clothes. He loves and marries her. She likes to bathe. One day a young girl sees her disporting in the water in the form of a serpent. Denounced to her husband and surprised in the bath, she disappears for ever; her descendants still live.

Jean d'Arras' Gervaise is Gervaise of Tilbury. The author of *Mélusine* names him five times. Without naming him, he takes from him an event in his tale of the appearance of sprites. They sometimes steal children from cradles. Then, translating word for word, he continues: *"And what is more the said Gervaise says that other phantoms appear at night in the form of women with wrinkled faces, of low or small stature, and that they do the housework in houses out of kindness and without doing any harm."*

Jean d'Arras was probably thinking of two stories of Gervaise when he describes the punishment of Mélusine's sisters – on the horrors of Mount Canigou, and on the lady of the Castle of the Hawk. But in Gervaise's *Loisirs imperiaux*, Canigou is the abode of demons, and the lady of the Castle of the Hawk is a demon that words of consecration put to flight – and her castle in situated in Arles and the bishopric of Valence. In *Mélusine* it is a thousand leagues from there, and the devils of Canigou and the Castle are replaced by two good Christians. Palestine watches over the treasure of the future crusade. Mélior opposes the laws of the Church to her great-grandnephew who asks for her in marriage.

These are matters of detail, but the following passage in the *Loisirs imperiaux* is rendered quite freely by Jean d'Arras and sums up the whole of *Mélusine*.

> *"Gervaise also says that faeries appear in the form of very beautiful women and that the men who take them for wives agree to certain conditions that they make them swear to. While these men hold to their agreement they have an abundance of good fortune. As soon as they break it they are deprived of all happiness, and some are changed into serpents on one or several days of the week. Gervaise gives the example of a knight called Roger du Chateau Rousset in the province of Aix, who by chance one evening found a faery in a meadow. She agreed to be his wife. They were together a long time and the knight saw his good fortune grow from day to day. Now it happened one day that he saw her dip her head into the water where she was bathing and become a serpent. She never returned and the knight, little by little, began to lose all his prosperity. What is more, Gervaise says that he believes that it is because of certain misdoings which nobody knows about except God, that God punishes these faeries so marvellously. How such things can be, no human being can know. All these things and many others God has kept secret, but he shows examples in places to people he chooses."*

In Gervaise's original text the knight of the chateau at Rousset is called Raimond. This is the name of Mélusine's husband. Raimond of the Chateau Rousset meets his faery on the banks of the river Laris. Raimond of Poitou finds his at the Fountain of Thirst. Each call the two Raimonds by name, who have never before seen them. The Provençal Raimond, like the Poitevin, loses his wife for having seen her in the bath. The two faeries are banished through violation of the oath made by their husbands, but they return at night to care for their small children. The nurses see them, the husbands never do. They weep for their fault. But they will be nonetheless punished for it, they and their lineage, by the diminution and final loss of their temporal happiness. Definitively, the essentials of the romance of Mélusine are in Gervaise. It is the marshal of the kingdom of Arles who is the first author of *Mélusine*. Jean d'Arras has transported a Provençal legend to Poitiers.

The travels of Marco Polo in the 13th century and those of Mandeville some years before *Mélusine* have a very different function in the work of Jean d'Arras. That of Marco Polo is almost imperceptible. This is because Marco Polo is an exact and truthful traveller. He puts before us what he has seen, to understand what he has understood. Although the preface of the *Devisement du monde* announces that he will find there "the greatest wonders of Greater Armenia, of Persia and of India and many other countries" they are more in the nature of natural wonders, like the fountain of oil in Greater Armenia – and not faeries such as in the Castle of the Hawk.

It is hardly credible that Jean d'Arras had not known Marco Polo in the French edition, read avidly and amply collected in the library of the Duke de Berry. He certainly alludes to the great explorer when he invokes the witness of these *"men voyaging through lands by whom are all things known"*. But the regions that Marco Polo visited were not those of Mélusine and the children of the faery of Lusignan.

However, Jean d'Arras seems to have borrowed from him. He applies to the Germans what Marco Polo said about the Kurds: *"There are bad people in that country who willingly rob travellers."* The great and beautiful palace of the golden king in the noble castle of Cathay, with its great hall entirely gilded, ornamented with beautiful pictures and portraits of all the kings who were formerly in China, singularly resembles the room at the Castle of the Hawk surrounded by painted images of the knights who have slept there.

Mandeville accords more with the author of *Mélusine*. Here everything is false, including the name of the author, supposed to be that of an English knight who died at Liège in 1372. The real author, from Liège, Jean d'Outremeuse, had probably never left his country. The book is only composed of borrowings, of which Vincent de Beauvais is the principle victim. Jean d'Arras treats the plagiarist in much the same way.

Urian and Guion arrive at the island of Cyprus at Cap Saint-André. "In Cyprus," says Outremeuse, "there is the hillock of Sainte-Croix and there is an abbey of black monks, and the cross of Dismas, the good thief." *"They see,"* says Jean d'Arras, *"an abbey on a cape under a mountain that they call the Black Mountain. Here they honoured Monseigneur St. Andrew. And they say that there is to be found there the cross upon which Dismas, the good thief, was crucified when Our Lord, by his holy grace, was put on the holy cross for our redemption."*

Jean d'Arras has also taken the story of the Castle of the Hawk from Mandeville. A long time after the disappearance of Mélusine and the death of her son Guion, first Lusignan king of Little Armenia, a successor to Guion attempted the adventure of the Hawk.

"*The history tells us that there was in Armenia a king who was a young man, in the flower of youth, brimming with strength and vigour, full of will and presumption, brave and violent as a young lion. He learned from some travelling knights that there was a rich castle in Greater Armenia and the lady of the castle was the most beautiful ever seen in the world, and that she had a hawk, and all the conditions of the adventure. The king said that he would certainly go and ask the lady for no other gift than herself.*"

The king, charmed by the marvels of richness that enclosed the castle, by its pictures, where one retraced the story of Elinas, of Pressine and their daughters, triumphed over sleep, despite the seductions of a table deliciously served.

On the morning of the fourth day, Mélior shows herself.

"*The dawn broke and day came, and as the sun rose, the lady of the castle entered. She was so beautiful that the king was ravished by her. She greeted the king and said: 'Sire, you are most welcome here and you have certainly done your duty well. Ask now for any gift you please that conforms to honour and reason, and you shall have it without delay.'*

Then the king, who was completely taken with love for her, said: 'By my faith, madam, I want neither gold or silver, nor inheritance, fine town, castle or city. God be thanked, I am a rich man, I have enough, and it suffices me. But I want to take you for my wife.'

'Foolish idle king,' replied the lady, 'you deceive yourself sir, for that is a gift you cannot have.'

'Grant me the promise of the adventures of his castle,' replied the king, 'for I believe I have truly done my duty.'

'I do not dispute that, but ask for something reasonable, and that you can have. But you cannot have me.'

'By my faith, I want no other gift but you, and no other will I ask for.'

'By God, king,' said the lady, 'if you ask for me again, it will be the worse for you, and for your descendants too, even though it were no fault on their part.'

'All the same,' replied the king, 'I want nothing but you. I did not come here for anything else.'

When the lady saw that he would not change his proposal at all, she became very angry.

'Fool king,' she said, 'you have lost both me and your gift, and have put me in the way of living here forever. Are you not descended from the line of King Guion, the son of Mélusine, my sister? Therefore I am your aunt, and even if I did agree to have you, the Church would not consent.'

And she told him point by point what you have heard in the chapter about King Elinas and also the chapter on the inheritors of Lusignan.

Then she said to him, 'Poor fool, your idling will bring great misadventure. For you and your own will lose land, possessions, honour and heritage until the ninth generation. And by your foolish enterprise the ninth of your line will lose the kingdom you hold, and that king will have the name of a dumb beast. Now go! You can no longer stay!'

Despite the lady's words, the king would not give up. He tried to take the lady by force, but she immediately vanished. Then the king felt blows and punches come down on him from all sides, as hard as rain falling from the sky. He was bruised all over, mistreated, pulled roughly outside the barrier and left there. He never saw anything of those who had thus served him.

As soon and as best as he could, he got up and cursed whoever had brought him the news of this adventure, and the hour he had set out upon it. He came to his men who saw plainly that he did not return as vigorously as he had left them.

'Sire,' they asked, 'are you wounded? Have you been fighting?'

'I am slightly hurt,' replied the king, 'but it was not in combat. I have been severely beaten but I do not know by whom. I saw no one, but I felt his blows very well. And know that I am not revenged, also that I had no combat at all, for he who gave me the first blows made no fight of it but did it for revenge.'

Soon after the king struck his tent, and went as quickly as he could back to his own country, thinking sadly of the words the lady had said. He was much afraid to have lost his good fortune, but he did not tell this to his people. But he told it to his brother when he made his will, who expected to inherit the kingdom from him. The king recommended he govern wisely, for he would have good need to.

After that, the king of whom I speak never had any joy in his heart. He reigned for a very long time, but day by day declined in many ways and in the end he died. His heirs have suffered since then many trials and pestilence, and as it appeared then, so it still appears up to the present time."

iii. Chronicles and histories

Chronicles and histories having resemblances to Jean d'Arras' book run from the beginning of the 13th century to the end of the 14th, but their influence is uncertain as there are commonplaces and formulae used in all works of that period. And Jean d'Arras takes great liberties with the chronicles whilst declaring that he conforms to them. He rarely translates them. But they suggest an idea or episode to him, that he lifts from a text in order to compose a long tale which does not contain much of the chronicle apart from the name of a place, a general idea or some analogy to the facts.

Jean d'Arras owes perhaps nothing to Villehardouin in *La Conquête de Constantinople* but he borrows much from Henri de Valenciennes, Villehardouin's continuator, such as when Urian addresses his men on confronting the Saracens at the battle of Famagousta. We can compare their discourse:

> *"Listen all of you, good sirs,"* says Urian, *"we meet here to defend the faith of Jesus Christ by whom we are redeemed. You know how he suffered a cruel death to save us from the pains of hell. Thus, seeing that he has granted us this grace, we must not jib at the perils that he pleases to put to us – to support the holy sacraments he administered to us for the health of our souls.*
>
> *"Our enemies are more than ten to one against us. But what of that? We are in the right. We must not hesitate. Jesus Christ took on alone the war for our salvation, and all who die in this war will have the glory of Paradise."*

In 1207 the Latins went to relieve the Valaques and the Comains at the battle of Philippopoli, and in Villehardouin their chaplain Philippe exhorted the crusaders.

> *"Lords,"* said the chaplain, *"have confidence in Our Lord who suffered pains and torments for us and who for the sin of Adam and Eve suffered martyrdom because of the piece that they bit from the apple, by which we will all go into the pains and shadows of hell, and by his own death in Jesus Christ we will be redeemed.*
>
> *"If they have more men, what does it matter? They are worth nothing. We know that the soul of whoever dies for God in this struggle, will go in glory to Paradise before God."*

Having spoken, Urian has his banner raised on high and carried by his brother, who is mounted on a great warhorse. He cries to all his forces, *"All who have the devotion to avenge the death of our Creator, to exalt his law and help the King of Cyprus, gather under my banner."*

The chaplain holds the cross of our redemption in his hand during his sermon, and when he has finished displays the cross of Our Lord to redeem his poor people and suffer death and passion.

Jean d'Arras knew Joinville's the *Vie de saint Louis*, for he bound a copy for the king. Would he not have read it as well? For a bookbinder as literate could hardly fail to throw a glance over the contents of the books on which he worked.

An incident of the war in Cyprus recalls the defence of the bridge of Mansourah. Urian and his army are camped on a meadow beside a river crossed by a bridge on the road to Famagousta. The Saracens occupy the other bank and attack the bridge. As at Mansourah, the defenders, at first less numerous, face the enemy, the archers and crossbowmen play havoc with them – "we were all covered with arrows" says Joinville. Urian calls up his reinforcements, the Constable of France and the crossbowmen of the King and the combat ends with the defeat of the Saracens.

Jean d'Arras has read many chronicles of his time. Guillaume de Nangis has been able to inspire him with the story of the surprise of the castle of Sion. The *"high rock"* on which Sion is seated, and which John of Arras locates in Ireland, is Mount Snowdon between England and Wales. It is the *"precipitous mountain"* that in 1276 Llewellyn, Prince of Wales, fortified to resist the King of England, Edward I.

It was learnt, says Guillaume de Nangis, that the King had arrested his fiancée, Eleanore de Montfort. He immediately took up arms. The King invaded his country. Llewellyn locked himself up in the fort of Sion. The siege lasted a long time. It was winter, many English perished in the swamps and defiles. But the King would not give up his enterprise and obliged the Prince to surrender, and the war ended, for the time being, with the marriage of Llewellyn and Eleanore, celebrated in the King's presence. The main theme in the history of Guillaume de Nangis and in the fable of Jean d'Arras is the revolt of a vassal against his suzerain, followed by punishment.

Yet another historical event gave Jean d'Arras the idea of his siege of Porrentruy. Renaud of Burgundy, Count of Montbéliard, had captured the town from its legitimate lord, the Bishop of Basle, Henri d'Isny. He claimed the help of the emperor, Rodolphe de Habsbourg, and in 1283 the Emperor laid the place to siege, took it after six weeks and returned it to the bishop.

Three Alsatian chronicles mention this war: the *Annales Colmarienses* (1211-1305), the *Gesta Rodulfi et Alberti regum Romanorum* of Godfrey d'Ensmingen (1273-1308) and the *Chronicon d'Albert de Strasbourg*.

Albert is the annalist of the two first emperors of the house of the Count/Dukes of Luxembourg, Henri VII and Charles IV. His book finishes with the reign of this emperor in 1378. The father of Charles

IV was Jean l'Aveugle. Jean de Berry and Josse de Luxembourg were the emperor's nephews. Thus it seems that Jean d'Arras had before him the chronicle of Albert de Strasbourg, provided by his patrons. It is yet more probable in that the chronicler relates the glorious death of the ancestor of the Marquis of Moravia and the Duke of Berry.

To other lines relevant to the siege of Porrentruy, Jean d'Arras perhaps joined a memory of an attempt the Count Egon of Furstemburg made in 1366, to take by surprise the town of Fribourg en Brisgau, the retreat of the burghers of Fribourg, soundly beaten at Endingen by Egon in league with several of his vassals on the marches of the Rhine, and massacred in hundreds in the combat and in their flight as far as the port of Brisac. He thus imagined an adventure which should please his distinguished patrons of Luxembourg and France – a King of Bohemia found honour there, as their ancestor had at Crecy forty-six years earlier.

Jean d'Arras is the contemporary of Guillaume de Machaut and of Froissart. Each of them gave service to a prince who dictated in some way his works to him. The Duke of Berry was, for the author of *Mélusine,* what King John of Bohemia had been for Machaut, and Wenceslas of Luxembourg for Froissart. Machaut composed the *Jugement de Jean de Boheme* for the King of Bohemia. Froissart wrote the romance of *Méliador* for Wenceslas. And Jean d'Arras wrote his book by order of his patron.

Another point in common is the place that the house of Luxembourg has in the lives of these writers. Froissart in his chronicles extends himself on the events which reflect on this house, and Jean d'Arras glorifies it by the tale of the exploits of Antoine and Renaud of Lusignan, one a Duke of Luxembourg and the other King of Bohemia.

Sharing the same clientele the three authors cannot have been unknown to each other. Machaut's book *La Prise d'Alexandre* was the biography of Pierre I of Lusignan, called the Valiant, *"the good king of Cyprus"* of Jean d'Arras. Perhaps *"those of Sassenage of Dauphiné"* owed it to him to be placed by John of Arras among the descendants of Mélusine, in memory of the lord of Sassenage, a war companion of Pierre I.

Froissart, like the author of *Mélusine*, liked the marvellous. His romance of *Méliador* is a faery tale and his chronicles contain tales of magic, enchantment, stories of revenants, and the famous legend of Orthon, familiar spirit of the lord of Coarasse. Like the Lusignan faery, Orthon is a beneficent spirit but also has his secret. Whoever transgresses it has no more right to his protection. The moral of the two stories is the same, curiosity punished and eyes opened after the sin.

The work of Froissart and of Jean d'Arras have so many resemblances that there is no doubt that the romancer, who imitates his formulae, was inspired by the tales of the chronicler. Several passages of the two authors can be identified that are similar.

[Here Louis Stouff quotes at length eighteen parallel passages from the two writers].

Legends

"To give our history the colour of truth we leave the authors for now," says Jean d'Arras, *"to tell what we have heard, and hear to this day, of things have been seen in the country of Poitou and elsewhere. These proofs are well known, without speaking of what the true chronicles and history books tell us. A person who never left their own country might not believe certain things that happened more than a hundred leagues away. They would find them very strange and say they cannot be. But those who haunt diverse lands and nations recognise the truth."*

If Jean d'Arras has not *"haunted"* many countries, he is informed of that which has been told of the story of Pressine and her daughters. John de Berry spoke to him of appearances of the lady of Lusignan. The King of Aragon and *"several others"* in his kingdom told him that Palestine showed herself on the mountain of Canigou.

The legends of Mélusine and her children are many. They abound in Poitou. "You find there," says Rabelais, "old witnesses of renown and good repute."

They have been carried far. *"Our story,"* says Jean d'Arras, *"is known in several places"*. Varied in detail, they have a common base.

Mélusine is a water faery. She appeared to Raimondin at the Fountain of Thirst. She caused a stream to run from the field at Lusignan at the moment the *"men"* sent by the Count of Poitiers finished measuring the land for Raimondin. Withdrawn to the castle of Breceleuf in the Autise valley under the Roc Cervelle, they see a little spring flow in a low hall of the castle, and a fountain springs intermittently from the rock. Three springs rise from the ground at the foot of the Baritaud Rocks near Châtonnay en Vendée at the moment she is thirsty there. In

Dauphiné she bathes in the cisterns of Sassenage and she has a spring at Montelieu. Everywhere they know her predilection for fountains. At Vouvant, in the 17th century, they solemnised her memory by building a monumental fountain. At Porrentruy, town of the German empire, a century before, they sculpted her image on a beautiful fountain that, since the change of sovereignty, has been called the Swiss Fountain.

The feasts given by Mélusine, *"the fine wines, foreign and others",* the hypocras she has served *"widely"* are worthy of the kitchens and cellars of a faery. The dinner at her marriage recalls the wedding feasts of Riquet á la Houppe. The dishes and the servants seem to come from the ground by virtue of a magic word and the guests marvel at the magnificence of the banquet and diligence of the servers. In the 17th century they still spoke of it. Corneille knew what he meant when he wrote the lines: "Urgande and Mélusine never spontaneously furnished their cuisine better, you go beyond their enchantment."

Another thing struck people's imagination and excited their curiosity – the ancient monuments they had before their eyes, in the midst of where they lived. It was natural to ask who built them. Mélusine, they often replied. She was for them the great mover of earth and stones. She flew through the air, building materials in her muslin apron and water in her mouth.

A large number of tumuli bear her name. Her apron tore, the materials fell out. Thus were formed the earthworks at Puyzay near Lusignan, and the mound at Montail called Mélusine's Apron. She let fall the three stones at Vouillé. The biggest was in her apron, the two others under her arms. She dropped, near Poitiers, on the heights of the suburb of Saint-Saturnin, the stones that ranged themselves to form the dolmen of the Raised Stone. It was she who planted the Raised Stone in the plain of Denans and the menhirs called the Baritaud Rocks.

Mélusine had rebuilt the Roman ruins at Saintes. The Roman roads of Poitou were her work. She had dug, on the way from Niort to Parthenay, the Fossé de la Mère Lusine. She had built the amphitheatres at Poitiers, even larger than that at Nïmes, the aquaduct that brought to the town the waters of Fontenay-le-Comte and the walls of the city. She was short of time again when the pick of the Poitiers workers struck some remains of a Roman construction – they accused Mother Lusine of obstructing their work.

On disappearing, she left a multitude of abbeys, priories and churches *"where they said prayers and masses and sang psalms, and kept vigils and anniversaries at her intention"*. She never ceased founding *"noble places in Poitou, Guyenne, Brittany and Gascony."* The *Castrum Julii*, like other strong points of the Romans, became a seigneural castle. But, according to the romance, it was Mélusine who had constructed the strong towers and thick walls and given it the name of the Châtel Aiglon. She built the castle and town of Melle, Vouvant (of which the keep, built in the 13th century, is still called the Mélusine Tower), Mervent, the town and tower of Saint-Maixent, the castle and town of Parthenay *"so strong and beautiful that it had no parallel"*, founded the castle at La Rochelle, and the towers that guard the sea and commence a part of the town. Saintes is no more in the romance, as in local legend, a Roman city rebuilt by Mélusine, it is one of the new towns. She built Pons and Mirebeau in Poitou, Talmont in Talmondois, and a number of other towns and fortresses. The fateful message that recalled her to her husband found her in Niort, where she wanted to build a fort. She had hardly finished the high twin towers, built in fact in the 12th century by the Counts of Anjou.

According to Jean d'Arras the legend adds the Tower of Guyenne at Béruges, the Salbert Castle at Niort, the castles of Exoudon and the Soubise Park in Poitou, Marmande in Touraine, Montelier and Sassanege in Dauphiné, and even the castle of the King of the Bretons in Sucinio.

Among the military defence works then in use was one that they used to surprise the rear of an enemy occupied in attacking a fortress, and also to serve as refuge. Underground tunnels, coming from the interior of the place, debouching in the country in the middle of bushes or thick copses to hide their exit. Mélusine built a tunnel six leagues long from Lusignan to the arenas of Poitiers. She dug a wide tunnel from the castle of Sucinio to the Trinitarian convent of Sarzeau. She journeyed there, sometimes in a boat, sometimes in an ox cart. It needed but a blow of her heel to open the ground. It was thus that, fleeing from St. Louis, who had chased her from Fontenay and from Vouvant, that she made an underground way that led to the Fumerie de Jazeneur where she returned to the light, sixteen leagues from Vouvant.

Mélusine only worked at night. She built by moonlight the towers and walls of the castle Salbart. She built in one night the chapel and abbey of Valence in Poitou. One night was enough to raise the seven towers of Vouvant. She took three to build the church at Parthenay.

Surprised by dawn or by an observer, Mélusine immediately suspended her flight, stopped work and made off. The rising sun caused the fall of stones at Vouillé which she had intended to complete the castle Salbart. There always lacked a stone at the chapel of Menigoute. Mélusine was going to place it when cock crow put her to flight. They say the same thing about the church at Parthenay. The masons could never fill the gap that Mélusine had left. The stone they put there always fell.

The faery escaped at a gallop on her horse and the imprint of the shoes of her mount could be seen on the last stones she had placed. They were building the castle of Ponzanges when in the morning the workers were astonished to find their work more advanced than where they had left it the evening before. One of them hid in the bushes. Mélusine came at midnight and started to build but saw the reckless one.

The works of Mélusine were often not completed. A caprice of the faery sometimes produced the same effect as the dawn of day or an intruder. The masons hired to build the church of Verruye gave up the work. Mélusine built it herself. It only lacked the keystone of a window of the bell tower when the faery, without anyone knowing why, abandoned it. The masons placed the stone several times, uselessly. It fell, taking with it all they had done since Mélusine's departure. It was necessary to forget the window. There was in the works of Mélusine, as in her sons, something that lacked completeness.

It was not enough for Mélusine, without relaxing, to build churches, towns and castles herself. She interested herself in other works that were done in her domains. She wanted to be their architect. A miniature represents her giving her orders to the stone cutters and masons. She supervised the work, and those that displeased her were never completed. A castle was in ruins on the way from Parthenay to Poitiers, near Vouillé. They never managed to rebuild it. Mélusine did not wish it. At Clussais near Melle, at Verruye, at Saint-Paul in Poitou, sometimes showing her opposition, sometimes giving her aid, she left the inhabitants to decide the position of their future church. But the work they did always had to be restarted. They did not find it there in the morning. She transported the sections of walls each night to a place she preferred.

Mélusine followed the destiny of her creations across the centuries. She was their providence and their guardian. *"This illustrious fortress,"* says Jean d'Arras, speaking of Lusignan, *"has gone from hand to hand and has become by law and conquest by sword that of my dear and redoubtable lord. And it is held for certain that ever since it was founded, it would never stay more than 30 years in the possession of any man who was not a direct descendant of Raimondin and Mélusine."* This Mélusine had wanted. The goods must remain in these families.

She is sorry when the castles are in danger of destruction. St. Louis, at war with the English, took the town of Béruge and intended to demolish it. But he heard a cry of sorrow, thought it was Mélusine and ordered, "Friends, no more destruction!" She also uttered great cries when the Duke of Montpensier ordered the demolition of Lusignan.

But she did not hesitate to destroy her works, or to abandon them to ruin, if she was unhappy about them, or if they fell into unworthy hands. In her anger against trouble at Pouzanges, she cried "Pouzanges, Tiffauge, Mervent, Chateaumur and Vouvant, each year, I swear, you will lose a stone!"

Mélusine, like St. Louis, was a friend of the poor. When the news of her departure became known in the country all the people sobbed and cried and regretted the loss of their lady. She learned that the Lord of Châtelaillon was hard on the poor. She turned up at his castle one stormy night in the appearance of a poor woman. He repulsed her. She cursed the castle, broke up the stones of the cliff on which it stood, prayed the ocean to continue the work of destruction, and as she added her efforts to those of the sea, the fortress fell stone by stone. She carried the stones to the abbey of Maillezais. But sometimes fatigue cased her to drop them and they became dolmens. Today the ocean has submerged the work of the Romans and those of Mélusine. Only the spring tides allow us to see the ruins of the seven towers that could still be seen at the beginning of the 18th century off the headland of Châtelaillon.

The most widespread legend is that of reappearances of Mélusine. Nowadays the traditions have disappeared but not long ago they told that when death was about to strike the lord of one of the old castles Mélusine would be seen in the midst of the ruins. In Franche-Comté she appeared to the Châtellaine and on the Keep of Vadans, former possession of the Poitiers family. The legend is the same in Bohemia and in Luxembourg where two sons of Mélusine reigned, and in Ireland, where Geoffroy á la Grand Dent made war against the rebel vassals of his father. In every place where Mélusine came as a messenger of Death, she made herself heard with lamentable cries. Her cries frightened those who passed during the night around Brécelay and the Roc Cervelle. "To make the cries of Mélusine" is a popular saying as common in the Jura mountains as in Poitou and Touraine.

When separating from her husband, Mélusine twice told him that he would never see her again *"as a woman, in the feminine form."* But she returned every evening to visit Raimonnet and Thierry. She held them to the fire and the nurses dared not say a word. She continued to make herself seen on the days of sorrow fixed by Pressine. She appeared for a long time at Lusignan. *"It is true,"* says Jean d'Arras, *"that there is a place at Lusignan near the wells, where in times past they fed poultry. She has been seen there several times by a man still living in the fortress, called Godart. She never did him any harm, and he swears this by God and upon his soul."*

Jean d'Arras cites other witnesses. The Duke de Berry had heard from certain French or English captains, Perceval of Cologne in Poitou, Yvain of Wales, and Creswell, who had been his prisoner, that the adventures of war had brought them to meet her.

Perceval was on the English side. He had fought under Pembroke, Chandos, and the Prince of Wales. He was captain of Thouars in 1372, when Du Guesclin besieged the fortress, and it was no doubt after the surrender of the place that the Duke de Berry spoke with him. Perceval had served elsewhere under Pierre I of Lusignan, and was both brave and intelligent. He showed this at the siege of Alexandria where he took the Customs House, and he was the third to land at the attack on Tripoli. His master had every confidence in him and asked his advice and charged him to organise the single combat that he proposed to undertake against Florimont de Lasparre. This combat would have taken place at Paris in 1367, where Perceval was well known, from whence he had come three years before.

"And before that," Jean d'Arras continues, *"there was a Poitevin knight called Perceval of Cologne, who was chamberlain to the good King of Cyprus. This knight swore many times to my lord that when he was in Cyprus the king had said to him 'Perceval, I am very fearful.' 'Why, sire?' 'By my faith,' said the king, 'because I have seen the serpent of Lusignan, who showed herself to me. I am much afraid she foretells a loss to me or to my son Perrin, for she appears when one of the heirs of Lusignan is about to die.' And within three days came the hard events that everyone knows and pities, for the king died, as he said, by great treason."* On 17th January 1369 the king had been assassinated in his bed by his barons.

The witness of Yvain de Galles, and of Creswell, refers to the siege of Lusignan, then an English fortress. The Duke de Berry had ordered the siege. The captain who defended Lusignan was the Englishman Creswell, whom Jean d'Arras calls Cersuelle and the chronicle of Du Guesclin, Cressonnelle. Alain de Beanmont the young conducted the siege. An illustrious war companion of the Duke de Berry came there. Yvain de Galles, the true Prince of Wales, son of Aimoin whom the King of England, Edward III, had killed after seizing his Principality. Yvain put himself in the service of France, fought the English with great ardour, spurred by his resentment, and was charged by Charles V with high commands. After many victories he was assassinated in 1378 on the eve of storming the English at Mortagne-sur-Mer in Poitou, that he was besieging. *"Item:"* says Jean d'Arras, *"Yvain de Galles swore to my lord that he had twice seen the serpent on the walls of Lusignan three days before the fortress surrendered."*

Mélusine appeared at the same time to the English captain.

"At the time the fortress was besieged by my lord, Cersuelle was spending the night with a woman called Alixandre, a native of Sancerre, whom he kept as a concubine. He saw a marvellous serpent appear before his bed. He did not know how it had entered, for all the doors were locked and barred. There was a great fire in the hearth. The serpent came and went, beating with its tail all around the bed and at their feet, but without hurting them. Cersuelle said to my lord that he had never been so frightened in all his life, and that he drew the sword that he kept by his bed. The woman who was with him said 'What, Cersuelle, are you, who have been in so many great places, afraid of this serpent? It is the lady of this fortress who first built it. She has only come to show you that you are about to lose it.' Some time later, the serpent changed into the form of a tall and upright woman, dressed in a rough brown robe belted under the breast, and wearing a white old fashioned form of headdress. She went and sat on a seat before the fire. At one point, for an hour, she had her face turned toward the bed, and it very much seemed she had been very beautiful – then she would turn her face back to the fire, and there was hardly any time when she did not make some kind of movement. She stayed like this until an hour before dawn. Then she changed back into a serpent as before. She returned to the foot of the bed, then disappeared so suddenly that Cersuelle did not see her departure or know how she had done so. And I have heard said to my lord and to many others that Cersuelle swore this by all the oaths that a gentleman could make, and after he had seen it, the fortress was surrendered to my lord, to whom God give joy by his grace and to all his descendants."

From all these tales is it not necessary to conclude that there is perhaps no faery whose renown has been so durable and also extended as Mélusine, who has left a brilliant memory in which most touching things have been told? "A lady," says Brantôme, "of the most noble lineage, in virtue, in mind, in magnificence, and in whose time there were even others about whom there are such tales. And even if they are fables can one not also say that all was good and beautiful about her; and if they wish to accept her as true, was a true sun of her times, from whom are descended brave lords, princes, kings and captains, bearing the name of Lusignan, of which the histories are full."

Among these fables is it possible to distinguish between those that were told before Jean d'Arras had written his book, and those which owe their existence to the success of his romance? And of these, how much have they sometimes been elaborated?

Brittany claims to possess the tomb of Mélusine, who would never have been there, and also that of Raimondin, whom Jean d'Arras buries at Montserrat. Mélusine, they say, founded the Trinitarian convent at Sarzeau (actually founded in 1341) and the married couple had chosen their sepulchre at the religious house, where they rest under a great stone.

Marcilly-le-Chateau, mentioned in a tragic scene in the romance, was, according to the people of the country, Mélusine's usual residence when she visited there. "Here she did her marvels and changed her form." They show on the front of the parish church an old sculpted stone representing a woman suckling serpents. The woman was Mélusine; the serpents her children, and she gave them suck of "the wisdom of the serpent."

The legends of Luxembourg and of Lutzelbourg are almost the same.

Sigefroy, first Count of Luxembourg, married a woman named Mélusine. He promised never to try to see her on a Saturday. Overcome by curiosity, he looked through a hole in the door lock. Mélusine, in a cellar, was combing her hair. Her body ended in the tail of a fish. Her husband's cry made her flee but she returned to the castle. They saw her coming out of the wells or on the round tower which bore her name. In some neighbouring houses she came and knocked three times on the night before a death.

If the legend of Lutzelbourg does not name Mélusine the events of the tale show her well enough. Count Robert de Lutzelbourg, out hunting, met the faery near a fountain. She agreed to marry him and declared she was of as high birth as him and imposed two conditions. The Count must not seek to know her origins. This is not in the romance. Raimondin married Mélusine without wanting to know of what lineage she was, and replied brusquely to his cousin the Count of Poitiers, who was more curious than he: *"Sir, as it suits me, it should also suit you. I do not take a wife for you, as far as I know, I take her for me. I will bear the sorrow or the joy as God pleases."* The other condition is that of the secret of the Saturday. The Count of Lutzelbourg will prepare an apartment where she will confine herself, and no one, not even her husband, may seek for her on that day.

The Count of Lutzelbourg, as with Raimondin, became the happiest of husbands and fathers. The goodness of the Countess made her loved by all her subjects. But if Raimondin had an evil brother, the Count had two. Their insinuations have the foreseen effect. The Count doubts the faithfulness of his wife and surprises her in the state we know. The next day the Countess, cold and severe, reproaches him for his lack of faith, and explains to him the transformation he has witnessed. Her mother, when pregnant with her, offended an old hermit, who put a curse on the child when it was born. The indiscretion of her husband prolonged the punishment of his unhappy wife for centuries. "Farewell Robert," she ends, "always love your children." She flies from a window, but is seen at certain times in a form of transparent whiteness.

The most well known legends are those which make the Sassenages the second family of Mélusine and the Sassenage lands her new country. The Sassenage family is one of the oldest and most illustrious of Dauphiné and of France. The lordship of Sassenage extends to all the mountains of Villars de Lans that with their formidable peaks dominate and overshadow the valleys of the Drac and the Isère. The deep defiles of the Engins and of the Bourne cross them from side to side. They enclose, at their summit, like a fortress, the dark forests, and the meadows of Corençon, Lans, Méaudre, Autrans and the Éconges. At the bottom of the gulfs crouches a happy countryside, the forests and lakes interspersed with high vineyards of the Royans, and at the rising Sassenage to the outflow of the Furon. Their castle is suspended over the gorge of the torrent before the grottoes and the cisterns – the seven wonders of the Dauphiné.

The lordship of Sassenage was for long an 'alleu', the lords possessing it outright. In 1297 they turned it from many lands with a multitude of owners of "alleux" and converted their domains into a fief, and avowing as their feudal lord the Dauphin of Viennois. Their land thus gained in honour and was the second barony of the Dauphiné.

The inhabitants of the Sassenage lands were persuaded that their lords were of the blood of Mélusine and that the faery took refuge in the grottoes of Sassenage. They cited as proof that cistern where she lived, and called the stone table where she ate Mélusine's table. But they did not agree in their stories.

Some told a legend put into Latin verse by Salvaing de Boissieu with many amplifications and embellishments. Mélusine had left Lusignan annoyed with her husband and came to sulk eternally in the caverns of Sassenage. However, she wanted to recompense the hospitality of the labourers who surrounded her refuge. Each year, on the day when black beans were introduced to dishes composed of herbs, garlic, cheese and wine at the custom of electing a king, she would announce the success of their labours by the quantity, more or less great, of the waters that poured from the vats. One day, her grand-nephews abandoned the lands of Lusignan to reign far away on the banks of the Isère.

A second legend is the repetition of the story of Mélusine at Lusignan. Mélusine, weary of being confined in damp caverns, crossed the Furon to marry the lord of Sassenage. They had a son who perpetuated the line of lords of the place but one Saturday her husband surprised her making her ordained penitence, and with a bound she threw herself from the great tower of the castle into the grottoes. They searched for her in vain. She was never seen again.

These tales add awkwardly to the story of Mélusine. They are fastidious, forced, *"difficult to believe"* says Jean d'Arras. But they show how lively an impression had been made by the story of Mélusine. They wanted to belong to this charming faery, even in disfiguring or skimming over her reputation. For in the peevish Mélusine of Sassenage we do not recognise the loving wife of the popular tales and the romance, leaving her husband tenderly weeping, pardoning him, assuring him that as long as he lives she will have *"recreation in him"*, but having pity for him because he will no longer see her. Then faithful to the memory of Raimondin over the centuries after his death, showing briefly in her widow's dress, a "very wise and most virtuous lady" whose memory moved Brantôme.

5: Historical Connections with the Romance

It is now a question of seeing if the Mélusine legend has any historical basis; if the characters of the romance really lived, and if in the events it contains there are any which really happened in which the Lusignans were concerned. And if among the domains attributed to Mélusine and her descendants there are any which belong to the Lusignans.

According to the romance, the Lusignans did not originate in Poitou. The family is Scottish and Breton. Mélusine is a daughter of Elinas (king of "*wild Albany*") and of Pressine, faery of a Scottish forest. Raimondin comes from a great family of Brute Bretagne, that of Léon. Lusignans established in the eastern Mediterranean did not forget their origins, as a son of Urian received the name of Hervé "in regard for his grandfather."

The Léons have a great estate in Brittany. Alain, Hervé's brother, is lord of Guéménéguingant. Hervé was seneschal to the King of the Bretons and had from the king a fief in the Léon territory, of Penthièvre, Guérande and other lands. "*I do not want you to lose the heritage due to you from your ancestors in Brittany,*" says Mélusine to her husband, dispossessed by Josselin du Pont de Léon. "*All that land must come to you.*"

So much for the fiction. Nothing in history attaches the Lusignans to Scotland. But in the 13th century they had great lands in Brittany, and as in the romance, they had been deprived of them. Hugues XI had become Count of Penthièvre by his marriage to Yolande de Dreux, daughter of Pierre Mauclerc, Duke of Brittany. She died in 1272 and her brother, Jean I, Duke of Brittany, put his hand on the country.

Equally, the domain of Porhoët, otherwise called the country beyond the forest of Brécilien, whose chief town was Josselin, belonged to the Lusignans. It was amongst a number that Philippe le Bel commandeered, and if they pleaded their cause before the parliamentary court of the King of France, it was without the success that Raimondin had at the court of the King of the Bretons.

In truth, the Lusignan family was Poitevin. The name of the faery of Lusignan is not Mélusine. Jean d'Arras always said *Mélusigne*, Couldrette *Mellusigne*, and the people *Merlusine* or *Mère Lusine*. If Lusignan derives from the Gallo-Roman *Liciniacum*, Mère Lusine could be the divinity of the Fountaine de Soif, the *Mater Lucinia*.

As far as we can penetrate the past, we find the Lusignans firmly installed in Poitou. Lusignan is, so to say, their lordly mansion. At all times the family to which it gives its name held it in fief from the Count of Poitiers. The son of Hugues le Veneur (the Hunter), Hugues II le Bel Aimé, the second lord of Lusignan, who lived in the 9th century, built the castle. The Lusignan lands remained in the family until 1308. That year Guy, son of Hugues XII, died without issue, and with him the Lusignan line ended in France.

In 1271 Philippe le Hardi had put his hand on the County of Poitiers, and thus the lords of Lusignan were for a long time vassals of the King of France. Guy had appointed his sister Yolande, wife of Elie Rudel, lord of Pons, as his universal legatee. But Philippe le Bel obtained another testament that annexed Lusignan to the crown. The lordship of Lusignan henceforth followed the vicissitudes through which the county of Poitiers passed. Given by Charles V to Jean de Berry in 1357, surrendered to England by the treaty of Brétigny in 1360, ceded to Jean de Berry in 1369, charged to win it back. None of these rapidly successive masters were *"issue of Raimondin and Mélusine through mother or father."* The will of Mélusine was finished.

From the naming of the domains that the romancer somewhat prodigiously gives to Lusignan, it is necessary to remove those of Guyenne and Gascony and most of the possessions of Aunis and Saintonge. They never held la Rochelle, nor Saintes nor Châtelaillon. And among their possessions in Poitou one must delete Niort, Saint-Maixent, Melle, Talmont, Pons and Mirebeau.

There remain Parthenay, Vouvant and Mervant. Mélusine bequeaths in her will that her son Thierry should be its lord, and in this there is some historical relevance. At the time of Jean d'Arras the house of Parthenay-Larchevêque possessed these three lordships.

Although it may be well to assume that the heroes of a romance exist only in the mind of its author, some have tried over several centuries to discover historical characters in the book of Jean d'Arras. Mélusine, Raimondin, and above all Geoffroy á la Grand Dent, have been the object of these attempts.

If one believes de la Mure, Raimondin is Raimond Count of Forez, third son of and successor to Guy II. Raimond married a certain Marie of Lusignan, and she is none other than Mélusine. The father of this Mélusine is Hugues le Brun, her mother Sarrasine. In fact one meets these two names in a series of Lusignans, but they do not correspond to the author's suppositions of the claimed Mélusine. What is more, it is not enough for Hugues le Brun to be lord of Lusignan, he is also Elinas, the King of Albany! Nor does he reign in Scotland – his kingdom is Albania on the Adriatic, a neighbouring country to his wife's lands. These reveries put in doubt the historiography of Forez.

The motives for such fantasies have long disappeared, but the same questions continue to be discussed. And the first, was there ever a Mélusine?

Some genealogists have hesitated between three great ladies of the 12th and 13th centuries who have some link to the house of Lusignan.

Two of them were called Mélisende (*Milesendis, Milisendis* in Latin). Mélusine and Mélisende are the same name, they claim.

The oldest was daughter of Baudouin du Bourg, third king of Jerusalem, and wife of Foulque d'Anjou, fourth king of Jerusalem (1131-42). Their two granddaughters, Sibylle and Isabelle, married two Lusignans. One Guy, ninth king of Jerusalem and first king of Cyprus, the other Amaury or Aimery, second king of Cyprus.[12]

The second Mélisende was the daughter of Amaury and Isabelle, and thus great granddaughter of the first. She married Boémond IV le Borgne, Prince of Antioch.

But there is some distance between Mélisende and Mélusine. The main action of the story of Mélusine took place in Poitou; the two Mélisendes were princesses in the east. The first was not even a Lusignan and nothing points to them for this excess of honour.

The third possibility is Eustache Chabot, only daughter of Thibaut Chabot II, lord of Vouvant, Rocheservière and other places, married to Geoffroy I, lord of Lusignan, who was a valiant warrior in the third crusade. She died in 1229. Her only claim is to be the mother of a son of Mélusine, Geoffroy á la Grand-Dent.

The descendants of Mélusine and the events of their life are not, for all that, completely imaginary.

The name of Geoffroy, like that of Hugues, appears to have been hereditary in the Lusignan family. Several lords of Lusignan had it and furnished diverse romances of chivalry in the 12th and 13th centuries with the character of a Geoffroy of Lusignan, *"adroit, valiant, vigorous*

---

12 In fact Guy was never king of Cyprus, but its governor. It did not become a kingdom until the time of his brother Aimery. Similarly, strictly speaking Guy was eighth, not ninth king of Jerusalem, as its first ruler, Godfrey de Bouillon, did not accept the title of king. G.K.

knight", redoubtable at Bordelais in the song of Garin le Loherain, indefatigable jouster in the passages of arms represented in the romances of *Flamenca* and the *Châtelain de Coucy*. But these romances say nothing of the tooth of a Geoffroy of Lusignan. It came to him much later.

The chronicles agree with Jean d'Arras in recognising in Geoffroy not only the tooth but the temperament of a boar. He is blasphemy incarnate. "There is no God" was the war cry of the historical Geoffroy, *"By God's tooth!"* the oath of the fabulous Geoffroy. Both had a distrust and hatred of monks, whatever colour their robe. The Geoffroy of the charters and annals persecuted with equal brutality the Benedictines of Maillezais and the Cistercians of Notre-Dame de l'Absie en Gastine in Upper Poitou.

At Maillezais he is the typical model of a false oath, carrying desolation to a house he had been charged to protect, the most cruel and most frequent abuses of that time. The whole Church suffered, it was said, from the insolence of its "protectors".

After Geoffroy ruined the establishments and lordships of Maillezais he was excommunicated.

The romance shows him even more culpable, burning down the abbey with all its monks, including his brother Fromont, and lighting the fire with one of the church lamps. Seized with remorse as sudden as his anger, he went to the Pope to seek absolution for his crimes. He obtained it, according to the romance, at Rome, on condition that he rebuild the abbey. But Jean d'Arras speaks of a Pope Benoït, and Couldrette of a Pope Léon. The last popes with these names were Léon IX, who died in 1054, and Benoït XII, who died in 1342. In reality it was Gregory IX from whom Geoffroy received his pardon, at Spoleto, on 15th July 1233, including the renunciation of his rights of protection.

In 1242 St. Louis was at war with Hugues X, Lord of Lusignan, Count of la Marche. Geoffroy was the count's cousin and held from him in fief Vouvant, Fontenay, Soubise and other domains. He took up arms against the king of France, but in April of the following year he transferred homage for his fiefs to Count Alphonse of Poitiers, thus making himself a vassal of his enemy's brother. He died before 1250 and left no children. On this point history and fiction agree. His tomb is in the church at Maillezais, says Couldrette, and his statue at the door of the church. Jean d'Arras says that he had it made after rebuilding the abbey, and of its grandeur and the nearest that they could to make a resemblance. Rabelais has described it in his fashion and states that they still possessed the head.

History does not know any other son of Mélusine. It knows nothing of Urian, King of Cyprus, Guion, King of Armenia, Renaud, King of Bohemia, Antoine, Duke of Luxembourg, Eudes or Odon, Count of la Marche, Raimonnet, Count of Forez, Thierry, Lord of Parthenay, Fromont, monk of Maillezais.

All the same, the first king of Armenia of the House of Lusignan was called Guy, but he reigned a century and a half later than the first king of Cyprus of this house. There was also perhaps a Raimond, brother of Geoffroy á la Grand Dent, a monk at Maillezais. This would be the Fromont of the romance. Finally, the county of la Marche truly belonged to the Lusignans. The romance founds their title on the marriage of Eudes, son of Mélusine, with the daughter of the last Count. History says that Hugues IX claimed to have the right of la Marche and profited from the death of the King of England, Richard Coeur de Lion, to take over the county. His descendants kept it until the death of Guy. The county then returned to the crown following the negotiations of Philippe le Bel with Yolande, sister of the deceased.

The romance attributes numerous posterity to the sons of Mélusine: the kings of Cyprus, Armenia, Bohemia, the dukes of Luxembourg, the counts of la Marche, the lords of Parthenay, the Pembrokes in England, the Sassenages in Dauphiné, the la Rochefoucaulds, the Cabrières in Aragon, and if one of the best manuscripts of *Mélusine* is not wrong, the King of Aragon himself, because he is a Cabrière. The Cadillacs, who would be the Quercys according to the English version of *Mélusine*, written about the year 1500, and equally descendants of the brothers of Lusignan. This version adds to the nomenclature the Château-Renauds, placing them in the first rank.

The Lusignans of Cyprus and of Armenia have left the most noble memories in history. Guy, the first king of Cyprus,[13] was son of Hugues VIII le Brun, eighth lord of Lusignan. The kingdom lasted until 1473.

The glory of this dynasty was Pierre le Valient. Facing the Saracens as the single champion of Christianity, the others lost in fratricidal wars, he dreamed of a new crusade. To try to reanimate fervour, he travelled twice through France and England, countries where his campaign in Egypt and taking of Alexandria had made him famous. He was a latter

---

13 see previous footnote.

day Godfrey of Bouillon.[14] His murder must have delayed his designs until the last years of the 14th century, which ended in the disaster of Nicomedia.

The kingdom of Lesser Armenia was founded in 1187. The Lusignans did not begin to rule there until 1342. They formed the third dynasty. But the founder of the kingdom, Léon II le Grand, married Sybille, daughter of Amaury of Lusignan, second king of Cyprus,[15] and Isabelle of Anjou, queen of Jerusalem and sister of the third king of Cyprus, Hugues I (1210).

In 1341, after the death of Léon V, the "nobles and commons" of Armenia elected as regent Jean of Lusignan, prince and constable of the realm. The first Lusignan king was Guy (1342-44). After an interregnum of twenty-one years during which two usurpers, Constantin IV and Constantin V succeeded, Pierre le Valient was elected (1365). He reigned until the "hard adventure". The second usurper possessed the kingdom until his death in 1373.

Léon VI of Lusignan, son of Jean of Lusignan, was crowned in 1374, with his wife Marguerite of Soissons. The following year, he lost his kingdom and his liberty. He was imprisoned in Cairo until 1382. The intervention of the King of Aragon freed him. After that he led a wandering life, in Venice, in Avignon, in Castille, in Aragon. He finally arrived in Paris in 1384, "having nowhere to live", says Froissart. He received from Charles VI a royal pension that never failed him and died at the Tournelles palace, the refuge that the King of France had provided him, on 29th November 1393, a few months after the completion of *Mélusine*. He was buried beside the high altar of the Célestins in Paris in a magnificent tomb, that was later transferred to St. Denis. With him ended the rule of the Lusignans in Armenia.

It had been very short and unhappy and the last king truly carried the name of the *"dumb beast"*. This was the punishment announced by Mélior to her great nephew who only wanted *"the gift of her body"* as reward for his nights of watching at the Castle of the Hawk. Mélior played on the name of Léon which, in Latin and Old French, was the same as that of the lion. The lion is a dumb beast, that is to say a wild beast, and is even the dumb beast *par excellence* as it is the king of the animals.

---

14 A leader of the 1st Crusade, elected ruler of Jerusalem in 1099.
15 See previous footnote. Amaury and Hugues I were first and second actual kings of Cyprus.

Of the families of Europe that Jean d'Arras claims to be Lusignans, Father Etiènne of Lusignan,[16] well placed to know the genealogy of the house to which he belonged, "and the most interested, it being natural for anyone to know the descent of his ancestors", recognised only two, the la Rochefoucalds and the Parthenay-Larchevêques. But he included the Saint-Gelais, the Saint-Severins, the Saint-Valliers, the Valences, the Montignacs and finally the Soubises, which he made a branch of the Larchevêques. "I have not found," he concludes, "any other families descended from the house of Lusignan."

His list is incomplete, for there are some that are found in the fantasies of Jean d'Arras. We have seen that the Counts of La Marche were Lusignans. The same with the Counts of Pembroke. The root of the Pembrokes was Guillaume of Lusignan, called de Valence, fourth son of Hugues X, lord of Lusignan and Count of la Marche, and Isabelle of Angoulême, widow of John Lackland, King of England.

The Parthenay-Larchevêques could come from the Lusignans. They bore arms broken with a band of gueules. Their house would have been founded at the beginning of the 12th century by Guillaume, son of Gilles of Lusignan (1100-1130). However it was, the two families were allied. Valence of Lusignan, daughter of Guillaume, son of Geoffroy I and Eustache Chabot, married Hugues III of Parthenay. It was by this marriage that the lordship of Vouvant, of which Eustache Chabot had been the lady, then Geoffroy á la Grand Dent the lord, and the lordship of Mervant that Valence's father had possessed, passed to the Parthenay-Larchevêques.

The la Rochefoucalds and the Luxembourgs also had Lusignan blood. From the marriage of Hugues III of Parthenay and Valence of Lusignan was born Létice, wife of Aimery I, lord of la Rochefoucald.

Towards the middle of the 15th century, more than fifty years after the appearance of Jean d'Arras' book, Louis, son of Pierre de Luxembourg, Count of Brienne and of Saint-Pol, and of Marguerite des Beaux d'Andrie, had "Lusignan" for a war cry. It descended to the seventh generation of Hugues I, king of Cyprus. Marie, daughter of King Hugues, had married Gautier IV le Grand, Count of Brienne.

In the 14th century their great-granddaughter, Isabeau, Countess of Brienne and Duchess of Athens, brought as her dowry the rights and the titles to Gautier IV, lord of Enguyen en Hainaut. The marriage of their granddaughter Marguerite to Jean de Luxembourg caused them

---

16 Author of *Histoire de Cypre, 1586.*

to enter the house of Luxembourg. Pierre de Luxembourg was the son of Jean and Marguerite. They were married about the time when Jean d'Arras wrote his romance and the marriage of this distant descendant of the Lusignans caused him to imagine a rapport between the lion of Luxembourg and the lion of Lusignan. Much later, the fame that the romance had given to the name of Lusignan put into the mind of their grandson to take up the war cry of the Lusignans.

There existed some affinity between the Chateau-Renards of Touraine and the families of Lusignan and Luxembourg. They were of the great house of Châtillon-sur-Marne of the branch of the Counts of Saint-Pol and of Blois. Marie de Châtillon, who lived at the beginning of the 14th century, had married Aymard de Valence, of the house of Lusignan. Her contemporary, Jeanne de Châtillon, was married to Gautier V, Count of Brienne, and Pierre de Luxembourg was their descendant.

There is perhaps no proof that the other families named in the romance, in particular the most well known, the Sassenages, were branches of the Lusignan family. Ismidon I and Hector de Sassenage, father of St Ismidon or Ismier, who lived at the beginning of the 11th century, were sons of Artaud, great lord of the Viennois. But this Artaud must be distinguished from his contempory, Artaud III, Count of Forez. What is more, the two Artauds, even if made into one, would not be Lusignans.

Ismideon I and Hector were the founders of the two Sassenage families, the first extinct in 1338, while the second, that of Bérenger, still exists. Two Bérengers took part in the expedition that Pierre le Valient conducted in 1367 to relieve le Cruq, attacked by the Grand Caraman. One, Raimond, grandmaster of the Order of St John of Jerusalem, brought his knights. The other embarked on a galley of the King of Cyprus, was "the lord of Sassenage, a wise and loyal knight" says Machaut. But nowhere is it said that the Lord of Sassenage and the grandmaster had been the king's cousins. Altogether, the Sassenages are an indigenous pure Dauphinoise family and are no part of the house of Lusignan.

Some other characters in the romance might appear in history. The *"heinous"* Mataquas, son of Elinas, is the Maccabeus of the Latin chronicles, the Macbeth of the history of Scotland and the Shakespeare tragedy. The tragedy of Mataquas was to destroy his own family. Pressine left with her children and Elinas went mad. Macbeth killed King

Duncan, but once master of the kingdom governed with a mildness and ability that was firm and just. The same Mataquas conducted himself *"vaillamment"* – which expresses in one word all the qualities of a good king.

We look in vain for the name of Aimery in the genealogy of the Counts of Poitiers. But memories surrounding Hugues le Veneur have served perhaps as a model for the tale of the adventure of the hunt with which the story of Raimondin starts, and for the portrait of Count Aimery. He greatly loved hunting, hounds and hawks. He had many *"braconniers et fauconniers, oiseaux de proie, chiens braques, levriers, chiens courants, limiers et chiens de grosse chasse."*

St. Guillaume, of whom Aimery is the great-great-grandfather, who abandoned all his possessions to serve God and joined the order of the white monks, is St. Guillaume, hermit of Maleval near Sienne en Tozcane, who died 10ᵗʰ February 1136. Jean d'Arras seems to have confused him, as have others, with three Counts of Poitiers and Dukes of Aquitaine of the same name.

The first was Guillaume I, called Tête d'Etoupe (Tow Head), who married the daughter of Rollon, first Duke of Normandy, and was the father of Guillaume II who became a religious as St. Cyprien at Poitiers and then at Saint-Maixent. He died in 963. Guillaume III le Grand married twice, founded the abbey of Maillezais and died in 1030. Guillaume VIII left no male heir. His daughter Eleanor married successively the King of France, Louis le Jeune, and the King of England, Henry II. Guillaume VIII was neither religious nor saint. Making off with church property, mistreating the canons of St. Hilaire at Poitiers, partisan of the anti-pope Anaclet, St Bernard converted him. He died on Good Friday on a penitential pilgrimage to Santiago de Compostella.

However, the romancer returns to history when he joins the memory of St. Guillaume to the Ordre des Blancs Manteaux. This order, whose actual name was the Servers or Servants of Mary, was not created until some time after his death, and not in Toscane but at Marseilles. But when St. Guillaume died, his disciples founded the order of Guillaumites who followed the rule of the Hermits of St Augustine and wore black robes. The Servers had a house in Paris in the Rue de la Vieille Parcheminerie and the road and the monastery itself received the name of Blancs Manteaux. In 1298 the convent was given to the Guillaumites, nonetheless the name remained. All these complications explain the further confusion committed by Jean d'Arras that his profession was conducted in the Rue de la Vieille Parcheminerie.

Saracens in the east and the Knights of Rhodes hold a large place in the romance, with adventures in Cyprus and in Armenia, where the sons of Mélusine fought and others helped them. Here again history is at the base of the legend.

Equally generous, brave, and loyal, the Christians and Saracens respected each other. At the battle of Famagousta, Urian sees the Sultan of Damascus cutting his men down with great blows of his axe. *"By my faith,"* he says, *"it is a great pity that the Turk does not believe in God, for he is very gallant. But he kills my men and we are not here to make long speeches."* He throws himself upon him and cuts off his head.

The second Sultan of Damascus is the nephew of the beheaded Sultan. Well beaten before his capital by the Lusignan brothers, he takes a great liking to Geoffroy who has, with a blow of his sword, thrown him and his horse to earth. He takes him to Jerusalem, loads him with jewels; and the Christian and the miscreant, on leaving each other, so embraced that they were in fear of transgressing the law. Anticipating Walter Scott in his *Talisman*, Jean d'Arras credits the Sultan with the greatness of soul and courtesy of Saladin, the noble adversary of Philippe Auguste and Richard Coeur de Lion.

The relations of Urian and Guion with the Order of St John commence at the beginning of their expedition, before their arrival in Cyprus, with the deliverance of two galleys from Rhodes pursued by Saracens. The grandmaster of Rhodes quickly arms many galleys and takes them to aid the King of Cyprus, besieged at Famagousta. The siege raised, the Lusignan brothers make a solemn entry to the town, with the grandmaster at the head of the procession.

Urian having become King of Cyprus, sends Guion and the grandmaster by sea to discover if the Saracens have returned to their country. They meet the Saracen fleet, destroy it, and disembark at le Cruq. In the middle of the festivities for their reception a brother announces that a great fleet has just passed before Rhodes and is on the way to Cyprus. They re-embark hastily and set off in pursuit, all sails spread.

They gain a third naval victory and throw overboard a number of Saracens. But Guion remits a hundred of them to the grandmaster to ransom some Christians and religious brothers who are prisoners of the Turks. He also gives him two of the conquered ships.

The war continues in Cyprus. The Kurdish admiral and King Bridimont of Tarsa besiege Limassol but at the news of the defeat of the Saracen fleet, they retire to the port at Cape St Andrew and land there. Guion and the grandmaster fall *"like a storm"* on their vessels and burn them, only six ships escaping destruction.

Then comes the last battle. The Lusignan brothers massacre the Saracens on the shore while the grandmaster, with his galleys, is on the watch to cut off their retreat. All their ships are taken and the pagans *"thrown into the sea."*

The campaign over, the grandmaster, in company with the barons of Poitou and Cyprus, attends the wedding of Guion with the heiress of the Kingdom of Armenia. Then they take the barons to Rhodes and give them good cheer.

After some years, the Saracens seek revenge. The Caliph of Baghdad and the Grand Caraman fall upon Armenia. The Caliph, King Anthénor of Antioch, the admiral of the Kurds, and the Sultan of Barbary swear an oath never to give up until they have destroyed Rhodes, put all to death in Armenia and Cyprus, crucified Urian and burnt his wife and children.

But there was a spy among them who was in touch with the grandmaster. He knew the Saracens' language so well that they never suspected he was not one of their own. He knew all their secrets, went to Beyrouth and took a boat that left for Turkey in search of trade.

The boat stopped at the port of Rhodes. The spy said he wanted to look around the town for a little. *"Come back in time,"* they said, *"for we will not wait for you." "I will be back soon,"* he replied, but as soon as he could, gave his news to the grandmaster.

Urian, quickly warned, sought with the grandmaster and Guion to embark with all their forces and to wait off the coast of Jaffa. It was in this port that the Saracens had assembled their fleet. The grandmaster took with him brother sergeants-at-arms and others, strangers who were in search of adventure.

On the way they struck up against the fleet of Anthénor and the admiral's advance guard. They would have been lost if God had not guided Geoffroy to the place of battle. He had learned, at Lusignan, of the danger into which his brothers ran, and Mélusine and Raimondin had equipped him with a fleet. This knight *"so forceful,"* said the Saracens, *"against whom nothing could stand"* saved Guion and the grandmaster.

The Christians took Jaffa and marched on Damascus, the grandmaster in the advance guard. Their victory at Damascus was followed with the conclusion of a truce of a hundred years, in which the grandmaster took part. He then accompanied the Lusignans to the Holy Sepulchre where they made their devotions together. On their return the grandmaster invited them to his island for great festivities.

What one can say about these romantic adventures is the harmony that reigns between the Lusignans and the Knights of Rhodes. It was not quite so cosy in history – the Hospitallers did not always like the Lusignans.

Three times in *Mélusine* we see Saracen chiefs furtively leaving a battle that is turning against them. Assailed by Guion and by the grandmaster, the admiral of the Kurds fled in a small galley so quickly that all marvelled. At the battle off Cap Saint André, the Caliph fled by sea, and the admiral invited him to his little galley in which he himself was escaping. When they saw danger coming upon them they fled, in full sail and with oars striking quickly. In Syria the second Sultan of Damascus left the mêlée, turned his shield behind his back, struck his spurs and fled toward the pagan camp. These desertions recall the evasion of the King of Cyprus, Henri II de Lusignan, at the siege of Acre in 1291. Standing down from the night guard and promising to return in the morning, he profited from the darkness to make it to the port and return to his island.

The Hospitallers, chased from the Holy Land by the fall of Acre, obtained from Henri II permission to retire to Limassol. Here they suffered such vexation from him that they determined to conquer the island of Rhodes to gain their freedom.

The wrong was on the part of the Lusignans. The Knights of St. John remained faithful to the second mission that Raimond Dupuis had assigned them, to defend Christianity by force of arms.

In 1187 their grandmaster Garnier de Napoli in Syria, at the battle of Tiberiad where the King of Jerusalem, Guy of Lusignan, was captured, by strokes of his sword opened a passage through the enemy ranks but died the next day from his wounds. Seven years later the Hospitallers wanted the King of Cyprus also to bear the title of King of Jerusalem, marking in this way their continued intention to wrest the Holy City back from the infidels.

Under the reign of Constantin IV, the Saracens of Egypt invaded Little Armenia. Constantin implored aid from the Knights of St. John, and despite all that could make the new king repugnant to them, a usurper and Greek schismatic, the grandmaster, Dieudonné de Gozon, placed the word Christianity before any other consideration and responded to his appeal. The Hospitallers only left Armenia when it had been purged of all infidels. They thus prepared the restoration of the last King of Armenia of the house of Lusignan.

The union of Hospitallers and Lusignans, renewed in the campaign of 1367, achieved the taking of Alexandria. No doubt the author of *Mélusine* thought above all of the expedition of Pierre I when he recounted that of the Lusignan brothers in Syria. Several details are the same. The Saracen ships left the port of Alexandria, giving chase to the Christian vessels and threatening the coasts of Syria. It was necessary to stifle them in their base. And is the taking of Jaffa by the sons of Mélusine and the grandmaster of Rhodes anything other than the taking of Alexandria by Pierre le Vaillant and Raimond Bérenger? The infidel fleet was burned in the port, the town taken by assault, the booty loaded into vessels. But after furious combat and enormous losses to both sides, the Christians retired.

Two things are remarkable in the romance of *Mélusine* when we consider it from an historical point of view. It is that several characters and certain events belong to the 14th century, and particularly to the time when Jean d'Arras lived. The author knew what interested his patrons and contemporaries by combining the story of the serpent faery with the people of his time. He also took care to make each of his protectors, and their high relations, play a definite part in these interesting events. Their fiefs and their kingdoms became the theatre for scenes in the romance. *Mélusine* was for all a book of current affairs.

The King of Aragon had in his territory Palestine at Mont Canigou and Raimondin at Montserrat. The barons of his court, the Counts of Empurias, Prades, Urgel, the whole royal house of Aragon, and the Counts of Cardone, were flattered to see their ancestry figure in the first ranks at Raimondin's funeral. Towards the end of the 15th century a Count of Cardone collected Thomas of Lusignan of the royal family of Cyprus, chased out by the Turks, and adopted him. Would it be rash to assume that the mention of the Cardones in a famous book might have played a part in this act of benevolence?

The Duke of Bar and the princes of the house of Bohemia/Luxembourg followed the journeys of the sons of Lusignan on the banks of the Meuse, the Rhine and the Elbe. In the *"most valiant prince"*

Asselin, Lord of Luxembourg, father of Cristine *"so beautiful and good"* they recognised "Wincelin", that is to say Venceslas, son of King Jean l'Aveugle and Beatrix of Bourbon, a brother of the emperor Charles IV, brother-in-law of the King of France Jean le Bon, and grand uncle of Charles VI. In whose favour Charles IV had raised the County of Luxembourg to a Duchy, marrying him to Jeanne, Duchess of Brabante and Limbourg in 1354. "The gentle and handsome duke," says Froissart, "and when he departed this life, they said that the highest and finest lineage of the most noble blood had died," and his widow "had never wanted to re-marry."

The knightly generosity of Duke Oste of Bavaria, spontaneously joining the Lusignans and the King of Alsace to save the King of Bohemia, pleased the courts of Lorraine and of France. The House of Bavaria was for a long time held in honour there, and Charles VI had asked Duke Frederick for his daughter Isabeau to make her Queen of France.

The Duke de Berry could not be other than attentive to whatever concerned Poitou, his noble and difficult conquest, and as it is glorious to triumph over valiant enemies, the author did not spare eulogies on the bravery of the Poitevins. Before Famagousta, at Cap Saint-André, under the walls of Luxembourg and of Prague, the most powerful battalions were pierced by their furious charges.

To intrepid and faithful nobles came dangerous tasks and missions of trust, although in the romance more so than in real life. Geoffroy á la Grand Dent took only ten knights with him from Poitou to defeat the Saracens before Damascus. *"Now, charge, my children!"* he cried. The knights dismounted, drew their fine swords and struck off arms and heads.

Antoine of Lusignan, leaving for Bohemia, delegated the Duchy of Luxembourg to a baron from Poitou called the Lord of Argenton. Geoffroy of Argenton, often named in Froissart, was a loyal knight but one whose loyalty was first to the King of England. He was in the raid by Chandos on the county of Anjou. He fought at Lensac. He held Raimond de Marueil, a French partisan, prisoner in his castle "and dare not disobey the King, his lord", but was prepared to free him when an English squire helped him to escape. He was present at the taking of Montcontour at the side of Perceval of Cologne and John Creswell. They called on him for the relief of Sainte Sévère. He is found in Thouars in 1372 with Perceval and a great party of knights of

Poitou. The English career of these Frenchmen ended here. The fortress surrendered, and Argenton and Perceval "turned French" along with their companions in arms.

The knight of Thoars in the romance, whether it be either the Viscount or the Lord of Thouars of the chronicles, was, on the contrary, a persevering Frenchman. The Viscount took part in the siege of Thouars; the Lord was in the company of Yvain de Galles.

One should not be surprised to see Jean d'Arras mention these French, some servants of France, others soldiers of England, without making any difference between them, not seeming to worry about offending the feelings of the French side. He had fine examples before his eyes. At the peak of high society indifference often ruled, political and national passions died or were dissimulated, opposing opinions tolerated or accommodated between themselves. Even in the midst of war, adversaries could live on good terms whilst still doing their duty. During truces, English and French lords were neighbours and jousted together. In London Froissart saw five kings, the King of England, the French king, Jean le Bon, his prisoner, the Kings of Scotland and Denmark, and the Lusignan King of Cyprus "frolicking" at the house of an inn-keeper who was Mayor of the city.

There are in the book of Jean d'Arras other names of persons and places which have not been put there without reason. He had his finger on the pulse of the people of the 14th century.

Duras was a victory for the French against the English. In 1377 the town had been taken by assault by the Duke of Anjou, and some days later the castle surrendered, by arrangement, to Du Guesclin.

To the name of Derval, the castle of the felon chatelaine, is attached the memory of one of the many atrocities of the Hundred Years War. The French besieged the castle, and besiegers and besieged each took hostages. By a castle window the English erected a kind of scaffold, made the hostages mount it, and cut off their heads; heads and bodies rolling into the moat in full view of the French. Immediately the French took their hostages and decapitated them under the eyes of the English.

Le Cruq, mentioned several times in the romance, was famous for the vigorous defence of the Venetians against the Saracens to preserve Christianity in the last port of the east.

One could compare Hervé de Léon, Raimondin's father, seneschal and counsellor of the King of the Bretons, *"wise and courteous knight, well spoken, of such daring, that as regards his honour, he was second to none in the world"* and another Hervé de Léon, on the French side, whom Froissart speaks of as a "noble and powerful man", so well regarded by his enemies that on becoming prisoner, Edward III granted his freedom by remitting him to deliver a challenge to King Philippe de Valois.

The two Alains de Léon remind us of the two Alains de Beaumont, French captains. All these Alains were equally wise, good and courteous.

The traitor Josselin du Pont de Léon, jealous of Hervé's good fortune, and by a calumnious homicide becoming a powerful lord in Brittany, along with his son Olivier *"who did not weigh an ounce less than his father"*, resembled the two Hugues le Dispensier, father and son. "They were", says Froissart, "the greatest masters of the Kingdom of England who wanted to surmount all the other barons through envy." The crimes of Josselin and the Despensiers are of much the same nature. The royal majesty is attainted by them and the denouement is similar. Queen Isabelle of England, like the King of the Bretons, had the felons judged and executed.

The lady of the castle of Valbruyant, a lady of intelligence and courage, energetic, shrewd, *"subtile"*, which is to say capable, personifies three great French ladies: the Lady of Soubise, the Countess Dauphine of Auvergne, and the Lady of Plainmartin. Their husbands away, alone in their castles, which had been entrusted to them to guard, they knew how to defend them and to conserve them by negotiation. Valbruyant itself, which Jean d'Arras locates in Ireland, was a French fortress, Chateaubriand, then known as Chastel Bruyant.

The Lady of Soubise, besieged by the French, having few men, seeing that the town was not strong enough to hold out for long, and with no hope of rescue, called the barons and knights in council, and sent them to treat with the enemy. She obtained a guarantee of safe conduct for the English wherever it pleased them to go, and swore from now on to obey the King of France.

The Dauphine of Auvergne, returning quickly in amazement as the news came to her of the surprise of the castle of Merquel, carried off by a trick of Aymerigot Marcel and the naivety of the chatelain Girardon, at once sent two squires to rouse the knights of the country to help reconquer her fortress, and the siege lengthening, obtained restitution and financial consideration.

In 1373, after the surrender of Niort and Lusignan, the Bretons and Du Geusclin presented themselves before Châtel Allart. "And soon," says Froissart, "the constable sent for the Lady of Plainmartin who was the wife of Sir Guichard d'Angle. She entreated him for a safe conduct to allow her to go and speak to the Duke de Berry at Poitiers. This the constable granted and had her taken there by one of his knights.

"When she was brought before the duke she curtseyed low. The duke raised her up and asked what she wanted to say. 'My lord,' she said, 'I am required by the Constable of France to put myself and my lands into the hands of the King of France. Now you are well aware that my lord and husband is a prisoner in Spain. Thus all the land is governed by me. But I am a defenceless woman, and I cannot make over my husband's heritage at my will, for if, by chance, I acted against his wishes, he would be rightly annoyed and the blame would rest on me. But in order to appease you, and to keep my land at peace and my people too – who are not warriors and do not wish to be – when my lord is released from prison and returns to England, where I believe he will go, I will inform him of this arrangement. He will let me know his will and then I will immediately answer you.'

"The Duke replied 'Lady, I agree, on condition that neither you nor your fortress purvey food or artillery, nor otherwise restore yourselves other than you are now.' The lady then returned to Chastel Allart and had them raise the siege."

It is the same at the end of the story by Jean d'Arras. The Lady of Valbruyant represents the Lady of Châtel Allart, and Geoffroy á la Grand Dent the Duke de Berry.

"The lady of Valbruyant had a graceful and beautiful daughter who was about eight or nine years old; also a handsome and well educated son of about ten. The lady mounted a splendid palfrey, along with her two children, who had two elderly gentlemen to lead them by the reins. Six maidens, also mounted, accompanied them. With this party she left the castle.

Before the gates she met the knight who brought Geoffroy's command. She greeted him courteously, and the knight responded with great respect, for he had been well instructed. The lady said to him in a calm and even tone:

'Sir knight,' she said quietly, 'my husband is not here, and for that reason I wish to see your lord to ask him what he intends, for it seems to me that he has come to make war. But I cannot believe it would be against my husband nor anyone in this fortress, for God knows, my husband and his men have never done anything that might displease my lord, his father. And if by chance

anyone to spite my husband has told Geoffroy otherwise, I would humbly like you to ask him to be good enough to hear my husband's explanation.'

When the knight heard her speak so wisely, he replied:

'In good faith, my lady, what you ask is reasonable, I will take you to my lord, and I think you will find him very amiable and will get satisfaction from him even if he has been informed about Guérin very unfavourably.' And they set out to where he was staying.

They came to Geoffroy's tent. When he was told that the lady was there, he came out to meet her. The lady, who was very well instructed and knew very well how to conduct herself, took her two children by the hands and knelt with them before Geoffroy, showing him great respect. Geoffroy bowed to her, raising her up gently, and said 'Madame, you are most welcome.' The two children also greeted Geoffroy with great respect, and when Geoffroy had raised them both up, he returned their greeting.

Their mother then began to speak, pretending not to know that he had come here with fierce intent. 'My noble lord,' she said, 'My husband is absent from our country just now which is why I have come to invite you, if it pleases you, to do my husband and me the honour of staying in your fortress. Bring as well as many of your men as you wish, for I assure you, my lord, you will indeed find everything there you might need, thanks be to God, and I and all my household will welcome you most willingly and joyfully, as we should to the son of our natural lord.'

Geoffroy was quite astounded that she dare make such a request, in view of all that he had heard about her husband. Nonetheless he replied:

'My dear lady, I thank you for the great courtesy you show me. But I cannot grant your request, for I have been given to understand that your husband, by his actions toward my lord father and toward me, does not deserve such. Nevertheless, I wish you to know that I have not come here to wage war against ladies or maidens. God forbid! You may rest assured, as well, that I would never permit any harm to come to you, to your people, or to your fortress since your husband is not here.'

'Many thanks to you, my lord,' she replied. 'But I pray you to tell me, if you please, why you are angry at my husband. I am sure that there is nothing that he or I would be able to think of displeasing you. And I believe, my lord, that if you agreed to hear my husband defend himself, you would find that those who have spoken against him have not told the truth. And I believe, my lord, on my life that you will find it just as I say.'

Geoffroy thought a little and then replied: 'Well my lady, if he can show that he has not betrayed his oath or transgressed the homage he owes to me, I will be most happy to hear his version of events, of himself and his companions. If they come, they may do so in complete safety. I will grant him safe conduct for eight days, with up to sixty of his men, apart from the time it takes for their journey. I do this for the sake of you and your children.'

'My lord,' replied the lady, 'May God, in His grace, reward you!'"

6: Mélusine as a Book for the instruction of Princes

Mélusine is already a book of knight errantry. We see a number of men of war and main characters of the romance pursuing adventures.

Foreigners of many nations confined in the city of Famagousta, surrounded by Saracens, make a vigorous sortie against the infidels. In the town of Prague were a hundred Hungarians, very brave knights, who often broke out, harrying the army of Zélodus and doing him very great damage. Foreigners joined with the Knights of Rhodes to fight the Saracens. It was through knights adventuring in Asia Minor that the *"foolish"* King of Armenia was led into temptation.

One day Urian and Guion came to their mother and Urian said to her very wisely, *"Madame, if you please, it will soon be time for us to go on foreign adventures to acquire honour, renown and the order of knighthood. We wish to conquer other lands and countries, for we are already eight brothers and if God increase our number, we are likely to be yet more! When your land is divided into so many parts, whoever succeeds as heir can hardly retain the estate as great as that which you and our father hold. So my brother Guion and I will abandon our share of whatever might come to us, excepting your good grace and any help that you give us for our journey."*

Father Etiènne of Lusignan, who wrote his *History of Cyprus* (1586) at about the time *Don Quixote* appeared, relegated the "old romance" of Jean d'Arras to the level of the insipid productions that abounded in his time, that did not see, like Cervantes, that their subject matter called for humour but wrote about it in tragic terms. They were nothing more than "lies, fictions and impostures fit only for little children or old women to read or tell over the fire." Their author, wanting to illustrate the noble race of the Lusignans, obscured the glory of that family "for it is no great honour for such a chivalrous line to be praised by so displeasing and lying a pen."

However, there are other things than "untruths" in *Mélusine*. Jean d'Arras aimed to produce a book to meet the taste of his contemporaries, and pleased them by writing about marvels. But educational books were also in fashion. In *La Livre du cavalier de la Tour Landry pour l'enseignment de ses filles* the knight dedicated to his own daughters a singular book for teaching young ladies, which enjoyed a great vogue in France and Germany. The Duke de Berry had no less than seven such works "for the direction or information of princes" in his library.

When Jean d'Arras called his book a treatise he spoke truly. For proverbs, with which he is prodigious, can be a means of instruction. Their brevity reinforces the expression of the thought and engraves it deeply upon the memory.

The first chapters of *Mélusine* contain a eulogy on the sciences. Jean d'Arras wants the knowledge of these "noble arts" to be reserved to nobles. "*In those times,*" he says, "*unless they were nobles, none dared have their children instructed in any of the seven arts that consist of the noble art of rhetoric, which includes grammar, music, physics, philosophy, geometry, and theology. In those days knowledge was more greatly prized than now and high princes understood their affairs more clearly. They accepted more readily the essence of advice given them because they had learned the knowledge required of the times. I believe that a man of noble extraction who has a knowledge of the noble arts at heart will ever be greater than one who has learned them through desire to enrich himself by pleasing princes through dissimulation or obscuring the truth and the right. For a gross nature cannot well apply itself to that which is noble.*"

Count Aimery of Poitiers lived in that golden age when all was noble. He was "*full of knowledge and especially the science of astronomy of which he was the wisest since Aristotle.*" His son Bertrand knew Greek, in which he discovered the origin of the name of Mélusine and of Albany. When Mélusine had built the castle of Lusignan, what name should be given to it? Bertrand invited her to choose one.

"*Sir,*" *said Mélusine,* "*since it pleases you that I give it its name, I shall call it Lusignan!*" "*By my faith,*" *says the count,* "*that name comes from two roots. You are called Mélusine of Albanie. In Greek, Albanie means something which lacks for nothing, and Mélusine marvel or marvellous. And on the other hand we see the building of this place has been marvellous, and I have no doubt that as long as the fortress lasts, it will be the site of marvellous events.*"

The two wise counts of Poitiers are models for the noble readers of Jean d'Arras. *Mélusine* is a worldly guide to the conduct of young men of high birth. The knowledge necessary to develop great lords is revealed here. They will find depicted here the society in which they will live. They will find the maxims of the honest man, the principles of good government, the elements of military art and the rules of war, lessons in good manners and even some advice on table manners.

Feudal Relationships

The society that Jean d'Arras describes is feudal, and there is a great need to note all the requirements of homage. One must never delay in paying homage nor question it.

Soon after the death of Count Aimery of Poitiers, the barons of the county are mandated on a certain day to renew their fiefs and pay homage to their gracious lord, Bertrand, the old count's son. This is the day that Raimondin receives from Bertrand the gift of the land of Lusignan. He alone does not pay homage, for the count gives it to him freely, thus he owes nothing to him or to his successors, neither faith nor homage nor any obligation.

The King of Brittany renders the barony of Léon to Raimondin, victor over Josselin. Raimondin immediately pays him homage. Then he asks the king's permission to grant the barony to his cousin Hervé. *"Hervé,"* says the king, *"receive this gift of the barony of Léon that your cousin presents you, and pay me homage for it."* Then Raimondin calls Alain, his other cousin, and says to him, *"Dear cousin, I give you the land that the king has given me, that was once that of Josselin du Pont de Léon, pay homage to the king."* The two cousins obey at the same time.

The King of Cyprus, when dying, takes the crown and places it on Urian's head, then calls the barons of the country and commands them to pay homage to King Urian, his son-in-law. This they do right willingly. Guion marries Florie, the heiress of the King of Armenia. Before the end of the marriage feast, all the barons pay homage to King Guion. The Duke of Luxembourg dies. Immediately all the country and the main towns pay homage to his daughter Chrétienne. The Count of Forez is hardly dead before the barons of his country, on Geoffroy's orders, pay homage to Raimonnet.

Raimondin has renounced the world, and is on the road to Montserrat. Geoffroy succeeds him from now on to the lordship of

Lusignan. Arriving at Toulouse, Raimondin writes many letters, seals them, and sends them to Geoffroy and to the barons of the country. They order Geoffroy to receive their homage and the barons to receive him as their lord.

A suzerain and his vassals were inseparable. The lord lived a patriarchal life in the great hall in his castle in the midst of "the barons of the country". He could not leave them. It was also a crime in their eyes for him to remove one of his men. *"By the faith that I owe to the soul of my father,"* says the King of Brittany to his barons, *"Josselin nor his son will ever again commit treason or cause me to banish gentlemen from my country."* And he hangs them both.

The vassal must aid and advise his lord. In *Mélusine* and no doubt in real life, the duty of advice had become the right to counsel and authorise the suzerain. It was no longer the lord who governed his country, not even his own person. It was the barons. They no longer counselled, they ordained. When Raimondin asks for land from the Count of Poitiers, he speaks to the barons first before approaching the Count. He takes them as witness of the request he is about to make, and when he has expressed it, the Count replies *"if it pleases my barons, then it pleases me."*

The barons of Albany give a wife to their lord Mataquas. The nobles of Forez provide Hervé with a "gentle lady", sister of the Count of Poitiers. The Duchess of Luxembourg, Chrètienne, solicited by the King of Alsace to marry Antoine of Lusignan, discusses it with her barons. *" I know,"* she says, *"that you who are my men see more clearly in my affairs than I can, and would not advise anything that was not to my profit or honour."*

This feudalism was sometimes a servitude for the lord but it was faithful and full of regard when he was unfortunate. The Count of Poitiers is dead. The barons go *"very gently to comfort the lady and her children as much as they can, and so much that they lighten their sorrow."* The King of Alsace, vanquished and impoverished, is all the same welcomed by his barons.

The single knights show no less attachment to their lords. Their life consists of following them in their campaigns, to perform the office of quartermasters, to preserve them from danger. The old knight that Mélusine had at the time of her wedding accompanied Raimondin to Brittany and revealed the treason of the chatelaine of Derval. The two Poitevin knights who came to Lusignan to bring the news of the siege of Famagousta went with Antoine and Renaud to Luxembourg, and many years after, took part in the war against the Duke of Austria. Philibert of Monmonet, who had raised and taught Geoffroy, did not lose sight of him in his adventures round Sion. But he follows him from afar, hiding under cover in the woods, so as not to offend his ferocious disciple. Geoffroy led his ten knights when he went to fight the giant Gardon in Guérande; to punish the monks of Maillezais; to deliver Northumberland from the giant Grimault; and finally on his pilgrimage to Rome and to Montserrat. *"My friend,"* says Geoffroy of the new knight who has saved his life in Ireland and at the battle of Damascus, *"such roses are good to wear in one's hat. The lord who has his party garnished with such flower of chivalry and gentility, loving and fearing honour, must and can surely rest easy."*

Vassals and knights place honour and candour to the fore of their feelings for their masters. Geoffroy surprises the Count of Forez, whose false report had lost him his mother, at Marcilly-le-Château surrounded by his barons. He shouts at him, and chases him to the top of the tower. When he comes down he tells the barons why he has killed his uncle. The barons calm down when they learn the crime their lord has committed. Geoffroy has proved his right to vengeance before the vassals of Forez.

The vassals of Ireland roughly recall to him the words of the obligations of a suzerain. *"Thou shalt do no wrong to any who are true and obedient subjects of Lusignan, for if anyone aims to molest or injure us, you must protect us."*

When Geoffroy sets fire to the convent at Maillezais, his ten knights leave him. *"They do not want,"* they tell him, *"to be guilty of such an infamy as to burn the house of God and of his servants."* And when Geoffroy, incendiary and murderer, begins to moan and feel sorry they tell him brusquely, *"Ha, my, lord, it is too late to repent when the madness is done. Think how to make satisfaction to God and the world."*

The loyalty of the old chivalry is thus always in honour. An episode in the romance shows it pushed to the point of heroism. Some vassals of Raimondin in Ireland are accused of having taken part in the revolt of Claude de Sion and his two brothers against Raimondin, their lord. Geoffroy comes to take Sion and to hang the guilty. He now has before him the presumed accomplices who seek to exonerate themselves. *"Make them swear on the Bible,"* his counsellors tell him, *"that if we should lay siege to Sion, whether they would help Claude against you. If they swear yes, they are your enemies; but if they swear no, you must not act against them."* In giving this advice, they have no doubt that these men will observe a religious oath, even at peril of their lives.

In the diverse traits that we come to see, we recognise once more in *Mélusine* 13th century society. But perhaps a new thing is how the bourgeoisie figure in a romance of chivalry. The commons of Poitou show great sorrow at the death of the Count of Poitiers. When King Urian and Queen Hermine visit their kingdom, the bourgeois of the great towns come to meet them outside the walls with great processions and musical instruments. Many of the bourgeoisie, both male and female, are present at Raimondin's funeral.

Jean d'Arras knows the powerful municipalities on the borders of the Rhine. The 'community' of Luxembourg swear with the barons and nobles that, since their lady does not wish to marry the King of Alsace, they will show him that he does wrong to the maiden and to themselves. And soon they man the forts and the country.

Antoine and Renaud, going to Bohemia, camp before Aix-la-Chapelle. The bourgeoisie give them very rich gifts. Antoine offers them his services. Arriving before Cologne, where there is a bridge over the Rhine, the Lusignan brothers come up against the refusal of the citizens to let them pass. They negotiate. The bourgeoisie meet in council with the elders. They come to an understanding. The Duke of Luxembourg comes to the city with his highest barons. He invites the ladies and maidens of the town to supper, along with the townsmen and many gentlemen who live in Cologne. The meal is followed by a fête. And at the end, there is no lady or maiden to whom the duke has not given a fine jewel. He does as much to many townsmen and especially to the gentlemen.

On leaving, the duke thanks the citizens for the honour they have shown him. *"Noble duke,"* they reply with one voice, *"the city and all of us are under your orders more than any other lord that we have for neighbours. Do not draw back from asking for anything we could do. We are all ready now and at other times."*

The next day the duke comes from mass and orders the trumpet call for raising the camp. Already the advance guard and the baggage train are on their way when four knights come from the city. They are mounted and armed like St. George, apart from not wearing helmets, and a great company of men at arms follows them.

The knights dismount before the duke. They salute Antoine and say to him, *"Most powerful duke, the noble and fine city of Cologne commends itself to your grace, and, dear sir, for the great honour and nobility that those of the city recognise in you, they wish to be your good friends. They convey to you four hundred men at arms and a hundred crossbowmen, paid for eight months to go with you wherever you please."*

"Great thanks, fine sirs," says the duke. *"It reminds me of your courtesy in other times and places."*

"Sir," says one of the knights, *"there are none of the four of us who are not familiar with all the roads from here to Prussia, throughout Esclavonia and in Cracow. If need be, we can guide you through the defiles, passages and rivers."*

"That will greatly help our affair," replies the duke, *"I will not refuse that when the time comes."* And he retains the men of Cologne under his banner.

On return from the war, the four knights take the advance guard to prepare the passage of the Duke of Luxembourg at Cologne. The great bourgeoisie and masters of the city ask them for news of their journey. The knights tell of the power of the Lusignan brothers and how Renaud is now King of Bohemia. Those of Cologne are most happy to have acquired the love of such princes. The notables go to meet Antoine, fête him and pray him to stay in their town. Antoine receives the ladies, the townsmen and the gentlemen to supper again. The farewells are such as are exchanged between equals and friends.

The place that the bourgeoisie occupies in the romance is not great. But they are shown blessed with the same qualities, and with privileges as advantageous as the nobility. The great towns at this time had become part of the feudal system.

The feudal spirit and knighthood is no longer the same that it was in preceding centuries. The simplicity, the austerity, the roughness of other times is replaced with exaggeration and artificiality. One might say romanticism. But does that not touch upon the epoch of gothic flamboyance? The nobility becomes worldly. It is refined in its sentiments, pretentious in its discourse, recherché in its fashions. High lords and great ladies are passionate for magnificence and sumptuous ceremonies.

At Mélusine's wedding they are none other than marvels and riches. Those who had seen them could never forget them. Mélusine received the Countess of Poitiers in a pavilion of cloth of gold ornamented with pearls and precious stones. The countess is dazzled at the sight of these jewels of the bride. *"In all the world,"* she says to herself, *"there is no queen or empress who could have the like of these.*" The chapel for the marriage is an inestimable treasure, with its noble books of splendid images, gold and silver censers, ornaments engraved with fine gold and enriched with pearl embroidery. Dinner is served in vessels of gold and silver. And after the feast, the ladies watch the jousting on scaffolds draped with gold.

Aiglentine, daughter of Frédéric, King of Bohemia, loses her father. The King of Alsace decides to marry her to Renaud of Lusignan. "*He has her abandon her black mourning clothes and put on her finest garments with costly jewels, enamels, brooches, precious stones, splendid belts and chaplets.*" When the maiden enters with her company "*the hall was lit up with richness and beauty.*" They soon hear the news in the city of Prague. Soon all the town will be hung with golden drapes covering the streets. When it was time to retire they led the bride to lie in a rich ornamented bed.

The gifts they give so readily on these occasions always "*content*" those who receive them. Mélusine makes a gift to the Countess of Poitiers of a golden clasp "*of which none could tell the price*"; to Blanche, the countess' daughter, a chaplet with pearls and sapphires, great rubies, diamonds and other precious stones. Raimondin offers the King of the Bretons a gold cup profusely studded with precious stones. Hermine gives Urian a golden clasp which contains a very rich gem, and to Guion a diamond ring.

The dead also have their luxuries and even ostentation. The funeral of Count Aimery is made "*very honourably according to the custom of the times.*" At the funeral of the King of Bohemia, and at Raimondin's, horses are caparisoned as one would expect for great princes. Even Horrible himself, the wicked three eyed monster that his mother condemned to death, did not lose the right to a rich funeral.

In the tomb of King Elinas at the centre of the chamber there is a great luminary of lamps and burning torches and great candelabra so that one can see as clearly as if it were broad daylight. Above is the statue of a knight with a marvellously worked crown upon his head. The tomb, the six columns that support it, the crown, the chandeliers, are all of fine gold. Precious stones sparkle there. At the foot of the tomb, on a column, is a life size alabaster figure of a queen, wearing a crown, and so beautiful that there could never be a being more ravishing. She holds a golden tablet on which is inscribed "*Here lies Elinas, noble king of Albany*" and explains at length how Elinas has been put there.

All happy events are celebrated with rejoicing. There are fêtes for baptisms, the churching of women after childbirth, the granting of knighthood, the presentation of homage, the completion of the castle of Lusignan, the return from a war. They last from eight to fifteen days. They announce them with criers, they are "cried". Eight days before those that Urian gives to celebrate his victory over the Saracens, the people begin to gather. The king is very pleased about that. According to 14th century custom, he has it cried *"on pain of losing liberty and possessions"* that none should take advantage by increasing prices.

These fêtes are *"great and noble"*. They are *"well jousted and well danced"*. They make very good cheer. The delicacy of the dishes, the fineness of the domestic and foreign wines, spices, sugared almonds, and sweetmeats they offer to the guests after the tables have been stripped of their cloths, dismantled and taken away, hands washed and grace said, the melodies of minstrels gathering the guests that have been heard throughout the feasting, all witness a generosity that was not limited to faery tales in the time of Jean d'Arras.

Religious Faith and Practice

Thoughts of God dominate the whole story of *Mélusine*. It inspires the teaching she gives her sons. *"The judgments of God are like bottomless deeps without sides. Human understanding is too crude to understand them. But one must remember to glorify He who ordains all things."*

All the misfortunes of Mélusine and her descendants, the physical stigma on her children, her sorrowful departure, the two murders committed by Geoffroy, the fortress of Lusignan passing into foreign hands, are merited punishments. Two commandments of God have been violated. "Thou shalt not take the name of the Lord thy God in vain," and "Thou shalt honour thy father and thy mother."

"Firstly," says Mélusine to her sons, *"love, fear and serve God your Creator continually. In all places you are, every day, hear the divine service before you do anything else."* The children of Mélusine never fail to be present at mass, whatever the circumstances, mounting arms, striking camp, going into battle. *"The mass was sung, the trumpets sounded, the army marched off."*

"Honour Our Mother, the Holy Church, support her, be her champions against all her enemies." The sons of Mélusine do not wear the cross on their shoulder like those who departed at other times for the deliverance

of the Holy Land. But fighting the Saracens in Cyprus, in Syria, in Bohemia, they have the right to say, like Urian, *"We are the soldiers of Our Lord Jesus Christ."*

Mélusine is a very great lady. It is also not surprising that she recommends humility to her children, presenting it to them as the first virtue of the great. *"Before everything, I forbid you pride. Be humble, gentle and courteous, offering a fine response to all. Do not act like a master or lord among your companions. Speak to each according to his quality, and as to the one so to another. Be thus to all."* She herself shows them by example in all her life. *"We lose today,"* cry the people of her house, *"the most humble lady, the most intimate and familiar with her servants and most compassionate to their problems."*

The duty of justice is the *raison d'être* of princes. *"Kings,"* says Raimondin to the King of the Bretons, *"have been established first to give justice." "Do right to the small as to the great,"* says Mélusine. Urian, visiting his kingdom, orders his officials to exercise justice without favour. He forbids them to molest their subjects or to commit any extortion. He commands them to go among them with true justice, or he will punish them severely as an example to others.

A man must be disinterested. After his father's death, Geoffroy governs the land of Lusignan in such way that for ten years his officials render him no accounts and he wants it to be so. When they tell him, *"Sir, hear your accounts to learn how you live." "What accounts do you want me to hear?"* he replies. *"When you and I are all at ease, my fortresses well maintained, all my affairs in good order, and you give me money when I ask for it? Do you think I have wanted to make my house of gold? Those of stone that my father and mother have left me are sufficiently good."*

"Be generous with your goods," says Mélusine. *"If God accords you good, give part to your companions."* The liberalities of her sons are as numerous as their victories. It is a point of honour with them not to retain booty other than things that are necessary for them to continue the war. Winning a naval victory, they give to the Knights of Rhodes the wood of the ships taken from the enemy, but they keep the artillery. The King of Alsace is vanquished and a prisoner. Antoine says to him, *"I free you and deliver all the men that we and our men have taken, and all your tents and pavilions, but the money that is shared between my companions, I cannot render to you."* Each one is held by good pay. Urian's men after the battle of Cap Saint-André are all *"made rich"* for which they greatly praise him. But there did not remain for their master anything worth a penny.

The Arts of War

Among the teachings of Mélusine, one single thing seems pointless: *"When at war, take the advice of brave men who have honourably pursued the profession of arms."*

She has forgotten for the moment that she had already given them talismans that assured them of victory as long as they fought in a good cause and upheld loyalty *"without trickery or malice,"* and that at a stroke by her faery arts she had endowed them with the whole science of war. Nor did she remember it when she placed Antoine and Renaud under the governance of two old knights. These children, of whom the eldest was eighteen, soon put these old campaigners to school. Jean d'Arras shows them practising the military arts in a series of tableaux so authentic that we might well assume that he had been a soldier himself. Were not the middle classes in those days to be numbered among the valiant? Like most of them the author of *Mélusine* had always lived in the midst of war and he was close to one of the most illustrious soldiers of his time.

The armies and fleets with which Mélusine equips her sons are those of the 14th century.

In the army the knights hold the first rank. They are called the men at arms, or bassinets, after the style of their headgear, and seem to have reserved to themselves the name of combatants. They had a suit of armour, which is perhaps the same thing as the hauberk, the helmet, the breast plate, the gauntlets, the bulky leg armour, the lance and the sword.

The foot soldiers are the *brigands* or *brigandiniers*, armed with shield and spear, the archers, the crossbowmen and "the rest". This disdainful expression signifies the varlets and pages. In his journey through Brittany Raimondin took pages with him. They carried the lances and helmets of the men at arms. But the pages were held in mediocre esteem until the reign of Charles VII (1422-1461). Mélusine did not provide any for the expedition of Antoine and Renaud, she replaced them, as they did at the end of the 14th century, with "hefty armed varlets with strong hooded surcoats."

Men at arms, archers, crossbowmen, were all gentlemen, squires or knights. Alain and Hervé de Léon brought four hundred of them to the aid of Raimondin when menaced by the chatelaine of Derval. They recruited them from their friends and relations.

All who served under the Lusignans were mercenaries. Mélusine when assembling an army for Antoine and Renaud *"had their wages cried"* through all Poitou and the surrounding districts. *"That all who wished to be engaged by her sons present themselves at Lusignan on the said day when they would be paid their wages for a whole year."* Men of war were paid in advance – as they were not sure of what the next day might bring.

The fleets of Mélusine's children, like those of the Knights of Rhodes and the Saracens, consisted of great ships, galleys and small vessels called galiotes. The Christians called their galiotes 'rampins'. The lesser sized of the big ships had two enclosed spaces or bridges, the larger ones three. The fleet that Urian and Guion received from their mother could carry three thousand men at arms.

The galiotes were vessels *d'avantage,* that is to say, very fast. They had eight or sixteen oars and were carried within the big ships. The rampin that Hermine procured for Geoffroy to save Urian went so quickly that it was soon lost to sight to the people of Limassol. It preceded the fleet and went on reconnaissance. In the battle off the coast of Jaffa it accosted the great vessels and rammed them at close quarters so that whose within did not realise it until they found their ships filling up with water *"and so they perished in the sea."*

The artillery on the ships consisted of *pavois* or *pavars* which were placed at the fore tower of the bridge at the approach of battle, along with the ladders to scale the fighting platforms of the masts; great *arbalètes* drawn up on the bridge; *espringales* that fired darts and stone bullets; and finally, alongside these old weapons, the cannons, a great novelty in the time of Jean d'Arras.

The rules of military service were exact and severe. Arms drill, exercises, marches, attacks, retreats, all movements of ordnance, were announced by trumpet call. There were calls for each one. Urian decided to break camp at dawn. They sounded the reveille and Urian rose. Then a trumpet to assemble kit and saddle the horses. At the third trumpet call they fed and watered the horses. And at the following call they took up their arms and marched.

Urian at the battle of le Pont in Cyprus, Antoine and Renaud at Luxembourg, went to encounter their enemies. Armed head to toe, a great baton in hand, ready to dismount and replace the baton with a lance, they went *"to the front line"* before their men, returning from time to time to keep order, so well unified and well kept together that they seemed not half the number that they actually were, and each was but a finger's breadth from the next man.

One never saw lack of discipline. They dare not refuse to obey their masters that all knew were rigorous. The least punishment was to lose horse and equipment and be banished from the company. The worst punishment was the gallows. Antoine, crossing Cologne, had it cried that none be so reckless as to take anything from the town without paying, under pain of the rope. The King of Cyprus threw himself at the Saracen army and did great damage to them, for he had ordered, on pain of the gallows, that they take no prisoners, but all should be put to death.

The army must always be on hand and ready to fight, some distance from what appeared to be the time and place of battle.

One day, Antoine and Renaud ordered that all ride fully armed, each one under his standard, in good order. They were surprised, for they were a hundred leagues from Luxembourg, and it would take another ten days to get there. Many were overburdened to be always in full equipment, especially as there was no need to be so dressed, and some of them murmured.

"*My lords,*" said one of the two old tutor knights to the two brothers, "*most of your men feel badly treated that you order them to wear all their equipment. It seems to them that there is no need until they are nearer your enemies.*"

"*Sir knight,*" said Antoine, "*do you not think that a thing one is long accustomed to is better known than when it is newly practised, and is thus less difficult to do. It is better that they learn to wear their arms at a time when they can be at their ease and in safety, to know they will bear them more easily when need arises. For if they have to learn it in the midst of their enemies and the miseries and anguish of war, their difficulty would be doubled. And, as you know, whoever does not learn his tread when young, will hardly make a good workman when he is old.*"

"*My lord, you are right and speak truly,*" replied the knight.

The following night they had hardly fallen asleep before the brothers made the call "*To arms!*" There was a great fracas in the camp, and all were greatly agitated. They assembled for battle before their tents under their standards. Many torches and lanterns made a great light as if it were day. The brothers went from rank to rank and if they found any fault they corrected it. The army stayed thus for a long time until the runners who had been sent out to search around returned to say that they had seen nor heard nothing. All then asked who had given the alarm and finally they discovered the truth.

The knights said to the brothers, *"My lords, is it not foolish of you to pain your men for nothing?"*

"When you try a new custom," said Antoine, *"do you not try to find if there is anything that needs correction?"*

And they replied, *"By my faith, my lord, that is true."*

"Thus," said Antoine, *"I was right to test my companies to see if they are ready to my needs. At least, if there is any fault, we can put things right with least damage than if we awaited the time for battle."*

"My lord," they replied, *"that is very true."* And they highly regarded the good sense of the brothers.

The day before a battle Urian ordered all his captains to present themselves before him with their men at arms of all kinds, so they could pass in review. They then said *"Have them mount arms."* They did so before his tent. One after the other the captains filed past, pennons in the wind, followed by their men. They ranged across the field and Urian passed through the ranks. He saw how all were armed and if they lacked any piece of their equipment. Also making a close examination of their countenance and bearing to keep in mind those who were most confident in their function.

The army of Antoine and Renaud crossed Bavaria. The Duke of Bavaria sent an old squire to identify the men who were travelling through his country. The squire saw the camp at the bottom of a valley. He saw horses and coursers running and foraging over the grassland. He heard them neigh. He saw the gentlemen in troops. Some jumping, some fighting. There were some who practised throwing a stone, an iron bar, a spear or a throwing knife. Others tested their swords or pieces of their equipment or helmets against darts or blows of swords and did other strong exercises. *"Here is an impressive sight of men at arms,"* said the squire, *"these are men ready for conquest."*

To surprise the enemy and not be surprised by him was one of the first rudiments of the art of war. *"Never be surprised by your enemy,"* said Mélusine, *"however weak they may seem, always watch them and do not be surprised."*

Urian appeared suddenly behind the fierce sultan at the assault of Famagousta. They came to tell the sultan, *"Sire, all the tents are taken, the camp guard is dead, the fiercest men one ever saw have overrun it."* The sultan turned and saw the banners and pennants of Lusignan, but before he had assembled half his men, Urian was upon him.

Under the walls of Damascus, Geoffroy penetrated the middle of the sleeping pagans as far as the tent of King Galafrin of Damietta. *"It is time to wake up him up this morning,"* he said to his men, *"he has slept too long."* With his hefty sword, sharp as a razor, he struck his head into his brain. But the guards outside never saw the Lusignans.

Camps were always placed by a river. The Aisne, the Meuse, the Rhine, the Elbe, the rivers of Bavaria, of Cyprus, of Syria, had seen the Lusignan pavilions dressed along their banks. It was a useful precaution against surprise attack.

Antoine and Renaud had not yet left Poitou. From their first step, they ordered a watch to be kept *"as if they were in enemy territory."*

Urian, warned that the Saracens had put to sea to invade his country, kept himself to the middle of his lands, like Charles V in the war against the English, to be closer to wherever the enemy landed. He placed guards at all the ports, commanding that, as soon as they saw the Saracens, they light a beacon. The nearest guard would see the signal, do the same, guard after guard repeating it, by means of which, in less than a night, the whole kingdom would know.

The romance of *Mélusine* gives many descriptions of battles on land and sea, off the coast of Rhodes and Sicily, Cyprus and Syria, the island of Cyprus, Luxembourg, Bohemia and the Rhineland.

The army ranked in line of deployment, men at arms in the centre, archers and crossbowmen on the wings. *"It was a great beauty to contemplate"* for the weather never lacked to be fine on a day of battle. There you would have seen helmets, armour, gold and blue, the colours of standards and pennants, resplendent in the sun. There one could see a fine company, the flower of chivalry, banners flying in the wind – hear the clinking of their harness.

The trumpets sounded quickly. The Lusignan brothers, lance in hand, shield against the breast, going *"at good pace and in fine array"*, their standard before them. The war cries resounding *"Lusignan! Alsace! Saint-Jean de Rhodes! Antioch! Barbary! Kurds! Damascus!"* The archers shoot their arrows. The crossbowmen tend to their good crossbows, quickly priming *viretons* or *carreaux en coche*, to fire their bolts all at once. The salvos continue ceaselessly. Men at arms and enemy knights charge fiercely. At the lowering of lances there is a great fracas, stirring, tribulation, great *peleterie*, abundance of fallen men. There will be many who wish they were back home in the place whence they had come. Lances broken, drawing their swords or seizing a battle axe to strike without pity. Many a man is killed in great pain. The ground is covered with dead. War horses run riderless across the field, leaping about, their reins trailing.

Indulging in fierce assaults, ten thousand Saracens follow their king or their sultan. The Poitevins are famous for their skill at arms, strong and tough, fierce as lions, and their lords so powerful that none, however brave, dare confront them. Victory is unsure. It must finish by means of a master stroke, to undo the enemy chief.

A son of Mélusine throws himself at the enemy ranks *"faster than lightning falling from the sky."* He cleaves them, striking to left and right. His men run after him, all astonished at what they see him do. He finds that which he searches for, Bradimont, King of Alsace, the Sultan of Damascus, and the Duke of Austria. With a well aimed blow he kills the Saracen, and stuns the Christian prince, takes his body by the arm and drags him from his horse, throwing him to the ground so roughly that his heart might have burst within his chest.

He turns to his own. *"Lusignan!"* he cries. *"Advance barons! Strike down all you can, the day is ours, God be thanked!"* The soldiers perform marvels at arms. The enemy lose their courage along with their chief, turn and flee. They are pursued without cease, massacred in the fields, in the thickets. *"Be sure that few escaped."* Thus is the battle finished. There remains only to clear the field of carnage, bury the dead, burn the carcasses of the horses that have perished.

The Christians see a Saracen fleet. They put out flags on ships and galleys, prepare their war machines, climb on the platforms of the masts, spears and darts in hand, and sound the trumpets. At the cry *"Lusignan!"* they run at the Saracens with force of rams, all sails spread, their ships flying like crossbow bolts.

The surprised Saracens recoil a little in putting themselves into formation. But when among the Christian vessels, some go around them and turn about with such speed that they are disconcerted. Others make a passage between the ships in such a way that there remain not four together. The cannons fire *"horribly"*. When they are carried, they throw darts so strong and hard that they seem like an iron hailstorm.

At their first encounter with the Lusignans, the Saracens prepare a ship they have captured from the brothers of St. John of Rhodes full of logs, oil, grease and sulphur, set it on fire and direct it toward the Christians. But they are keeping watch. They assail their enemies from the other side, and the flaming vessel ends up burning three Saracen ships.

Finally the Christian fleet approaches the pagan ships. It shocks them violently and sinks them or engages them with pots of fire. They throw themselves onto the Saracen ships. At the battle before Jaffa, Geoffroy jumps into the vessel of King Athenor. The pagans are lost. Their ships, emptied of miscreants, pillaged of anything worth taking, are burnt and sunk. But when a vessel is full of *"very fine things"* it is taken into port.

Here are "beardless" youngsters who know as much as the most experienced captains of the Hundred Years War. So well that in following the tale of their expeditions one can learn how they conducted war in the 14th century. The holding of men in a state of readiness at all times, exacting complete obedience and submission, the ensemble and precision in manoeuvres, establishing encampments, ruling the order of march, the ordering of battles.

They also know the laws of war. It must be chivalrous. Their mother has only to repeat what they have heard throughout their childhood.

"Be intractable to the wicked. Be hard and have at heart the fierceness of a lion toward your enemies. Show your power and your lordship over them. Do not give up until they are reduced to obedience. However, I recommend you do not make it a point of honour to punish them. If you are courteous to them it will turn great honour to you."

Zelodus, after having killed the King of Bohemia, has burned his body. The King of Alsace burns the body of Zelodus. *"By my head,"* says Antoine, *"you have done well there. Truly Zelodus was too cruel. When a man is dead it is great shame for his enemy to strike him again."*

One does not strike an enemy in the back. The Sultan of Damascus flies before Geoffroy. *"Saracen,"* cries Geoffroy, *"you are a coward, to be so well mounted and nobly armed, and afraid to face a single man. Turn or I will kill you flying, even though I dishonour myself."*

All war must be declared. It is not permitted to attack an enemy until he has received a challenge. *"Lord king,"* says the messenger of Antoine and Renaud to the King of Alsace, *"I challenge you by the two young men of Lusignan and all their followers."*

"Well," replies the king, *"I will guard myself from surprise and loss."*

"You will have good need to!" says the messenger.

The Lusignan brothers go to attack the Germans. *"We must not,"* says Geoffroy, *"fall upon these men without a challenge. It is necessary to warn them to take guard against us."*

"That is quite right," they reply.

Then they write one of those letters of which the 14th and 15th centuries have left us many examples. *"To you, Duke of Austria, Count of Fribourg, and all your allies, we, Antoine of Lusignan, Duke of Luxembourg; we, Odon of Lusignan, Count of la Marche; we Raimonnet of Lusignan, Count of Forez; and I, Thierry of Lusignan, Lord of Parthenay, warn you that through these letters read, you defend yourself against us, for we will bring you damage as soon as we can."*

The brothers put their seals upon the letter. A herald remits it to the Duke of Austria who has it read in audience.

"Why," say the Germans between themselves, *"has the Devil brought such as the Lusignans to this country!"*

All single combat, whether or not judicial, is preceded by a verbal challenge. Raimondin before the King of the Bretons calls Josselin and his son Olivier to battle and throws down his gage.

"I challenge you by Mahomet my god," cries the Sultan of Damascus to Geoffroy.

"By my head," replies Geoffroy, *"I do not prize you or your god any more than a head of rotten garlic."*

Geoffroy even challenges the giants that he has searched out in their lairs. *"Wicked creature,"* he says to the giant of Guérande, *"I hold you for dead where you stand, and I challenge you by God, my Creator."*

"Defend yourself, I challenge you" he cries to the giant of Northumberland. He spurs his horse, couches his lance and strikes the giant so hard that he is thrown to the ground with his legs in the air.

Social Etiquette

These hardened warriors *"like hawks that fall on skylarks or hungry wolves that throw themselves on sheep"* know the customs of good society. They show deference and delicacy. Of a man of their character and education they used to say *"He knows good and honour well."* Some centuries later they would say *"He is a gentleman."*

At the marriage of Renaud and Aiglantine there was very fine jousting. But as no knight could hold against Antoine or Renaud, when the brothers saw that the jousting was weakened because of them, they left and disarmed, and this, the King of Alsace, the Duke of Bavaria, and the other barons remarked. Thus they continued jousting for a long time.

One could hardly imagine men more ceremonious then the characters in *Mélusine*. On all occasions when they met there was nothing they did without form. Acts, words, obeying complicated rules with the most punctilious awareness, pushed to the point of humility. On approaching to speak to someone they gave greeting. On leaving them they took their leave. *"I commend you to God,"* they said. *"May God keep you,"* was the response. Welcomes and farewells are innumerable in *Mélusine*.

It is the same with paying respects. They made a match of it from one party to the other. Geoffroy arrives at Limassol. Hermine, the Queen of Cyprus, awaits him, holding her son Hervé by the hand. She curtseys low before her brother in law Geoffroy who does as much, raising her up and embracing her gently saying *"Madame, may God grant you all the joy your heart desires."*

There are cases where respect is not enough. The messenger bringing news of the burning down of Maillezais; the old knight announcing to Mélusine that dinner is served; Raimondin asking Count Bertrand the charter of the gift that the count has made him of a part of the forest of Colombiers; Alain thanking his cousin for having given him the barony of Léon; the sons of Mélusine when they thank their mother for the help she has given them for their wars; Hermine herself witnessing her recognition of the Lusignan brothers – all speak on their knees. The little Hervé, beside his mother, puts one knee to the ground before Geoffroy. His uncle raises him in his arms. *"Good nephew,"* he tells him, *"God keep you and bring you increasing fortune,"* and the child replies *"Great thanks, good uncle."*

No circumstance dispenses with marks of courtesy. Urian and Hermine, two lovers, exchange many honours. Aiglentine married in the morning abases herself before her husband and thanks him for having deigned to take for wife so weak a maiden as she is. Antoine vanquishes the King of Alsace by stunning him with a sword blow to his helmet. The death or life of his prisoner is still in his hands. He has not decided. But they are no longer at the battle. They go to eat at table in the castle at Luxembourg. The captive king is still a king. Antoine has him called, invites him to sit first, then the lady of Luxembourg, Renaud next, and after that four leading barons of the country, and finally in the hall each one takes their place according to their rank. Thus the French king Jean le Bon, a prisoner in London, daily received royal honours.

These are the ordinary observances of politeness. In great circumstances the ceremonial becomes majestic.

The Count of Poitiers approaches the place where the wedding of Mélusine is to take place. An old knight, wearing a belt decorated with precious stones and pearls, mounted on a tall dappled grey palfrey, followed by twelve men of honour nobly dressed, advances joyfully to him. He sagely pays his respects: *"Good sir,"* says the count, *"Be most welcome. Tell me whom you seek."*

"Sire," replies the knight, *"the lady Mélusine of Albany commends herself to you, such as she can, and thanks you for the great honour you have given to your cousin Raimondin and to her, in coming to her wedding."*

"Sir knight," says the count, *"you can tell your lady that there is no need for thanks, I am held to honour my cousin."*

"Sire," says the knight, *"you speak courteously, but my lady is wise enough to know that we are in your debt, and sire, she has committed me and my companions to acknowledge this."*

After that the countess comes, the count's mother, with her daughter. Mélusine sends before her the old knight and several ladies in waiting of high estate and receives them with the melodies of many instruments.

The two entries of the Lusignans to Luxembourg, that of Antoine and Renaud the day they have defeated the King of Alsace, and that of Geoffroy, Eudes, Thierry and Raimonnet going to fight the Duke of Austria, are equally of high ceremonial.

Antoine rides a great Liard courser. He is dressed in a coat of crimson velvet, embroidered with pearls and small gems. He wears a chaplet of pearls on his head, his sword at his side, baton in hand. His brother, next to him, is similarly attired. Two hundred knights accompany them.

A hundred gentlemen and barons of the country come to meet them and pay their respects. The brothers enter the city. Before them are heralds, trumpeters and fiddlers in abundance. The townspeople have decorated the streets up to the castle with rich hangings.

At the foot of the steps of the castle, the maiden Chrétienne awaits them, surrounded by ladies, knights and squires. She takes the brothers by the hands and places herself between them. Together they pass through the great hall, which according to custom is hung with beautiful tapestries, then enter a splendid chamber.

The major domos kneel before the maiden to say *"My lady, all is ready when it pleases you to wash your hands."*

"When it pleases my lord," she replies.

"Lady", says Antoine, *"we are ready whenever it pleases you."* The brothers take the hands of the maiden and take her to the table.

They do not say which prince is served before the Duchess of Luxembourg. At the dinner of their betrothal, Hermine and Urian are seated at a table near the sickbed of the King of Cyprus, and Guion is served before Hermine. During the dinner at the funeral of Raimondin, the King and Queen of Aragon regard Bernadon, the son of Eudes, with pleasure, for he serves the lords so gracefully that they marvel.

At the start of the expedition to Austria, Antoine and Renaud, who were then at Luxembourg with the Queen of Bohemia, learn that their four brothers are staying nearby.

The Duke of Luxembourg cries *"To horse, and alert the whole town."*

They mount on horseback in a great company of knights and go to meet their brothers, and the ladies to their rooms to make themselves ready.

Geoffroy sees his brothers coming, and clears a space of at least two lance lengths where none dare approach more closely. Many men at arms before and behind hold others to order. Renaud and Antoine greet their brothers and make them graciously welcome. They take the road together, two by two, the eldest to the fore, and ride back to the castle.

There the queen and the duchess and their ladies and maidens come straight away to pay their respects to the brothers. Great joy follows, the tables prepared, the dinner ready, all washed and seated.

And after all have dined, Geoffroy tells of his adventures.

ⲓⲓⲓⲓⲓⲓⲓⲓⲓⲓⲓⲓⲓⲓⲓ

Altogether, the author of *Mélusine* is singularly original, because he has built upon a Celtic legend a book of the genre of *Télémaque* and transformed the faery of a fountain in Poitou to a Christian Minerva. The adventures of the sons of Mélusine – apart from Geoffroy á la Grand Dent – show morality in action. Her wise children practise perfectly the lessons of their mentor. Their obedience is royally rewarded and the penitence of Geoffroy beings him a peaceful life and the love of his subjects.

The Castle, Church & Town of Lusignan

I have collected together and translated here some interesting odds and ends about the Castle, Town and Church at Lusignan. The first from a 19th century history of the House of Lusignan by the Canoine Pascal, and the rest from the local church bookstall and tourist bureau when I last visited there.

X X X X X X X X X X X X X X X X

The Town

by Office du Tourisme, Lusignan

The Lusignan region has been inhabited since the time of the Gauls. We can say that after the Roman conquest, life was organised from Pranzanium-Pranzay and that a military camp existed at Châteliers. Then the name of Licinianus appeared, that after a number of transformations became Lusignan, in the 17th and 18th centuries. The region has known the passage or settlement of many peoples – thus the tribe of Scythes in the 5th and 6th centuries, having for mother goddess a woman with the tail of a serpent.

In the Middle Ages, after the reign of Charlemagne, the lands became the property of the Counts of Lusignan. Between the 10th century the beginning of the 14th they built the castle and the church. Near the castle, a town grew up on the plateau, protected by ramparts. At the site of the Fon de Cé was the village of Curzay, the suburb

The town of Lusignan

of Enjambes extending toward the northwest and the Lower Town developed along the Bourceron brook. Lusignan was then formed of three parishes: Notre Dame, Pranzay and Enjambes.

The Hundred Years War did not spare the region. Around 1350 the English invaded Lusignan and twice occupied the castle. Du Guesclin finally evicted them in 1374.

After a period of peace during which Jean de Berry tried to repair the war damage, the coming of Calvin, preaching the reformed religion, was a source of new conflicts. The castle and town passed to and fro under the domination of Protestant or Catholic armies. The bloodiest episode was the final siege. In 1574 the Protestants entrenched the town; fire ravaged the Lower Town and the Fon de Cé. The royal army, commanded by the Duke of Montpensier, attacked, and the decimated and starving Protestant garrison surrendered. Peace was signed on 15th January 1575 but the castle was demolished. A new period of peace was established until 1685, when the revocation of the Edict of Nantes outlawed the Protestants. In the harsh period of the Dragonnades they were persecuted to obtain their conversion. Lusignan and the region were depopulated as some Protestants preferred to emigrate.

In the 18th century things changed. The Promenades were built by the Count de Blossac, the market place created at the foot of the church, a new road crossed the river Vonne by a bridge at Pranzay, on which turned the mills of la Touche, Vauchiron and Envaux. Two oil mills, Chédau and Payré, worked on the Bourceron.

In 1790 Lusignan became the centre for the district, as it is today.

But the Revolution brought more trouble to the town. The nobles of the region emigrated while two families confronted each other: the royalist Tilberts, and the revolutionary Villeneuves, motivated by personal ambition as much as political ideas.

Modern times arrived with much building, including the railway and its two viaducts in the 1850s. They speak of the installation of a

telephone service and a meteorological station. In 1886 a fire service was equipped with 60 pails and a hand driven pump. In 1908 oil lighting was replaced by electric light. Security was assured by mounted police while a court and prison functioned at the Place du Bail.

There remained however a population often destitute. An office of charity and philanthropy – a veritable bank of mutual help – tried to help the poorest. Between 1878 and 1882 a hospital was built, replacing the hospice that had existed since 1695.

In 1836 a school was opened, and at the end of the 19th century Lusignan possessed a mixed public and private school. There was also an amateur musical group – the Mélusine Lyre.

An important project for laying on water was launched. Industry was varied and prospered: a mustard factory, drapers, wheelwright, blacksmith, carpenter, rope maker, chair maker, serge maker, candle maker … trade flourished. Lusignan then had about 2200 inhabitants.

The 1914-18 war slowed up growth. The population and industry diminished. The town suffered 92 dead and many prisoners.

Technical progress continued: the telephone, a departmental railway joining the villages of Jazeneuil, Lavausseau, and Béruges to the Poitiers/La Rochelle line. Lusignan developed a modern spirit of the times.

The 1939-45 war brought its difficulties, even if Lusignan suffered only light bombardment and the constraints of Occupation. After the

A street sign depicting 'la fée' in Lusignan

liberation, things developed rapidly. A camping site was opened in 1960 and a public bath and shower establishment in 1956. The population attained 2855 inhabitants in 1982, this growth bringing the creation of the surrounding suburbs.

The Castle

by Canoine Pascal

Raymondin of Forez, a native of Poitou, was the first head of the House of Lusignan; his wife Mélusine inspired the poets of France and Germany.

In the 10th century Hugues I, called the Veneur, contemporary of Louis d'Outre-Mer, was the head of the noble family; it was under his son, Hugues II, called the Bien-Aimé, that the castle of Lusignan was built. His descendants took the title of Lords of Lusignan; their glorious exploits are told in the poem of Jean d'Arras and in the chronicles of Froissart.

The famous castle of the Lusignans, whose ramparts, over the centuries, held the authority of the kings of France in check, was finally taken by the Duke of Montpensier in 1575 and destroyed; there remain only ruins today.

Here are a few retrospective details of this building.

Situated near the town of Lusignan that it dominated, it was enclosed by a triple belt of walls ten feet high. A wide and deep moat separated the first from the second, and a wide space of at least two hundred paces the second from the third. These three walls, and especially the first, were flanked with towers surmounting a crenellated parapet with many firing positions. The strong high towers in the form of truncated cones served as magazines, with rooms containing munitions and arms stores, and protected the pierced posterns at their foot. Before the castle, facing the town, was a bastion called Porte-Geoffroy, whose front was decorated with a crude sculpture representing Geoffroy á la Grande-Dent, which caused, incorrectly, the foundation of the castle to be attributed to this lord. The arms of the first Lusignans, bands of silver and blue, surmounted this imperfect bust.

On passing the two lines of walls one came to the Poitevin Tower, communicating with the courtyard that contained the stables, several wells, a deep pond and the servants' quarters.

In the centre, towards the west, was an artificial high mound, on which stood the keep. With a wall all around it, and its elevated front surmounted by a glittering helmet, symbol of hospitality, it oversaw not only the castle, but a great distance over the surrounding countryside.

The keep had a square tower, with turrets at the four corners; these turrets contained stairs, and one of them had a well called the Well of Despair, because of its unknown depth. The belfry, which crowned the centre and the platform, held the bell which was rung in times of alarm.

At Lusignan the casement windows were wide, high, and so as to conserve the light, the wall had been chamfered above the opening.

But on the ground floor was the Hall of the Ancestors, a long gallery with dark hangings, before which stood crude and stiff statues of the Lusignan line. During the day fitful gleams through the little leaded windows surcharged with paintings lit this monotonous room as if with regret. All here was sombre: the woodwork of blackened oak, the steel weapons, the suits of armour all mounted, hanging beside each statue, could make one think that the warrior was about to move and to walk. The sun never penetrated this room where, on entering, one breathed the humid and penetrating air of the cellars.

The chapel, joined to the keep by a corridor, raised its bell tower into the air whose delicacy made an pleasant contrast to the rest of the castle.

The parade ground extended before the keep, on the other side of which rose the Mélusine tower, two hundred and sixteen feet high, surmounted by the famous battlements on which the faery spreads her white wings when lamenting a coming catastrophe. One could see, at some distance, a natural fountain prettily shadowed by weeping willow trees, where it was said Mélusine often bathed. The country folk never tired of talking about the marvellous properties of the spring and of the strange things that had been seen here.

A recent event had above all impressed their minds. The Kône having dried up during some very hot weather, the women of Lusignan asked the Countess permission to wash their laundry in the fountain; but the laundry they took from the water became bewitched and flew

The site of Lusignan castle

from their hands before they returned home. What is more, the varlets and the watchman swore that they nearly died of fright the following night on seeing winged washerwomen skimming over the waters of the fountain wildly beating otherworld laundry. Since that day, everyone avoided the marvellous spring, even though at the request of the Countess the chaplain exorcised it.

They still claim that the Mélusine tower gives access to an underground tunnel leading as far as Poitiers, but no one has ever explored it, and some whisper that the faery, not being able to die, remains captive there during the day, leaving it at night, to go and beat on the battlements.

The faery appreciated music. They say that once, at the end of the day, the Count had come with his pages to the fountain and started to sing a ballad. And as he sang, they saw the water become agitated, and from it rose a white mist that, taking form, became the faery herself. She hovered over the water with the grace of flower dancing in the wind, then, when the Count had finished, she disappeared.

The Church

by Suzanne Devillards & D. Sabourin

Origins

The origin of the church is connected to the powerful Lusignan family. Hugues IV, le Brun, decided to build a church near his castle. There was thus a bill of exchange of land between the canons of St. Hilaire at Poitiers and Hugues of Lusignan. This was signed in 1024.

In 1025, King Robert le Pieux confirmed this exchange and its intention, which was to build a church in honour of the Virgin.

Hugues IV had earlier wanted to found an abbey near the church but the refusal of the monks of Nouallé led him to establish a simple priory. On the death of the lord of Lusignan, the church had got no further than the north transept, the sanctuary above the crypt and the first two bays. The building of the church was continued by Hugues VI, called "the Devil", who wanted to earn God's favour by a striking magnificent gift for His worship, and in thanks for having escaped death in the course of a crusade.

According to Monseigneur Cousseau, bishop of Angoulême and Monseigneur de Longuemar, Hugues VI would have finished the

church in seven years, from 1103 to 1110. A charter of this time stipulates that offerings at the church of Our Lady of Lusignan must revert to the abbey of Nouaillé.

History

From 1168 the passage of the army of Henry II Plantagenet, husband of Eleanor of Aquitaine, caused some damage to the church.

Come the Hundred Years War, the English took possession of Lusignan, then Du Guesclin besieged our fortress in 1373. The English crossbowmen fired from the bell tower, while the French riposted so well that part of the tower collapsed, followed by the roof. Jean de Berry, Count of Poitou in the 14th century, restored it in 1377 and also built a solid buttress to the south wall and had a window remade, inspired by the Gothic style.

In the 16th century the religious wars broke out. According to St. Bartholomew, our church suffered much. The Protestants occupied the castle and town, while the Duke of Montpensier, on the King's orders, organised a siege from 1574 to 1575. Montpensier fired cannon at the church and priory, which were fortified. The latter was destroyed, and the west façade of Notre Dame was damaged.

During the Revolution the church served as a warehouse. It was restored to worship in 1802, by a concordat between Bonaparte and the Pope.

Illustrious Visitors

In 1140 the Papal Legate and the Archbishop of Bordeaux stopped at Lusignan and prayed in the church.

St. Louis came to the castle and the pious King made his devotions at Notre Dame.

In 1305 when Bertrand de Got, Archbishop of Bordeaux, meditated in the church, representatives of the council came to tell him he had been nominated Pope. He took the name of Clement V and was installed at Avignon some time later. In 1307 he returned to Lusignan when he went to Poitiers to meet the King Philippe le Bel.

Exterior of the Church

The church of Notre Dame, which on the whole is in the Romanesque style, is in the form of a Latin cross, of which the nave forms one part and the transept the other, two apsidal chapels open directly on the arms of the transept.

The Bell Tower: The whole is dominated by the bell tower, square and in two storeys, separated by a cornice of modillions. The lower storey, like the upper, presents on each side four blind semicircular arcades separated by small columns with sculpted capitals.

The Turret stairway: At the southwest corner of the transept a turret stairway is covered with a conical roof of stone tiles.

The Walls: The lateral walls present an irregular type of 11th century masonry known as *á petit appareil* in which the stones are cemented with a mortar containing much earth.

The Buttresses: The thick walls are supported by powerful buttresses, particularly in the north, where the building is not far from the edge of the plateau.

The Bays: The bays are in the Romanesque style, and generally grouped in pairs in the north. In the south they are less numerous and have no

decoration. On the other hand the bays of the transept, of the apse and the apsidal chapels are ornamented. Toruses, mouldings, folded ribbons, diamond points are the principal elements. The columns framing these bays present sculpted capitals of leaves, knot work, animals or fabulous characters such as Mélusine. A simple bay escapes the Romanesque style of the whole by its ogival form with a stone upright separating two trilobial arches.

The Porch: A striking porch on the south façade opens on a triangular gable surmounted by a cross. Two doors are separated by a stone mullion

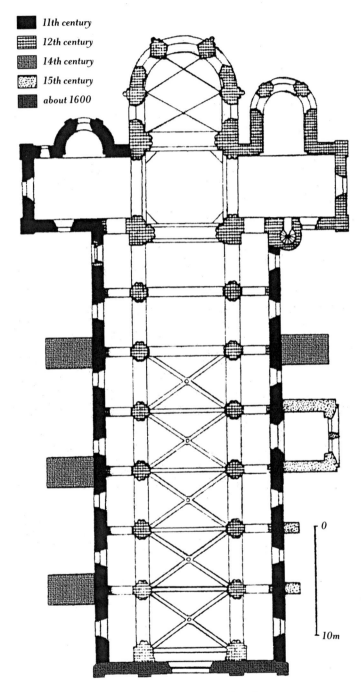

11th century
12th century
14th century
15th century
about 1600

0

10m

Interior of Lusignan church

framed by a deep arcade of arches broken by several projections, ending at the archivault and at the summit by a rosette frieze. The archivaults are staggered toward the interior, supported on short columns reposing on stone ledges. Framing all, two primatic needles are sculpted in their top half. Above the pier and the doors, ornamented lamp brackets once held statues that have now disappeared. The one in the centre presents half length a character carrying a parchment. He is surrounded by angels with coats of arms effaced by time. This vast porch was added to the south side of the church in the 15th century.

Back of the Porch: At the back of the porch a door opens on the nave; it is of thick nailed oak and has two leaves. Three archivaults fall at each side on two columns and a console with capitals sculpted with leaves. This door seems to be 14th century.

Lateral North Door: This once connected the priory to the church and opens today on the sacristy. It is a Romanesque arch formed from two archivaults disposed on the same level and resting on a cornice as if upheld by two pillars of large diameter whose capitals are ornamented with confronting animals and bundles of vegetation. A wide illuminated bandeau is surmounted with a torus ornamented with diamond points, while the lower archivault presents only concentric toruses.

The wide half circle is sculpted, with 23 figures of men and animals on many of the stones of the arch.

The one in the centre shows a human head with long beard and a faun's ears. Beside this, to its left, are two characters; one dressed in a long robe carries a book at the level of his chest, the other seems naked and hopping on one leg. The springing of the arch to the right is sculpted with two non-contiguous figures, one below dressed in a robe carries a baton in his hand, the other, crouching, with clawed feet, appears to have his arms tied by a cord. The many and various animals represent almost a complete medieval bestiary. We can identify a goose, a unicorn, a dragon, a leopard, an elephant... This ornamental bandeau represents the work of the Creation and the virtues and vices of man. The fine framing of the door is of the 12th century.

The Nave: This is of majestic aspect, its length 57 metres, and width 16 metres. The transept is 29 metres long. The central part of the nave is 7.5 metres wide and 15.6 metres high. The side aisles 4.25 metres wide and 13 metres high. The cupola is 20 metres high.

The two bays closest to the choir are barrel vaulted, broken arched and separated from each other by double arches in the same form, resting on high columns engaged in supporting pillars, which come equally to engage on columns less elevated than the first. They support the arches which join the nave to the side aisles. Between the groups of columns the intersections of the supporting pillars are charged with projecting fleurons, and the angles at their base are rounded out to form a paw.

The five longest spans of the choir are vaulted with prismatic ribs intersecting with escutcheons at the crown. The vaulting of these spans has been reconstructed at a higher level, no doubt at the beginning of the 16th century; the records do not give any precise date. M. Eygun, Poitevin archaeologist, gives several indications on the crowns of the vaulting in the nave decorated with escutcheons, one of which recalls royalty, another the marriage of Charles VIII to Anne de Bretagne in 1491 (fleur de lys and ermine). Another also carries the emblem of royalty surmounted by two facing hawks, which are the arms of the Fou family, having had connections with Lusignan. The fourth escutcheon has not been positively identified, while the fifth is indecipherable.

The Collaterals: Less high than the nave, and much narrower (4.5 metres compared to 7.5 metres) they have a barrel vault supported by double arches, on one side leaning on the pillars of the nave, the other side on the projections of the guttering wall. The collaterals, or side aisles, can be considered as veritable buttresses of the nave, being less high.

The Transept: The crossing of the transept is defined by four strong pillars destined to support the bell tower. They present four half columns on each face, supporting the preceding arch of the barrel vaulting. An octagonal cupola on squinches covers the square of the transept.

Choir Aisle: Raised on nine steps, the choir composes a straight span and a semicircle lit by five windows that are embrasured with projections and framed by two little columns with simple capitals. The vault is oven shaped and supported by flanges that rest on high columns rising as far as the cornice, like the church at Jazeneuil.

The two sides aisles are different. The north crosspiece barrel vaulted semicircle is endowed with a very simple semicircular oven shaped apsidal chapel. Lit by a single window, a single semicircular arch precedes its embrasure. The capitals of primitive character are 11th century as also the North crosspiece and its apsidal chapel.

The southern arm comprises a deeper apsidal chapel. The entry arch is lightly broken and double rolled, three windows light the semicircle, and small columns support their arches and their capitals, and are of the 12th century.

The Crypt: This supports the sanctuary which is more elevated than the floor of the nave, as we have said. It is an underground chapel divided into three parts by two ranks of columns that support the barrel vaulting. At the end of the crypt of seven metres by seven is a very simple altar behind which an ambulatory permits the faithful to circulate. Two beautifully scrolled capitals with clawed bases between two toruses define the ensemble as 12th century. The seven little windows are embrasured in steps. This crypt served as the burial place for the priors of Notre Dame, and some knights and captains of the castle of Lusignan.

Ornamentation of the Church

Capitals in the Sanctuary: Some capitals at the meeting of the apse and the two arms of the transept are remarkable; they reproduce symbolic animals of the Romanesque school: doves drinking in a vase, separately a lamb, wild beasts eating or disputing their prey. In the first two spans the capitals are sculpted with bodies of animals, and volutes like straight stems surmounted by very simple florets; further on leaves in the form of lance heads, knot work, palm leaves and crosspieces ornament other capitals, while the last shows a decoration hardly sketched out.

Chapel of St Anne: (south east apsidal) Two pillars ornamented with a silver dove holding a branch in its beak and perched on a branch with a blue background.

Nave: In the nave is an oak chair in octagonal form decorated with trunk columns and running foliage.

Side Chapels: The decorated background of the altar still apparent is of Lourdine stone, and although recently executed (19th century) presents Roman arcades framing religious scenes.

Stained glass: These are of the same epoch and have been presented by Mélusine families in memory of dear ones. The central stained glass window of the choir is consecrated to the Assumption of the Virgin, patroness of the church. She carries an escutcheon similar to that which recalls, in the Hall of the Crusades in the Museum at Versailles, the high dignitaries of Lusignan. The left window is consecrated to St. Peter and carries the arms of Pope Pious IX; that on the right represents St. Martin and carries the arms of Cardinal Pius, Bishop of Poitiers. Apart from these historical bays we find some pretty *grisailles*.

The Statues: The stone statue that dominates the Sanctuary is that of the Virgin and Child, and is of the 17th century. On a console is a small ancient pieta of polychrome wood. Low along one side is a recumbent figure in very poor condition that was brought from the Promenades some years ago.

Paving: The paving of the church was relaid in 1795, with a few tombstones from the crypt violated in the 16th century and some from the deconsecrated cemetery of Notre Dame.

An Historical Outline of the Lords of Lusignan

• Gareth Knight •

In his analysis of the Mélusine romance Louis Stouff comprehensively describes the culture of the 14th century inherent within it, but does not find a great deal of correspondence between characters in the romance and individuals in history. It is arguable, however, that he did not go back quite far enough – that is to say to the 12th century – and even to 11th century roots. Three lines of enquiry seem worth pursuing in this respect.

- First, the commitment, generation after generation of Lusignan lords to **the Crusades.**
- Second, the founding of a Lusignan dynasty in **Cyprus** that later married into that of **Lesser Armenia.**
- Third, the role of **Eleanor of Aquitaine and the Plantagenets** with the Lusignans.

The Crusades

The on-going commitment of Lusignan lords to the crusading movement runs from Hugh VI who went on the Duke of Aquitaine's ill-starred crusade of 1100 and became a comrade in arms of King Baldwin I.

His son, Hugh VII, accompanied Eleanor of Aquitaine and King Louis VII of France on the 2nd Crusade in 1142, in which he lost his life. Whilst *his* son, Hugh VIII, went on armed pilgrimage with his neighbour Geoffroy Martel of Angoulême, in support of the campaign

175

of King Amalric I in Egypt. He was captured in a skirmish at Antioch on the way home in 1165 and spent some years as a prisoner in Aleppo where he ended his life.

Nonetheless his sons Guy and Amalric became Kings of Jerusalem in 1186 and 1198 respectively, through marriage to successive heiresses, Sibylle and Isabelle of Jerusalem.

Their elder brother Geoffroy, a hero of the 3rd Crusade, returned home in 1193 to father another Geoffroy who was a fair approximation to Geoffroy Great-Tooth of the romance.

Successors in the main branch of the Lusignan line, in the succeeding three generations Hugh IX, X and XI lost their lives on later abortive crusades in 1219, 1249 and 1270 respectively.

Cyprus

After the fall of the Holy City to Saladin in 1187, Guy and his brother Amalric founded a dynasty on Cyprus. The island was raised to the status of a kingdom in 1198 that lasted until the Lusignan line died out, when it became a Venetian colony in 1469.

One of its later Lusignan kings, Peter the Valiant, who is mentioned by Louis Stouff, was something of a firebrand. From the age of 16 he was urging rulers of Western Europe to start another crusade, and on becoming king raided Alexandria in 1365. After appalling atrocities on both sides, his fellows in arms decided not to press on with his plan to invade the rest of Egypt and were content to retire with their booty. Peter the Valiant was assassinated in 1369, foreshadowed by an appearance of Mélusine, as related by the Prince of Wales to the Duke de Berry, as Louis Stouff records.

The Lusignans of Cyprus later married into the royal family of Lesser Armenia, a Christian kingdom on the coast of Asia Minor just north of Cyprus. It was overrun by the Seljuk Turks in 1375, and its last king, Leo V, was a prisoner in Cairo for seven years before being ransomed. His last years were spent in France attempting to raise interest in another crusade to regain his kingdom. He died in 1393, the same year that Jean d'Arras completed the Mélusine romance in which the original cause of Leo's misfortunes are attributed to an ancestor's attempt to possess the faery Mélior at the Castle of the Hawk.

Eleanor of Aquitaine

There was an on-going involvement between the Lusignans and Eleanor of Aquitaine, Queen of the Troubadour Minstrelsy and patron of the cult of Courtly Love. As Duchess of Aquitaine she was their liege lord but this did not stop the Lusignan brothers from attempting to abduct her on three occasions in 1168, 1199 and 1202, in order to further their interests.

On the 3rd Crusade, Guy and Amalric of Lusignan became closely involved with Eleanor's favourite son, Richard Coeur de Lion. It was he who enabled them to take over Cyprus. Amalric also benefited from the accidental death of Eleanor's grandson, Henry II of Champagne, who fell from a high window, enabling Amalric to marry Henry's widow, Isabella of Jerusalem.

Back at home events were less fortunate. Eleanor's youngest son John, on becoming King of England, made off with the 12-year-old beauty Isabelle of Angoulême on the eve of her marriage to Hugh IX of Lusignan. Although after King John's death in 1216 she returned to marry Hugh X of Lusignan, the son of her jilted fiancé!

IIIIIIIIIIIIIIII

But to go back to the 11th century, there is a claim made in *L'Histoire de la Maison Royale de Lusignan* (1896), by Chanoine Pascal, that there was a Lusignan interest in the Holy Land even before the 1st Crusade, when Robert of Lusignan made a pilgrimage to the East in 1062. His goal was not Jerusalem however, but Mount Zion, in the Sinai desert south of the Dead Sea. Here, where traditionally Moses had received the Tablets of the Law, Greek monks had founded a monastery, and Robert of Lusignan established the knightly order of St. Catherine to provide protection for pilgrims there. To quote from Chanoine Pascal's account:

> Attracted to Mount Siniai by the talk of miracles about the tomb of St. Catherine, virgin of Alexandria, he was struck by the abandoned state in which he found numerous pilgrims who came to venerate the saint's relics. Helped in his pious enterprise by his noble and faithful companions he founded at the place of this famous pilgrimage a hospice on the model of that

at the Holy Sepulchre. He established a body of religious here who devoted themselves to the care of the sick and undertook to defend pilgrims and guard the tomb of the illustrious martyr. In 1063 these knights embraced the rule of St. Basil and this was the origin of the humanitarian and hospitaller Order of St. Catherine of Mount Sinai.

These knights, reports Elias Ashmole, in his work on the Order of the Garter, published in London in 1672, made an oath to the grandmaster and the abbot of the monastery; they made a vow of chastity and swore to guard the tomb of the saint for two years.

Robert, whose renown became widespread in Palestine, hurried, although old, to the side of the Duke of Lorraine, Godfrey of Bouillon, to fight against the infidels, and, when the Duke was elected King of Jerusalem in 1099, Robert was created Count of Jaffa and Ascalon. That is how the Lusignans were first established in Palestine.

Actually the pious Godfrey of Bouillon (to whom we shall return) did not accept the title of king, on the grounds that he would not accept a crown of gold where his Saviour had been content with crown of thorns. But he was the first ruler, and upon his death the following year his younger brother Baldwin, having no such scruples, was crowned King of Jerusalem at Bethlehem on Christmas Day 1101.

Robert is not mentioned in any of the current histories of the early years of the Kingdom but Hugh VI of Lusignan was certainly closely involved.

Although not a participant in the 1st Crusade, upon news of the capture of Jerusalem in 1099 Hugh VI joined the hastily recruited army of Duke William IV of Aquitaine that left for the Holy Land in 1100. The army came to grief in crossing Asia Minor and was virtually wiped out by the Turks but Duke William and Hugh VI of Lusignan managed to survive and were formally welcomed by King Baldwin I at Beyrouth, then the northernmost point of the newly formed Kingdom of Jerusalem. After celebrating Easter at Jerusalem, Duke William took the first ship home but Hugh stayed on, to become a companion in arms of the newly established king.

In his short reign King Baldwin I had already delivered a mighty Egyptian army a crippling blow when they tried to invade. This, along with taking the coastal town of Caesarea with the assistance of Pisan ships, had given him a false sense of security. Now, in company with a handful of knights, including Hugh VI of Lusignan, Baldwin roved out on a routine raid to the south of his country, harassing various nomadic tribes and assorted Arab villages, which gave some sport and useful booty.

Then suddenly they came upon another Egyptian army marching north, even greater than the last. Before they knew it, the gallant band was surrounded. With little alternative they did the thing they knew best, charged straight at the enemy, and forced their way through to the little town of Ramla.

But this was a refuge that could not last for long. Barricaded in a tower in the centre of the town, the king and his knights were caught in a trap. The Egyptians stood guard outside and waited till morning to smoke them out and put them to the sword. There followed an anxious debate between the knights. Should some attempt be made to break out under cover of darkness in order to find and bring rescue? Such a possibility was remote. Simply to escape with one's own skin would be an achievement – let alone gallop all the way back to Jerusalem or down to Jaffa to bring up reinforcements. The rest would all be dead or enslaved by then. Much discussion centred about the king. If he were killed, it would mean the end of the kingdom too, weak and small and barely established.

It is said that in the middle of the night an Arab chieftain crept up secretly to the tower. Apparently Baldwin had recently performed a chivalrous act. After raiding and scattering an Arab encampment he discovered the wife of the chieftain to be in the last throes of labour and about to give birth. He went out of his way to protect her and see that the child was safely born. For this act the Arab felt he owed a debt of honour to his enemy. Hence he offered to act as a guide through the enemy lines for the king to escape in the night. One may imagine the doubts that were raised by this unlikely offer. Should it be taken at face value or was it only a trap?

Anyhow, at dead of night, King Baldwin slipped away from the tower, escorted by a couple of companions to act as decoys in event of pursuit, and after some hair-raising adventures in the mountains, made his way to the little port of Arsuf and some days later sailed down the coast to the comparative safety of Jaffa. The others were left to await the events of the morning.

These turned out to be for the worst. The Egyptians lit a fire round the tower, the Frankish knights charged out, and were slain by the awaiting cohorts. By all accounts only one or two survived, to make their way home after years of captivity in Egypt. It seems that Hugh VI was one of these, and in the end made his way back to Lusignan, where by way of thanksgiving he spent the rest of his life making improvements to the church, as Louis Stouff records.

It should perhaps at this point be admitted that in the historical record neither church nor castle at Lusignan were built personally by Mélusine, with or without the help of elemental spirits. Although if the function of a tutelary spirit is to influence and watch over her human family, she might perhaps be considered to have inspired them to do the work themselves! As indeed to commit themselves to the Crusades over half a dozen generations. The castle, originally a wooden affair, was constructed by Hugh II and later rendered into stone by Hugh III along with the church.

We might best turn for an account of early beginnings to Chanoine Paschal, which however may contain some inaccuracies and inconsistencies with other reports.

- **Hugh I**, called the Hunter, was head of the Lusignans in France. He was the younger brother of William I, Count of Poitou in 935 and Duke of Aquitaine in 950;[17] also called Tow Head, because of his thick fair hair, and who finally took the nickname of Lesignem. He was a contemporary of Louis IV d'Outre-Mer, King of France (936-954).
- **Hugh II**, called the Well Beloved, under whom, according to the chronicle of Maillezais,[18] the marvellous castle was built by the faery Mélusine.
- **Hugh III**, called the White, living in the reigns of Hugh-Capet and Robert.[19]
- **Hugh IV**, called the Brown, who undertook a war against William IV, Duke of Guyenne.[20]
- **Hugh V**, called the Debonair. Killed in 1060 in combat against another Duke of Guyenne, Guy-Geoffroy.[21] There is cited among his brothers Robert of Lusignan, who made the journey to the Holy

---

17 This seems doubtful, as the Lusignans were vassals, not blood relations, of the Counts of Poitou/Dukes of Aquitaine.

18 Maillezais abbey, founded in 989, features in the romance as having been burnt down by Geoffrey Great-Tooth.

19 Hugh Capet 987-996, Robert II 996-1031.

20 William Fierebras (Proud arm), Duke of Aquitaine and Count of Poitou 937-994.

21 Guy-Geoffroy, Duke of Aquitiane and Count of Poitou 1058-1086

Land, and the convent of St. Catherine on Mount Sinai, and ended up establishing himself in Palestine.

+ **Hugh VI**, called the Devil, on account of his great strength. He made the journey to the Holy Land where he perished in 1102.[22]
+ **Hugh VII**, who died in the crusade of Louis the Young, in 1148.
+ **Hugh VIII**, also called the Brown, who took the cross like his fathers and was made prisoner in 1165. Nonetheless he was father of seven children among whom were some important sons.
+ **Hugh IX**, son[23] of Hugh VIII, Count of la Marche in 1190, recovered the Lusignan domains from the English, and followed Richard Coeur de Lion on crusade,[24] married Matilda, daughter and heiress of Vulgrin, Count of Angoulême, and died about 1208. Among his brothers were: Geoffroy of Lusignan … Guy of Lusignan … Amaury of Lusignan…

We shall have much to say about these brothers, whose exploits are mirrored – albeit in a very distorted fashion – in the activities of Mélusine's sons Urien and Guy, and later Geoffrey, in the romance. They did not sail off in a great fleet from La Rochelle to harry the Saracen. Their approach was rather more subtle, although it did involve marriage to susceptible and suitable heiresses.

Their story begins back at Lusignan in their close involvement with Eleanor of Aquitaine in the year 1168. Eleanor by this time, after being Queen of France, had divorced her husband Louis VII, and married Henry Plantagenet, heir to the English throne. She was now Queen of England, adding her vast domain of Aquitaine to Henry's possessions of England, Normandy, Maine, and Anjou.

Things went well enough at first until the southern lords, including those of Lusignan, did not see why they should pay taxes to finance Henry's disputes in the north. To teach them a lesson Henry marched south with an army of Flemish mercenaries, slashing and burning as he came. Lusignan castle was until then thought to be invincible, but nonetheless it fell!

This was probably due to Henry's remarkable ability to get from one place to another in what seemed impossible times. Some put it down to

---

22 Although also reported to have returned to Lusignan to refurbish the church.
23 Actually grandson.
24 Actually he went on a later crusade led by John of Brienne and died at Damietta in 1219.

witchcraft but it was more due to tactical genius, savage discipline and irrepressible energy. By whatever means, he must have taken the castle by surprise, for the Lusignans and their followers were reduced to living in the greenwoods while Henry ransacked their castle. The fact that they got away suggests they were taken by surprise and not besieged or captured. Nonetheless their situation was none too comfortable. Forests were inhospitable places best left to wild beasts and faeries.

But Henry was never one to stay anywhere for long, and he had scores to settle back in the north. So it was not long before he departed, leaving Eleanor behind, perhaps with the thought that she would be best able to contain and even pacify her own subjects. It did not take long for either of them to be disabused of that!

Soon after, as Eleanor was riding through the woods, the merry men of Lusignan were lying in wait. Their thought no doubt being that having Henry's queen in their hands would be the best way to get their castle back. But things did not turn out quite as they had hoped.

Whoever led the affray at this time has never quite been made clear. Some put it down to Guy of Lusignan, the youngest of the sons, handsome, young and impulsive although not too bright. It was not a very chivalrous encounter. Before Eleanor's protector Earl Patrick of Salisbury could even arm himself he was killed in the first surprise onslaught.

In the resulting confusion Eleanor, who was no mean horsewoman, broke away and escaped. This was under cover of a remarkable young man who fought like a cornered beast. He turned out to be the young William Marshal, who later made a good living on the tournament circuit, and eventually rose to become Earl of Pembroke and even for a time Regent of all England. Although outnumbered, he stood with his back to a briar bush and defied all comers. It was not until one of the Lusignans cut a hole in the thicket behind him, and thrust a spear through his leg, that his display of desperate gallantry was ended.

Eleanor having made her escape, the Lusignans were no better off than they had been before. They continued wandering the greenwoods, going from place to place, carrying the wounded William Marshal until they could raise some cash for him. This indeed did happen in the end. Eleanor, who had been much impressed by the way the young man had aided her escape, eventually paid his ransom. He joined her at her court at Poitiers, where he became tutor in arms to her eldest son Henry. And in the end the Lusignans got back their castle.

Although the details have been lost to history, in the negotiations that surrounded all this it seems possible, if only through circumstantial evidence, that as a guarantee of good behaviour, the younger sons, Amalric and Guy of Lusignan, might have been held as hostages at Poitiers. It was certainly a remarkable opportunity for the two young Lusignans to become familiar with the most fashionable court in the western world, an asset which it seems they later put to very good use. Eleanor's court at Poitiers was remarkable despite the short time it lasted, from about 1168 to 1174.

It was based upon Eleanor's determination, at a time of estrangement from her husband, to make her court as great as it had ever been in the days of the earlier Dukes of Aquitaine. What is more, to make it a centre for the Troubadour minstrelsy and the celebrated Courts of Love. She built upon a firm traditional base of her forefathers, for even old William IV (the first recorded Troubadour) for all his failings, had made it a place to be reckoned with. It was he who encouraged the likes of Bleheris, a loquacious knight from Wales, to tell his fund of stories of ancient times of greenwoods and all who dwelt within them. Of ancient things once known but now only misremembered. Tales of faery happenings and a greater interchange between the human and the faery worlds.

Along with Eleanor and her poets, jongleurs, musicians, entertainers and troubadours came high lady friends and relatives, attracted by this efflorescence of new values that were expressed in terms of appreciation of the feminine. In particular Eleanor's eldest daughter, Marie of Champagne, who kept within her entourage the Arthurian romancer Chrétien de Troyes[25] and Andreus Capellanus (André the Chaplain) who wrote a famous guidebook to the art of Courtly Love.

What is more, some young men gathered as youths or boys at this time would meet up again as men some twenty years later for remarkable happenings in the Kingdom of Jerusalem in the aftermath of the 3rd Crusade. Apart from Amalric and Guy of Lusignan, there was Richard Coeur de Lion, Eleanor's favourite son, and her grandson Henry II of Champagne, the son of Marie of Champagne.

However, on the wider stage, things were slipping out of control. Eleanor was plotting against her husband and encouraging her sons to revolt, with the support of her former spouse Louis VII, King of France.

---

25 For the influence of Celtic faery lore on Chrétien de Troyes see *The Faery Gates of Avalon*, Gareth Knight (R.J. Stewart Books, 2008).

The upshot was that in 1174 Henry led another punitive expedition that destroyed the court of Eleanor, and imprisoned her in England for sixteen years. However, not before Amalric and Guy of Lusignan were safely out of the way. The whereabouts of Guy until 1180 is not known, but by 1173 Amalric was on his way to Jerusalem.

The Lusignan family in Jerusalem, Cyprus and Lesser Armenia

At the time of his arrival his namesake King Amalric I was campaigning on his north eastern borders rather than in Egypt as he had been when supported by Amalric's father, Hugues VIII of Lusignan some ten years before. The young Amalric of Lusignan seems to have welcomed the chance to prove himself in battle, perhaps rather too enthusiastically, as he was shortly captured. However, he had sufficiently shown his mettle for King Amalric to pay the ransom of his young namesake – and perhaps the record of his forefathers Hugh VI, VII and VIII, who had loyally served the kingdom, did something to encourage his redemption.

It is possible Amalric of Lusignan may have picked up some of his skill at arms (he was later to become Constable of the kingdom) at Poitiers in the company of his former adversary William Marshal. But another accomplishment that would have stood him in good stead in courtly circles was the high and fashionable education in courtesy he could have picked up at Eleanor's court, including a first hand knowledge of the cult of Courtly Love. Because of his combination of talents and family connections it seems that Amalric was regarded, despite his lack of funds, as an eligible young man, to the point of being offered the hand of the young Eschiva of Ibelin, daughter of a powerful local family. This was followed by being awarded a post at court as Chamberlain, in which capacity it was not long before he found himself preparing the coronation of a new boy king. For in the midst of his campaigning King Amalric had been taken ill and died.

The thirteen-year-old Baldwin IV who came to the throne turned out to be of invincible courage and saintly character but suffered the dreadful condition of being a leper. When, at the age of fifteen, Baldwin took up the full burden of kingship his mother Agnes de Courtenay returned to court to support him. Not that in the early years of his reign, before his leprosy caught up with him, the young Baldwin IV needed any cosseting. He showed himself quite capable of military leadership in the battle of Montgisard, when with a tiny army he scored a remarkable victory against the mighty Saladin, who was lucky to flee back to Cairo. The result may have been due to a fit of overconfidence on Saladin's part, but the young king and his troops were in no doubt they had won with the help of the relic of the True Cross that they took into battle, and the heavenly intervention of St George, who was seen fighting on the Christian side after the Saracens had ill advisedly desecrated his shrine when they sacked the nearby town of Lydda, birthplace of the saint.

However, with or without heavenly aid, and however admirable his courage, it was obvious that Baldwin, as a leper, was destined for a short life (he died nine years later) and an inability to father an heir. All hope was therefore placed on finding a suitable suitor for his elder sister, Sibylle. That is to say, someone powerful and wealthy to act as regent/consort and defend the impoverished kingdom against its enemies.

Choice fell upon William of Montferrat, nicknamed Longsword, eldest son of the Marquis of Montferrat, from a famous and well connected Piedmont dynasty. He duly arrived escorted by a Genoese fleet, his marriage to Sibylle was solemnised and for a romantic young girl brought up in her aunt Jovetta's nunnery he must have been all that she could have wished for. A tall, good looking young man with reddish-gold hair, brave but quick tempered, he had, in addition to his father's wealth, from earliest youth been trained in the arts of war. But however promising his qualities they became redundant when he fell prey to a fever and died. Not, however, before begetting a child upon the princess Sibylle.

But although the child turned out to be a son, another husband needed to be found quickly for the royal widow, to act as ruler of the kingdom until the infant heir-apparent grew to manhood.

Local sentiment among the barons now favoured Sibylle's marriage to one of their own, Baldwin of Ibelin, but whose hopes suffered a major setback when in a skirmish he was captured by Saladin. The prospect of Baldwin of Ibelin being in line to be a future King of Jerusalem was not lost upon Saladin, who put a king's ransom on his head. As this would have come close to beggaring the kingdom let alone the assets of a single lord, Saladin released him on part payment, to give him the chance to raise the rest by going begging to the Emperor of Byzantium. But not before pulling out two of his teeth as a reminder of what might be in store if he failed to deliver the cash. Baldwin accordingly went to Byzantium and threw himself upon the generosity of the Emperor Manuel, who in the power politics of the day, felt it might be a worthwhile investment to put a future ruler of Jerusalem in his debt.

However, the prospect of marriage to a local baron almost twice her age did not appeal to the Princess Sibylle after her brief marriage to the dashing William Longsword of Montferrat. In any case she was already half-promised in marriage to the Duke Hugh III of Burgundy, not that this dignitary seemed keen to desert the comfort of his duchy to take on the challenge of an impoverished and threatened petty kingdom, whatever its celestial connections.

The situation turned out to be a golden opportunity for the Lusignans.

It happened that Sibylle, as well as her mother Agnes, were quite intrigued with the new court chamberlain, Amalric of Lusignan. For he still bore the glamour of having been an intimate (whether real or claimed or assumed) of the world famous court of Eleanor of Aquitaine, Queen of the Troubadour Minstrelsy and Patron of the Courts of Love. An echo of which she may already have experienced with William Longsword, for the northern Italian court of Montferrat also had a reputation for encouraging Courtly Love and the Troubadour Minstrelsy.

Amalric was of course already married to Eschiva of Ibelin but he now took the opportunity to laud the merits of his younger brother Guy, who being distant was all the more attractive, given such romantic tales as that of Jaufré Rudel, Prince of Blay. Rudel, a lordly troubadour, traditionally conceived a great passion for "a far princess" whom he had never met, allegedly the Countess of Tripoli. So much so that he set off on a hazardous sea voyage to meet her, at the end of which he died in her arms.

This of course was all fantasy but in particular circumstances fantasy may prove more compelling than fact. And so it seemed in the romantic dreams of Princess Sibylle for this far off ideal lover, Guy, the younger brother of the personable Amalric of Lusignan. Abetted by her mother Agnes de Courtenay, she begged that he be brought to Jerusalem.

The story goes that Amalric took the long voyage back to Lusignan to fetch the young Guy, although this takes no account of the treacherous seas of winter which put a stop to shipping and travellers for some months of the year. Guy may already have been closer to hand but it no doubt heightened the passion of the young Sibylle to think that an epic journey had been undertaken for the courageous and incomparable Guy to be brought close to her. And indeed she was not disappointed, for by all accounts Guy was an exceptionally handsome and presentable young man.

So despite Baldwin of Ibelin returning from Byzantium with his ransom to pay for his liberty from Saladin, Sibylle decided that she was not for him and declared that she would marry no one but Guy of Lusignan. It is rumoured that Sibylle got her way – at some risk to herself and to her intended – by allowing it to be put about that the two of them were already intimately connected. At any rate a wedding was hastily arranged even though unheard of in the holy days of Easter. But another reason for haste may have been the rumour that Prince Bohemond of Antioch and Count Raymond of Tripoli were bent on deposing the leper king to lay claim to the kingdom themselves. With Sibylle married off, however, this plot, if indeed it existed, evaporated swiftly.

And so life settled down in Outre-mer with Amalric of Lusignan as Court Chamberlain and Guy of Lusignan wedded to the mother of the heir-apparent, the infant future Baldwin V.

It is perhaps to be expected that those who felt their prospects to have been blighted by the success of the Lusignans should have painted these events in the most pejorative terms. This was based upon the alleged low moral character of Sibylle's mother Agnes de Courtenay, said to be using her position at court to advance the prospects of her secret lovers – which included Amalric of Lusignan and even Heraclius, the Patriarch of Jerusalem. Thus Agnes, the natural mother of King Baldwin IV and his sister Sibylle, has suffered grievously at the hands of later chroniclers.

The seed for this defamation came from the fact that when, on the sudden death of his brother Baldwin III, Agnes' husband Amalric came to the throne, the high court of barons insisted that she be put aside. The official reason was the old chestnut of consanguinity, for Amalric and Agnes were indeed 'third cousins' (that is to say, shared the same great-great-grandparents) but more to the point was what lay behind the equivocal statement from the High Court of barons that Agnes "was not such as a queen *should* be of so great a city".

This seems but a veiled device of required diplomacy, which was the need to cement ties with Byzantium by finding a new queen from there – and this King Amalric proceeded to do, with Maria Comnena, the Emperor's niece. (In this he was but following the example of his brother Baldwin III, who on succeeding to the crown had married the 13-year-old Byzantine princess Theodora, although he died before she reached child bearing age and his young widow returned to Byzantium.)

However, slander mongers put the worst possible light on this ruling by the barons to put aside Agnes, citing it as evidence of the moral turpitude of a manipulative slut. These allegations come from a late chronicle by Ernoul, a servant of the Ibelin family, who after the catastrophic fall of Jerusalem were doing their best to distance themselves from the Lusignans.

This version of events has been routinely described in the standard histories, such as Stephen Runciman's *History of the Crusades* (1951) and René Grousset's *Histoire des Croisades* (1935), and the otherwise excellent biography *Baudouin IV de Jérusalem, Le roi lépreux* (1981), by Pierre Aubé. The rehabilitation of the reputation of Agnes de Courtenay, Amalric of Lusignan and Patriarch Heraclius has however more recently been effected by Bernard Hamilton in *The Leper King and his Heirs* (Cambridge University Press, 2000).

As the leper king's physical condition deteriorated Guy of Lusignan was appointed Regent of the kingdom for a time, but on proving somewhat lacking in diplomatic skills was soon removed from the position. Eventually, in 1185, Baldwin IV died, and Sibylle's sickly young infant became Baldwin V, only to die after a few months.

This left Sibylle directly in line for the throne, with Guy of Lusignan as her consort. A number of barons found this prospect intolerable and sought to stage a coup, advancing the cause of Sibylle's half-sister Isabelle, the daughter of Amalric I and his second wife, the Byzantine princess Maria Comnena. However, Isabelle and her intellectual and somewhat effeminate young husband, Humphrey IV of Toron, had no wish to be involved in this chicanery, and affirmed their allegiance to Sibylle and Guy of Lusignan. In the confusion that followed, Sibylle was crowned Queen of Jerusalem in a hastily arranged ceremony, and then astounded everyone by passing the crown on to Guy, decreeing him to be no mere consort but King of Jerusalem in his own right!

The local shock was tremendous. It was a bitter setback for the local aristocracy such as the Ibelins, who had come to power and been born and bred over three generations in the kingdom. It would have been hard enough to see one of their own set aside for some great powerful outsider such as William of Montferrat, but to accept some apparent fortune hunter from the backwoods of Poitou was a different matter. Even back in Lusignan, Guy's nephew Hugh IX declared that if Guy could become a king, there seemed no reason why he himself could not become God!

But within a year, disaster struck the crusader kingdom. The surrounding Saracen states, after decades of fighting between themselves, found unity under the charismatic leader Saladin. The inexperienced Guy, ill-advised by squabbling power factions that surrounded him, led the army of the kingdom to major defeat at the Battle of Hattin in 1187. He and most of the crusader leaders were captured and the city of Jerusalem fell, along with most of the kingdom's towns and castles. And everything might have been lost but for the fortuitous arrival of Conrad of Montferrat, a young brother of Sibylle's late husband William.

In retreat from some dangerous adventures in the stormy politics of Byzantium (in which his elder brother Boniface lost his life) he happened to arrive at the port of Tyre to find it on the brink of surrender to Saladin. He took over from the dispirited leaders of the city, rallied the troops and held on to the town. This effectively saved the kingdom for another hundred years but for the moment Tyre seemed an isolated outpost of little significance apart from being a possible port of departure for refugees.

Within a year Saladin released the Lusignans and other western lords from captivity, on condition (immediately reneged upon) that they did not take up arms again. Indeed they seemed in little condition to do so, and he probably felt that they might now pack up traps and go home, even though many of them, as locally born colonials, had nowhere else to go.

What is more, the crusaders were bitterly divided between themselves. When Guy of Lusignan presented himself before Tyre, he was turned away by Conrad of Montferrat, who challenged his right still to regard himself as king. If anyone deserved that title to the remains of the kingdom Conrad of Montferrat thought it should be himself.

But Guy of Lusignan was not without courage and determination. In an astonishing act of bravado he announced he would go and besiege the major port of Acre, currently held by the Saracens. This he proceeded to do, in what turned out to be three years of vicious trench warfare, with Guy and his army besieging the Saracens in Acre, and they themselves encircled by another army of Saracens.

During this time however, the 3rd Crusade was being mounted in the west, led by the Kings of England and France, the former being Richard Coeur de Lion. It was agreed that on arrival the kings would arbitrate between Guy of Lusignan and Conrad of Montferrat as to who should be rightful king of the kingdom – not that there was much of it left for anyone to rule.

Guy's chances decreased with the death of Sibylle and their two daughters in the intolerable conditions of the crusader camp at the siege of Acre, while Conrad strengthened his hand by marrying Sibylle's half-sister Isabelle, who was forcibly divorced from Humphrey of Toron. Isabelle's mother Maria Comnena persuaded her it was her duty to do so, and Humphrey's objections evaporated when he was challenged to a duel in single combat to decide the issue.

As Richard Coeur de Lion, after considerable delays, approached the Holy Land, the Lusignan brothers set off to meet him and lobby their cause. They met him on Cyprus, an island not far offshore that was still nominally part of the Byzantine empire but currently held by an opportunist Greek usurper. One who made the mistake, however, of trying to ransom Richard's womenfolk, his future queen Berengaria of Navarre and his sister Joanna, after their ships had been forced to put into Cyprus by storm. As a result the usurper Isaac found himself deposed in short order and clapped in irons and Richard, with the help of the Lusignans, took over the island.

On arrival at Acre, which had recently fallen with the assistance of the navies of the Italian city states, Richard was inclined in the choice of kingship toward the Lusignans; the family after all were his vassals back in Poitou. But the local barons wanted nothing of Guy, whom they blamed for most of their troubles, and despite Richard's wishes, opted for Conrad of Montferrat. (Who incidentally has been portrayed as a villainous and unsympathetic character in modern popular fiction).[26]

However, their wishes came to nothing very soon after, as Conrad was assassinated. The killers turned out to be followers of the Old Man of the Mountain, leader of a drug driven extremist sect that specialised in this kind of thing fairly indiscriminately. Nonetheless the finger of suspicion pointed at Richard, who realising that nothing would induce the locals to accept Guy, decided to back a fellow crusader leader and

---

26 For example Graham Shelby's celebrated *The Kings of Vain Intent* (1970)

close blood relation, his nephew Henry II of Champagne. There is, in all of this, a strange echo of the court of Poitiers twenty years before, for both Richard and Henry had been there (along with Amalric and Guy?) as children.

Within a week of Conrad's death Henry was married to Isabelle, even though she was pregnant with Conrad's child – the future heiress to the throne, Maria of Montferrat.

By way of consolation Guy of Lusignan was given the island of Cyprus, or at any rate granted the right to purchase it, and took up residence as its ruler. Guy's rule however did not last long. He died in 1194, perhaps from a broken heart. His elder brother Geoffrey (father of the historical/legendary Geoffroy Great-Tooth) might have succeeded him, as he had played an heroic part in the 3rd Crusade, in which most of the Mediterranean coast was won back, although not the Holy City itself, and he was appointed Count of Jaffa and Ascalon by Richard Coeur de Lion, although all inland remained in Saracen hands. But Geoffrey decided to return home to Lusignan where he married and fathered the prototype of Geoffroy Great Tooth of the romance.

It thus fell to Amalric of Lusignan to take over the island. Amalric was still married into the prominent Ibelin family, and had three children by his wife Eschiva. But now things took a dramatic turn which pulled him back into the ambit of the Kingdom of Jerusalem. In 1197, when receiving a Pisan delegation and reviewing troops, Henry II of Champagne fell from a high window and was killed. The distraught already three times married Isabelle of Jerusalem now needed a new husband.

A local lord, Raoul of Vermandois, was quite favoured by the local barons although he had little power or money, having lost his estates in the war with Saladin. The lot fell to Amalric of Lusignan after a fortuitous sequence of coincidences.

It so happened that just prior to the death of Henry of Champagne, Amalric's wife Eschiva died, possibly in childbirth, and in this same year Amalric had sworn allegiance to the Holy Roman Emperor, the highly ambitious Frederick II, who was keen to establish a power base in the area and raised the island to the status of a kingdom. Amalric of Lusignan had thus become King of Cyprus, which led to the proposal that he should marry Queen Isabelle of Jerusalem.

As rulers of Jerusalem and Cyprus, Amalric and Isabelle ruled wisely and peaceably until their deaths in 1205 and 1206, although the kingdoms were never completely united. Amalric's son by Eschiva of Ibelin was ten years old when he succeeded his father to the throne of Cyprus as Hugh I. The Kingdom of Jerusalem passed to Isabelle's daughter Maria of Montferrat and was, for the time being, out of Lusignan hands. Maria was married off to an astute and capable diplomat and warrior, John of Brienne, and her daughter Yolande to Emperor Frederick.

Hugh of Lusignan died at the young age of 23 but managed, just in time, to produce a male heir who came to the throne of Cyprus as Henry I at the tender age of 8 months. Nonetheless, good regents such as Philip and John of Ibelin were on hand, which was just as well for the rapacious Holy Roman Emperor, Frederick II, was bearing down aiming to appoint himself King of Cyprus as well as King of Jerusalem. He was prevented from taking over the island, although not without a fight, but made himself, through a series of financial deals with the Egyptians, nominally King of Jerusalem. Not that he stayed there long, leaving a bailiff to run things for him.

In Cyprus itself, Henry I of Lusignan ruled until 1252 and although he married three times only produced one child, late on, who succeeded as Hugh II at the age of two months, only to die when 14 years old. The crown passed to his uncle, who had already been acting as regent for the past six years, and became Hugh III (also called Hugh the Great, as he became King of Jerusalem as well as Cyprus in 1268 at the death of Conradin, grandchild and last descendant of the Emperor Frederick.)

Hugh soon palled of this honour and duty, as the Kingdom of Jerusalem had deteriorated into an ill-organised rump of separate towns with quarrelling lords. In 1276 he gave up in disgust and returned to Cyprus. He had no less than eleven children and in 1284 was succeeded by the eldest, John I, who reigned for only a year before he died, unmarried and without issue, some said poisoned by his brothers.

If so, this marked the start of a rot. John's brother came to the throne as Henry II but was the last King of Jerusalem in real terms, for in 1291 the kingdom fell to the Saracens. Henry was actively present fighting the Egyptians in the final siege of Acre, and after being driven out became the first of a long series of mere 'titular kings' of Jerusalem.

To add to his problems, he was epileptic, and his brothers conspired against him, as presumably they had against John. He put his brother Guy to death in 1303 for this very reason, but in 1306 his brother Amalric with the help of the Templars managed to remove him. He was exiled to Lesser Armenia, where the Lusignans had married into the royal family, but was able to return in 1310, and the usurping brother was killed. This was with the aid of the Knights Hospitaller and it may well be that the role of the Knights of St. John in the romance of Mélusine is a dim memory of this.

This was also the period that saw the winding up of the Knights Templar and Henry oversaw their dissolution in Cyprus and the transfer of their property to the Hospitallers. He did not carry through the full force of enmity against them however, as decreed by the Pope and the King of France. In a trial in Cyprus they were acquitted, and although a new trial was demanded the Templars did not suffer as they had elsewhere. Henry had many problems with his brothers, and when he died he was succeeded by a nephew, the son of the Guy he had put to death twenty years before.

This nephew, Hugh IV, who came to the throne in 1324, proved to be a moderate, well educated patron of the arts, literature and philosophy, and content to rule without any desire to stir up conflict with the surrounding Muslim nations. Indeed he severely punished his 16-year-old son Peter, who went off on his own initiative to Europe to try to raise a crusade. He also tried to balance the rival claims of the powerful Italian city states, by ceding trading rights to Venice, although this did not go down well with the merchants of Genoa. In 1358, after a long peaceful reign, he resigned the throne to his son Peter and died a year later, at what was then considered the advanced age of 63.

When he came to the throne at age 30, Peter I was no less a firebrand than he had been as a 16-year-old, and took it upon himself to try to regain the lost kingdom of Jerusalem. His first action was to go to the aid of Lesser Armenia which was badly threatened by the Turks and had appealed to him for help. He did this so successfully that many emirs in Asia Minor accepted his suzerainty and paid him tribute. However, it provoked an almighty reaction by the Turks against Cyprus, which he fought off with help from the Knights Hospitaller now based at Rhodes (an involvement that receives oblique acknowledgement in the Mélusine romance as one of Geoffrey Great-Tooth's exploits). Additional help came from the Pope and even from pirates – although it was alleged that much piracy was carried out by Cypriot lords themselves.

In 1362 Peter embarked on a grand tour of Europe. This was initially because of a challenge to his right to the throne by his nephew Hugh, which was supported by the King of France. He appealed successfully to the Pope in Avignon and, after his nephew was virtually bought off, Peter continued to visit heads of state in Europe, including England, where Edward III gave him a ship and a great deal of money to pay his expenses – which however he lost on his way back to the coast when waylaid by highwaymen. Anyhow, at the end of his extended trip Peter had successfully organised support for a crusade against Egypt.

This took place in 1365 and as already mentioned, Alexandria was sacked but without any follow through, as Peter had hoped, to march upon Cairo and coerce the Sultan into ceding Palestine to the Christians. In the end he was obliged to make peace, but was never forgiven or trusted again by the Egyptians, who now helped to turn the screws against Lesser Armenia, which soon fell. There was not a lot that Peter could do. He continued to raid the Palestinian coast, rather pointlessly, for all the old ports and immediate hinterland had largely been laid waste. And his abortive crusade and destruction of Alexandria severely disrupted trade between east and west for some time – which did nobody any good.

Nor had things been going well in Cyprus. During Peter's absence there had been many problems, including severe epidemics, famine, raids by Turks, problems with Genoese merchants, and even the unfaithfulness of his queen, Eleanor of Aragon. Peter retaliated fiercely against her favourite nobles, which included his own brothers, and in 1369 was assassinated, apparently with their collusion.

We have now reached the period when Jean d'Arras was writing the romance of Mélusine at the behest of the Duke of Berry. The Poitevin branch of the Lusignans had already died out and although the Lusignan dynasty continued in Cyprus for another hundred years, from now on things were all downhill. Peter of Lusignan's 15-year-old son succeeded him, but his mother, Queen Eleanor of Aragon, invited the Genoese to invade in revenge for the assassination of her husband, for which she particularly blamed his brother John. This turned out to be a very bad move as the Genoese came to stay, taking over the main ports. John was put to death as she had hoped, and the other brother, James, ended up a prisoner in Genoa for nine years, whilst Eleanor eventually returned home to Aragon. Her son Peter (called "the Fat") died in 1382 at the age of 25.

His surviving uncle was now released from Genoa and allowed to take the throne as James I. At his death in 1398 the eldest of his 12 children came to the throne as the 24-year-old Janus, under whose rule things continued to go from bad to worse. New epidemics, plagues of locusts, civil war with the Genoese, and raids from Egypt, where Janus was taken as a prisoner, paraded in chains on an ass before the Sultan and made to kiss the ground before him. He was eventually ransomed by donations from Europe, although during his captivity there was a major rebellion in Cyprus that was, however, put down on his release. He died in 1432 to be succeeded by his 18-year-old son, John II.

There is little record of John's reign except that he had a bastard son called James who was the apple of his eye and whom he made Archbishop of Nicosia at the age of 16. However, as the youth promptly murdered the Royal Chamberlain, he had to be divested of his obviously inappropriate ecclesiastical office. Nonetheless he was forgiven by his doting father, who would also have appointed him as successor to the throne had he not died before he could do so. Therefore in 1458, upon John's death, it was his 14-year-old daughter Charlotte who succeeded. She was nonetheless challenged by James, with Egyptian support, and after spending three years under siege in Kyrenia, was forced to flee the country, ending her life in Italy.

James the Bastard of Lusignan now ruled as James II and, seeking support from Venice against the Genoese, married a wealthy Venetian merchant's daughter, Catherine Carnaro. However, he died shortly afterwards in suspicious circumstances, apparently at the hands of Venetian agents. The couple's baby automatically succeeded as James III but died in equally suspicious circumstances before his first birthday. The Lusignan dynasty on the island had come to an end. Catherine Carnaro continued to reign as nominal queen but the island was now controlled by Venetian merchants, who called upon her to abdicate, and in 1469 Cyprus became a Venetian colony prior to being overrun by the Ottoman Turks in 1571.

The Lusignan family in Poitou

One of the closest links to history within the romance of Mélusine is the matter of fact statement about Eudes being Count of La Marche. And although little further is said beyond this bare statement, this county played a significant role in the fortunes of the Lusignan family.

The County of La Marche was a region of strategic importance situated at a concourse of ways between central France, under the suzerainty of the Capetian royal family, and western France, ruled by the Plantagenet kings of England. At a more local level it had been claimed by the Lords of Lusignan and the Counts of Angoulême since the tenth century. In 1177 however, it was seized by Henry Plantagenet for the benefit of his youngest son John Lackland. As a consequence, early in 1200, immediately after John came to the throne, Hugh IX of Lusignan waylaid John's mother, Eleanor of Aquitaine, when she was on her way through his territory to fetch her eleven-year-old granddaughter Blanche of Castile for betrothal to the twelve-year-old Louis Capet, heir to the King of France. The price of her freedom was the restoration of La Marche to the Lusignans.

This was a rather more successful outcome than the Lusignans' previous attempt at abducting Queen Eleanor in 1168. However it did not play too well with Count Aymar Taillefer of Angoulême and was mitigated with an arranged marriage between his daughter, Isabelle of Angoulême, and Hugh IX of Lusignan. This alliance of the two powerful families would form a redoubtable powerbase in the heart of Aquitaine. The plan however came to an unexpected and humiliating end as far as the Lusignans were concerned. A little before the marriage ceremony was arranged King John was staying as a guest at Lusignan, and at a reception given in his honour happened to meet the young Isabelle. Although only twelve years old she was of remarkable beauty – compared by some to Helen of Troy!

The king was completely smitten, and although arrangements were underway for him to marry the daughter of the King of Portugal, his desire for Isabelle overcame all that. It would also be politically advantageous, as close ties with the county of Angoulême would give him mastery of an important region in the heart of France.

Isabelle's father Aymar Taillefer was easily persuaded that it was better to have his daughter become Queen of England rather than a neighbouring Countess. Consequently, having diverted the attention of the Lusignans elsewhere, John seized the opportunity to carry off the bride, and a royal marriage was celebrated a few days later at Chinon. The danger represented by the outraged Lusignans served to hasten their departure, and in September the royal couple embarked at Cherbourg on the way to England where on 8th October Isabelle was crowned queen at Westminster Abbey.

The daughter of the Count of Angoulême had become Queen of England and Ireland, Duchess of Normandy, Countess of Maine,

Anjou, Touraine, Poitou, Aquitaine and Gascony. Prestigious titles that gave birth to immense pride and arrogance in later life. And the Lusignans had salt rubbed into their wounds when the marriage was followed by John taking back the county of La Marche.

This drove them back into the arms of the King of France and to an armed uprising against the Plantagenets. John was forced to return to France to meet the threat by diplomatic overtures to the King of France with whom he signed a peace treaty on 31st May 1201. Then he went with Isabelle down to Chinon where, having recruited some doughty champions to fight for him, he challenged the Lusignans to a judicial duel against them.

The Lusignans declined this loaded invitation and took their cause to the King of France, arguing that John had acted contrary to his obligations as a suzerain towards his vassals by carrying off the fiancée of one of them and depriving them of La Marche and other lordships in England and Normandy. Certainly they were vassals of the Plantagenets but the Plantagenets were in turn vassals of the King of France in respect of their continental domains. Instead of negotiating, John chose to follow a hard line by confiscating Moncontour from Geoffrey of Lusignan.

At the beginning of 1202 Philippe Auguste decided to act and called John to appear before his court to answer these charges. The insolent John, thinking he held the advantage, refused to go. This played into the hands of the French king, who proclaimed that by John's refusal to attend, and neglect of his duties as vassal and suzerain, his domains on the continent – apart from Normandy – were forfeit and bestowed upon Prince Arthur of Brittany, who, as the son of John's deceased elder brother Geoffrey, had a valid claim to the English throne.

But in August John achieved an unexpected success. Seeking to press their advantage by the old tactic of seizing John's mother, Eleanor of Aquitaine, who had taken refuge in the castle of Mirebeau, the Lusignans besieged the castle, which seemed due to fall next day. But in a surprise attack worthy of his father, after a forced march of his men, John captured not only Prince Arthur but the Lusignans and their followers as well.

After due humiliation of being driven on asses with ropes round their necks, Hugh IX of Lusignan was incarcerated in the dungeons of Caen castle, and a number of his supporters died in prison, victims of ill treatment. The Lusignans were released in November, after payment of heavy ransoms, but Prince Arthur was never seen again until his body, weighted with a stone, was discovered in the waters of the Seine. It was widely believed he had been strangled by John himself in a fit of rage after his orders to have Arthur castrated and blinded had been disobeyed.

These attacks of rage and fury (similar to those of his father Henry II) were succeeded by periods of apathy which soon cost him his empire. His only care now seemed to be to find more money in order to lead a lavish life with the young Isabelle, with whom he returned to England.

At this Philippe Auguste attacked the pride of the Plantagenet fortresses, Château-Gaillard in Normandy, which fell in March 1204 after five months of siege. Everything after that happened quickly, the Duchy of Normandy, and the counties of Maine, Anjou, and Touraine declared for the French king, and in August even Poitiers opened its doors to him. But Philippe Auguste did not push any further; he consolidated his conquests, and apart from the town of Poitiers did not hold anything south of the Loire. The Anglo-Anjevin empire was but a shadow of its former self, and retained nothing but the County of Angoulême, along with La Marche, and holdings in the southwest of France down to Bordeaux.

When Poitiers fell, Isabelle's chagrin was immense. The relations of the couple deteriorated, to the point of John turning his attention to other ladies of the court, and at the same time accusing Isabelle of adultery, hanging before her eyes those whom he claimed were her lovers. Then, reproaching himself for being the cause of all these misfortunes, his moments of madness passed, he would turn back to her, more tender and passionate than ever. Isabelle bore him five children, the first being the future Henry III of England.

In 1214 John finally attempted his revenge, spending more time in his possessions in France and organising an alliance with the Holy Roman Emperor, Otto of Brunswick and the Counts of Flanders, Holland and Lorraine. While the Germans and Flemings attacked the north in France, John aimed to conquer lands in the south and west. He prepared for his coming with gifts of gold and silver. No alliance was too expensive, even with the Lusignans who, up to now, had remained implacable. But now the County of La Marche was returned to Hugh IX of Lusignan, and John even offered the hand of his daughter Jeanne to Hugh's son, Hugh X of Lusignan. She was left at the castle of Lusignan until such time as she was of an age to marry.

By grants of territory John made his former enemies masters of western France and he was unsuccessful elsewhere. Philippe Auguste won a great victory over the Germans and Flemings in the north, and so John never recovered Normandy, Maine, Anjou or Tourain, and on his return to England John found himself faced with virtual civil war. The English barons sought to put a brake upon the tyranny of his arbitrary conduct and excessive taxes, and on 15th June 1215 he was constrained to sign the Magna Carta, limiting his powers, and a year later he died.

His death left Isabelle very much on her own, disliked, even hated by the English barons and her subjects, who blamed her for much of the indiscretions, debauchery and dissolute life of King John. She tried to claim the role of regent in the minority of her ten-year-old son Henry III, but the lords of the realm preferred William Marshal, Earl of Pembroke (whom we have met before!) and sent her back to Angoulême.

There she was enthusiastically received, but although she tried to maintain her titles of Queen of England, Ruler of Ireland, Duchess of Normandy and of Aquitaine, Countess of Anjou and Angoulême, the local lords were not ready to recognise her as their suzerain.

Hugh IX, whom she had previously spurned, decided to embark on the Fifth Crusade in 1218, while his son Hugh X, still affianced to Isabelle's daughter Jeanne, sought to make the most of his forthcoming marriage to the King of England's sister, on the strength of which he even persuaded Henry to appoint him guardian of Aquitaine, with authority over all vassals of the King of England in France.

Isabelle now began to think that her best plan was to ally herself with the Lusignans. She was still Countess of Angoulême in her own right, and if she married Hugh X of Lusignan, they would create between them a powerful veritable principality, as had originally been planned by her father Aymar and Hugh IX of Lusignan twenty years before. Accordingly the marriage took place, with Isabelle justifying her action to her son King Henry III by representing it to be in the interest of Plantagenets on the continent.

Setting aside the princess Jeanne in favour of her mother was explained to be on account of Jeanne being still too young to marry. Nonetheless, on her repatriation to England she was married to the King of Scotland the following year.

As masters of southern and southwestern France, Isabelle and Hugh had effectively set up a great personal state, free from both Capetian and Plantagenet interference, whom they were able to play one against the another. At 34 years of age, Isabelle became more authoritarian and audacious than ever, insisted upon being called a queen and treated like one, so that all bowed before her, including her husband.

She eventually overplayed her hand, as a result of being incensed at her treatment by the Dowager Queen of France, Blanche of Castile.[27] Summoned to the French court to swear fealty to Alphonse, younger brother of King Louis IX on his investiture as Count of Poitou, Blanche declined to recognise Isabelle as a fellow Queen Dowager and ranked her as a mere Countess. Mortally stung by this snub Isabelle began to foment a great rebellion, enlisting the support of her son Henry III of England and her son-in-law the Count of Toulouse. This ended disastrously. After losing a great battle at Saintes in July 1244, she and Hugh X of Lusignan, accompanied by their three sons, were obliged to prostrate themselves before King Louis and beg for mercy.

The county of Angoulême remained in the hands of the Lusignans for which they paid homage to the King of France, and Isabelle and Hugh oversaw the division of their lands between their children. Their eldest son, Hugh XI, received the Counties of La Marche and Angoulême as well as Lusignan. Isabelle retired to the abbey of Fontevraud where she died in June 1246. Hugh X survived her by three years, and in 1248, crusading in Egypt with King Louis of France, he was killed at Damietta.

At the beginning of the 14th century the powerful house of Lusignan came to an end. The last count, Guy, brother of Hugh XIII, had the affrontery to make the King of England, Edward I, his heir, but at his death in 1308 King Philip of France, citing enormous debts owed to him, reattached Lusignan to the French crown, and in 1314 it was the turn of the counties of Angoulême and La Marche.

However, to go back a century or so, we find a couple of historical characters, father and son, each called Geoffrey, who by their lives contributed to the legend of Geoffroy Great Tooth in the romance.

The first Geoffrey was the elder brother of Guy and Amalric of Lusignan who became Kings of Jerusalem. He played a major and heroic part in the 3rd Crusade, helping Richard Coeur de Lion

---

27 Blanche of Castile was the granddaughter of Eleanor of Aquitaine, whom she had gone to fetch to the French court to marry the Dauphin, back in 1200 when waylaid by Hugh IX of Lusignan. She and Isabelle were about the same age and bitter rivals.

recapture most of the coastline of the Holy Land for which he was rewarded by being made Count of Jaffa and Ascalon. He might in turn have succeeded to the rulership of Cyprus had he not decided to return home in 1193, where his nephew Hugh IX was currently head of the Lusignan family.[28]

Once he had arrived home the old crusader became lord of Mervant and Vouvant in Bas-Poitou and married Eustache Chabot, by whom he had a son, Geoffrey, in 1198. This son had a number of characteristics in common with Geoffroy Great Tooth of the romance. Whilst he was no giant killer, and probably had no "great tooth", he was such a fiery character that he was excommunicated for his rough treatment of the monks of Maillezais abbey who were forced at one point to evacuate. Although he did not burn the place down, or kill a brother or all the monks, his behaviour was such as to bring excommunication down upon his head and, in 1232, the obligation to make a penitential pilgrimage to Rome. Which must have been something of a climb down or change of heart if the story is true that his war cry up to that time had been "There is no God!" However, Geoffroy Great Tooth of the romance had similar swings of extremism and penitence.

The elder Geoffrey had had a hard time of it in the affair at Mirebeau back in 1200, where it seems that his complacency may have allowed the capture of Prince Arthur and Hugh IX, and the subsequent disaster. The younger Geoffrey had similar problems when supporting the insurrection of Isabelle of Angoulême and Hugh X of Lusignan in 1242. He was driven out of Mervant and Vouvant by King Louis IX but after a time on the run was pardoned and restored to his domains. He died in 1248 at the age of 50, some fifty years before Jean d'Arras wrote his romance, in which vague memories of both father and son became conflated in the giant killer Geoffroy Great Tooth.

An interesting footnote is that the elder Geoffrey married again after the premature death of Eustache Chabot and had two children, a boy called William and a girl, Valence, the latter inheriting and marrying Hugh of Parthenay l'Archeveque, who were to commission Couldrette to write a version of the Mélusine romance favourable to their interests, as a counter to that of Jean d'Arras writing for the Duke de Berry.

---

28 Hugh IX was the grandson of Hugh VIII, whose eldest son Hugh (brother to Geoffrey, Amalric and Guy) died young.

Faery Tradition
and the Kingdom of Jerusalem

• Gareth Knight •

We have for the most part dealt in a very rational way with a long standing romance and tradition, but as it is based upon a belief in faery/human interconnections it is likely to have an irrational side to it. But this does not mean that it should be too readily dismissed. What follows is an examination of historical and cultural curiosities, a brief examination of various recurring beliefs, traditions and coincidental circumstances that have an irrational side to them – on the basis of never quite knowing what we might turn up!

In short, do persistent beliefs, coincidental patterns or happenings point to some kind of source of hidden influence? After all, in astronomy as in particle physics, invisible bodies have been discovered through the perturbation of visible ones we know about. Admittedly this is all on one plane – the physical – or at any rate the extreme limits of it. But what might we intuit if we allowed ourselves a suspension of brute disbelief in the irrational?

The first pattern of coincidences is the remarkable record of the lords of Lusignan, generation after generation, going off on crusade. The question might be, were they being driven on or inspired by a tutelary spirit – conceived to be their family ancestor and founder – the faery Mélusine? And if so, why? Faeries and the bloody business of armed crusades seem an unlikely mixture. Why this concern with Jerusalem and the Holy Sepulchre?

And was Mélusine, or some inner source of influence, actively at work to see that matters turned out right for them? This is particularly noticeable in the case of Amalric of Lusignan, who would not have come to the throne as Amalric II had not a chain of coincidental happenings served to propel him there. If his wife Eschiva of Ibelin had not died at a 'convenient' time, just after Henry of Champagne had fallen from a window, and when Cyprus had been raised to the status of a kingdom, he would not have been in a position to marry the heiress, Isabelle of Jerusalem.

Admittedly the circumstances suggest that there might well have been some skulduggery afoot, but no hint of such has been made by any contemporary chroniclers, a class not usually reticent in personal or political innuendo. But any crime novelist could make a very convincing tale based upon the fact that Amalric had previously fallen foul of Henry, who had imprisoned him and banished him from the role of Constable of the Kingdom on account of him taking up the cause of some Pisan merchants, and Henry having fallen to his death when receiving a delegation of Pisans.

Or on the other hand, the whole Lusignan record begs the services of some historical novelist to take the faery hypothesis seriously. There have been some attempts, notably in France, but unfortunately they shirk from taking up a transcendentalist side and do their best to explain Mélusine away rationally.

Yet the Lusignans were not the only crusading family with a faery tradition. So too were the founders of the Christian Kingdom of Jerusalem – Godfrey of Bouillon, who was elected its first ruler with the title of Advocate (i.e. Protector) of the Holy Sepulchre in 1099, and his brother Baldwin who became its first king in 1101. Both were in direct line from a female ancestor said to have been married to a faery. One generally called the Knight of the Swan – named by some Helyas, and later developed by the Graal romancer Wolfram von Eschenbach as Lohengrin.

The earliest version of the story tells of a King Lothaire who one day out hunting met a beautiful maiden in the forest who became his wife. While Lothaire was away at the war, she died giving birth to seven children in a single pregnancy, six boys and one girl, each born with a golden chain about the neck. Her mother-in-law, who had always opposed the marriage, substituted dead puppies for the children, whom she ordered to be taken back to the forest and abandoned. However, they were cared for by a lone hermit until, some years later, the queen mother, learning of this, sent a servant to steal the chains as she suspected they were related to the children's existence in some way. When he did so, however, the children turned into swans – except for the girl who managed to escape and retain her human form.

Seven years later, in the city where their father lived, great curiosity was aroused by the close relationship of a little girl and six swans. On learning her story Lothaire ordered that the chains be returned to the swans, who were thus restored to human form, apart from one, whose chain had been melted down, and had to remain a swan.

Four of the boys grew up to become knights and no more is heard of them, but the fifth became famous as the Knight of the Swan, sailing down the Rhine one day in a boat drawn by his swan brother. He arrived at the Emperor's court in Neumagen just when the Duchess of Bouillon was seeking protection from the Duke of Saxony. The Swan Knight volunteered to be her champion in judicial combat, and having slain his opponent, married the Duchess's daughter Beatrix. But on condition that she never ask his name or that of the country from whence he came.

A daughter named Ida was born to them but when she was seven years old, her mother, no doubt concerned over the child's marital prospects, asked the forbidden questions as to her lineage. The Swan Knight immediately left, returned to Neumagan where the swan boat was waiting, sailed back up the Rhine and was never seen again. He did, however, leave an ivory horn for his wife which could exercise protection over her in some way. But the horn was forgotten about, until one day the castle caught fire, at which a swan appeared and plunged into the flames to save the horn and flew away.

The story identifies Ida with the saintly Ida of Lorraine (c.1039 – 1113) who married Eustace II, Count of Bologne, and by whom she had three sons, Eustace (the next count), and the pioneer crusaders Godfrey and Baldwin.

There is obviously a conflation of time periods here – as in the story of Mélusine, whose origins must date back to before the start of genealogical records, to Hugh the Hunter or beyond (early 900s) – and so with Ida's ancestors, back to or beyond King Lothaire of Lotharingia (855 – 869). However, our concern is with the historical record of their 12th century descendants in the Holy Land.

When the armies of the 1st Crusade were being mounted, the first group to be ready was commanded by the current Duke of Lower Lotharingia, Godfrey of Bouillon, accompanied by his younger brother, Baldwin of Boulogne. Against all the odds, Godfrey was to become the first ruler of the Christian Kingdom of Jerusalem, and at his death Baldwin became its first king. How did these two rise to the fore despite the challenges of mightier lords leading other armies, such as Raimond of St Gilles, Count of Toulouse, Duke of Narbonne and Margrave of Provence, or Bohemond, Prince of Taranto? They were as unlikely candidates for such high rulership as were Guy and Amalric of Lusignan, almost a century later.

The circumstances lie in the events of the long journey from the first calling of the Crusade in 1095 to the lengthy and weary way to Jerusalem, culminating in its fall four years later. Godfrey was a valiant fighter and achieved a certain reputation when he cut a Turk in two with a single blow of his sword outside the gates of Antioch. Whilst to impress his neighbours and his vassals, he was willing to repeat the trick in a somewhat less bellicose way by decapitating a camel. He was free from all pretension, and later impressed his Arab neighbours by receiving them sat on the ground in a tent. Off the battlefield he was a pious pilgrim, full of charity and Christian humility. Some indeed thought him rather ineffectual, as he seldom sought to impose his will, but this turned out to be his strength. On the way to Jerusalem his self-effacing nature often allowed a resolution of difficulties in the violent quarrels between the other lords. He came to represent a safe and reasonable compromise. And so it continued until it came to who should rule the Holy City, when Godfrey – *faute de mieux* – was elected.

In some respects it might have been thought that he was too good – or too simple – for this world. He refused to be called King of Jerusalem, on the grounds that "he would not wear a golden crown where his Saviour had worn one of thorns." This attitude had its debit side for he came close to letting an ambitious cleric called Daimbert usurp his power and make Jerusalem into a kind of rival Vatican. But before this ecclesiastic folly could gain ground, Godfrey conveniently expired.

The other great lords, still quarrelling, had left to make their presence felt elsewhere, and so at Godfrey's death the natural choice seemed to fall upon his brother Baldwin of Boulogne. The two presented a striking physical and moral contrast. Godfrey, not very tall, but broad chested, had very fair hair and beard. Baldwin was much taller, with jet black beard and hair and a very pale face, an imposing hauteur and a love of splendour. His gravitas came from his youth when he had studied for the priesthood, but the religious life hardly accorded with his temperament. He was proud, fiery and avaricious and a lady's man. Nor was he handicapped by personal modesty.

The only problem was that he was not close at hand! Ever with an eye to the main chance, he had turned aside from the last stages of the crusade to establish himself as the ruler of some Armenian Christians between the Tigris and Euphrates rivers, far to the north of Jerusalem, which later became known as the County of Edessa.

Nonetheless on the death of his brother Godfrey, and the invitation to take his place, whether by personal ambition or urged on by faery intimations, he made his way to Jerusalem, at the considerable risk of travelling from the north to the south of Saracen-held Palestine, where the Emir of Damascus lay in ambush for him. But, by brilliant cavalry tactics and superior intelligence sources he avoided the trap laid for him in a narrow defile near Tripoli and duly arrived at the Holy City. Here, after dealing rudely with ambitions of the Patriarch Daimbert, he had no hesitation in being crowned King of Jerusalem at Bethlehem on Christmas Day 1101.

He soon showed his qualities by defending the tiny kingdom from a mighty Egyptian army, and extending his grip upon the coast, at Jaffa and Caesarea. And soon after, as we have recorded, he shared the hair-raising adventures at Ramla in the company of Hugh VI of Lusignan.

Baldwin had already taken an Armenian wife but, as was later to become a pattern, although she was a Christian it was considered that a more prestigious queen was required for such a holy kingdom, preferably with a sizeable dowry, for the kingdom was desperately short of cash. Repudiating Queen Arda seemed no very great problem. So with the ecclesiastical blessing of Arnulf, the new Patriarch of Jerusalem, who was more malleable than the deposed Daimbert, Arda was put into a local convent and the task begun of finding a replacement for her.

Choice fell upon no less a lady than Adelaide, widow of Roger I, the Norman ruler of Sicily. Despite being of a certain age Adelaide had been one of the beauties of her era, and what is more, was of enormous wealth, being a daughter of the immensely powerful and well connected Boniface, Marquis of Montferrat. (His grandsons William and Conrad were later to marry Jerusalem heiresses, at least for a short time. Neither survived for very long. Not sufficient faery in the family?!)

Adelaide arrived at Acre in August 1113 in such great state as to rival Cleopatra. The prow and masts of her ship were brightly gilded and shining in the sun, accompanied by two triremes each carrying 500 knights, along with seven other ships, laden with gold, silver, purple cloth, jewels and precious stuffs. Another ship carried an escort of Arab archers clad in brilliant white, for at that time in Sicily, Christians, Arabs and Jews all had equal rights and lived in harmony.

Baldwin received his bride with equal pomp, as expectations were high of a grand alliance between the kingdom of Jerusalem and the well established Norman kingdom of Sicily. Between them they could dominate the eastern Mediterranean in rivalry to the merchants of Pisa, Genoa and Venice, and in defiance of the Egyptian fleet.

But it was not to last. The repudiation of Queen Arda, although a convenient local arrangement, was not well received by the rest of the world, and it was not long before Adelaide realised she had become involved in what was generally perceived as a bigamous marriage. As a consequence she sailed away and the anticipated alliance between Sicily and Jerusalem was no more.

In the end Baldwin died without issue, and although his eldest brother, Eustace, Count of Boulogne, was still alive, despite desperate attempts to lure him to the East he could not be prised away from the relative safety and comfort of the West. He was eventually cajoled into a half hearted effort to make the trip, but was only too happy for the excuse to turn back when he heard that the barons in Jerusalem, losing patience, had invited the next closest relative, Baldwin de Bourg, to take the throne. All the same, being only a cousin of Godfrey and Baldwin, he was not of the direct faery line.

As it turned out, Baldwin de Bourg was also Count of Edessa, having been presented with the territory when Baldwin of Boulogne had left to become king of Jerusalem. He also had taken an Armenian wife, Morpha, but was very content with her and saw no reason to follow his cousin's attempt at marital reorganisation. As it happened however, the couple produced no male heir to the throne, but had four daughters – Melisende, Alice, Hodierna and Jovetta.

This turned out to be a fairly neat arrangement, for the three units of the growing kingdom could, at least in theory, be knit more closely together. Consequently, Alice was married to Bohemond, Prince of Antioch, and Hodierna to Raymond, Count of Tripoli, whilst the youngest daughter, Jovetta (who had the stigma of having spent a year in childhood as a Muslim hostage) became abbess of a sparkling new monastery at Bethany, perhaps in an attempt to cement relations of the kingdom with the heavenly world.

Greatest attention however was focussed on Melisende, the eldest of the four daughters, and the need to find a suitable husband who would one day become king, and hopefully the sire of future kings. Choice fell upon a very powerful, doughty and recently widowed old warrior, Fulke V of Anjou. He was extremely well connected, wealthy, and a proven warrior, all great advantages to the kingdom, although the red-headed, wiry and somewhat raddled veteran might not have been love's young dream as far as Melisende was concerned. Nonetheless old Fulke genuinely loved his young bride, and engendered two future kings upon her, Baldwin III and Amalric I.

What is particularly interesting from our point of view is the coincidence that his family also happened to have the reputation of faery ancestry. Thus it might be said that, with Fulke of Anjou, faery blood returned to the royal line of Jerusalem. However Fulke's faery antecedent did not have quite the spotless reputation of Mélusine of Lusignan.

The story goes that a former Count of Anjou, returning from a mysterious journey, brought with him a beautiful lady with no known relatives, whom he married. The couple had four children, two sons and two daughters, and although the countess was credited with the name of Mélusine, she had none of the avowed Christian piety of the Lusignan faery. Indeed it came to be noticed that she would always avoid being present at the consecration of the host at the celebration of the mass. In the end the count was persuaded to make sure she attended by force, with the stratagem of having four knights stand around her, treading on the train of her cloak, so that she could not leave at the crucial point of the ceremony. As the priest raised the host on high she struggled to leave, but being unable to do so, shrieked as if in great pain, broke free and flew out of a window (or through the ceiling) of the chapel, taking two of her children with her. Neither she or these children were ever seen again.

From the two children that remained were descended all later Counts of Anjou – including Fulke V who married Melisende of Jerusalem, and indeed all the Plantagenet kings of England who became known as "The Devil's Brood". Indeed Richard Coeur de Lion tended to boast of it with jocular pride as the reason for the internecine fighting within his family – to say nothing of his father's martyrdom of the Archbishop of Canterbury, or his younger brother's murder of Prince Arthur of Brittany.

Some of the earlier Fulkes of Anjou had a reputation for bizarre cruelty and wickedness, as for instance Fulke III, known as the Black, who burnt his wife at the stake in her wedding gown for alleged adultery with a goatherd. Indeed Fulke III is often cited as the husband of the Anjou water sprite, but his relationships are historically accounted for, and so, as with the Lusignan and Lorraine families, the original faery contact must have been back in the unrecorded "dream time", some time before Ingelger in 870, the father of the first Fulke.

Anyhow, by virtue of these three family traditions – of Lorraine, Anjou and Lusignan – we find the incumbents of the throne of the Kingdom of Jerusalem having claim to faery origins. While most of this may be too speculative for any orthodox historical thesis, what does remain of serious cultural interest is the faery element in crusader literature and legend from the mid 12th century through to the 14th, including the development of the Arthurian and Grail legends – which certainly grew out of a culture in which faery tradition was paramount[29] – and so on to imaginative forms of the old *chansons de geste* – such as *Huon of Bordeaux*, *Le Roman d'Auberon* and *Le Bâtard de Bouillon* – in which there is a conflation of Crusader traditions with those of faery.

Le Bâtard de Bouillon seems to have been written to tell a wished for outcome of the 1st Crusade to the greater glory of the Bouillon-Boulogne family. It tells (quite unhistorically) how Baldwin I, King of Jerusalem, set out to conquer Mecca and the whole Saracen world. Then having fought his way across the Arabian peninsula he came to the Red Sea, asked what lay beyond it, and was told it was Faeryland, ruled by King Arthur and his sister Morgan le Fay.

Baldwin immediately embarks with twelve companions to explore this country where they find themselves separated from each other by a thick mist. However, one of them, Hugues de Tabarie (a convert from Islam), finds a horn which only the bravest knight in the world can blow. He succeeds in sounding it, whereupon King Arthur appears with all his court and the adventurers are reunited and led into a garden full of faeries and thence to an orchard, where Hugues de Tabarie is invited to pluck a rose as further indication that he is the greatest knight in the

---

29 *cf.* my study of the secularisation of faery material by Chrétien de Troyes in *The Faery Gates of Avalon*, R.J. Stewart Books, 2008.

world. King Arthur presents Baldwin with a magical suit of chain mail and tells them it is time to leave, after which they discover they have spent five years in Faeryland without realising the passage of time.

Baldwin then returns to Jerusalem and the rest of the story is taken up with the picaresque adventures of his bastard son – the result of a liaison with Sinamonde, a Saracen princess at Mecca, hence the title of the romance. Apart from occasional events that one finds cropping up in some faery or Graal stories – such as using a chess board as an offensive weapon, or a boar hunt – the bastard's further adventures are somewhat mundane and far from glorious. As Robert Francis Cook, the editor of a critical edition of the work remarks, "The Faery episode is a sort of Arthurian romance in miniature", and "If the Faery episode reminds one of Arthurian literature, the misadventures of the Bastard are more in the nature of *fabliaux*[30] or satiric literature."

Huon of Bordeaux, on the other hand, deals in a more serious way with the adventures of the hero, who is sent on a bizarre and virtually impossible quest to "Babylon" in order to atone for his inadvertent killing of a son of Charlemagne. He would certainly have found it impossible had he not been helped by Oberon – King of the Faeries, whom he meets on the way, somewhere between modern day Austria and Hungary. So popular did this faery figure become that it spawned another romance completely devoted to him, *Le Roman d'Auberon,* a kind of prologue to *Huon of Bordeaux.*

We might remark a certain similarity in the plight of Raimondin and that of Huon. In each case their meeting with a faery follows upon their being cast into an extremely difficult situation on account of an inadvertent killing. (As indeed was the situation with Raimondin's father Hervé de Leon!) The main difference with Huon being the gender of the faery helper.

Like Mélusine, Oberon is a very moral character, and when Huon meets up with a beautiful Saracen princess, Esclarmonde, Oberon discourages any carnal intimacy until they are married.

We do not need to take too literally the alleged parentage of Oberon, which is that he is a twin brother of St. George, their father and mother being Julius Caesar and Morgan le Fay, and ultimately descended from Judas Maccabeus! What is intended here is not so much a personal historical genealogy but an archetypal positioning of the nature of

---

30 short, usually comic, coarse, and often cynical tales in verse, popular in the 12th and 13th centuries.

the Faery king. He is on a par with a great Christian saint, directly descended from a great warrior and empire builder on the one hand, and magically gifted faery queen on the other, with ultimate roots in heroic Biblical tradition.

The faery powers that Oberon demonstrate come along with particular magical artefacts, which include a horn, a *hanap* (a large drinking vessel) that replenishes itself with wine, an invulnerable suit of mail that fits perfectly whoever wears it, and a musical bow that causes those who hear it play to sing and dance. The magic horn is of ivory, with bands of gold, made by the faeries, and can be heard throughout the whole world by the vassals of its owner, to call them immediately to arms by his side, whilst its sound restores health to whoever hears it and revives those who hunger or thirst. Huon finds himself in some trouble at first when granted the loan of the horn, by using it in vain, not when he really needs it, but to see if it works.

An interesting fact about Oberon is that although supremely handsome, he is only three feet tall. This the result of an obscure incident of faery ill-wishing at the time of his birth, but beyond this is the odd fact that in later tradition faery folk began to be depicted smaller and smaller. The great originators of faery, the Tuatha de Danaan or the Sidhe, were mighty creatures – but by the time of Shakespeare they had become diminished. Shakespeare's Oberon and Titania may well be of human size (and quite stroppy with it!) but others such as Peaseblossom and Mustardseed – and even Puck, and Aerial in *The Tempest* – are diminutive by comparison, whilst Shakespeare's contemporary, Drayton, takes us into the realm of spider's web whimsy.

However, let us turn to romance literature contemporary with the Crusader Kingdom period, and in particular that of the Graal, of which the first recorded example is Chrétien de Troyes' *Conte del Graal* which, he tells us, was based on a manuscript vouchsafed him by Count Philip of Flanders. This intriguing document spawned a whole tradition of continuations and elaborations, and, as we have demonstrated in *The Faery Gates of Avalon,* has obvious faery elements.

It may thus be worth our while to turn our attention to Count Philip of Flanders himself – for his actions provide some fascinating grounds for speculation about faery elements in the history of the Kingdom of Jerusalem. His family were not of any recorded or claimed faery origin but they were certainly deeply committed to the kingdom in one way and another.

Philip of Flanders was the youngest son of Duke Thierry II of Lorraine, who had a remarkable record for crusading. Duke Thierry, who was born in the same year as the foundation of the Kingdom of Jerusalem, went on his first crusade in 1139 and married Sibylla, a daughter (by his first marriage) of Fulke V of Anjou, King of Jerusalem. He later joined the 2nd Crusade of Louis VII of France and Eleanor of Aquitaine (the same one that Hugh VII of Lusignan joined), in 1142. On his third crusade, in 1157, he was accompanied by his wife Sibylla, who declined to return home and became a nun in the convent at Bethany ruled by Jovetta of Jerusalem, where she died in 1165. Thierry himself took part in an unsuccessful siege of the Syrian city of Shaizar. His final and fourth crusade was to join King Amalric I in the attempted invasion of Egypt in 1164/6, after which he adopted the image of a date palm upon his seal.

He died on 17th January 1168, whereupon his son Philip of Alsace became Count of Flanders. He had married Elizabeth of Vermandois, a daughter of Petronilla of Aquitaine – the flighty sister of Eleanor of Aquitaine – who seems to have followed in her mother's footsteps, for Philip discovered she had taken a lover, Walter de Fontaines, whom he had beaten to death. As this occurred in 1175, very shortly after the break up of Eleanor of Aquitaine's court in Poitiers, it might be reasonable to assume that Elizabeth had been one of the high ladies who embraced and encouraged the cult of Courtly Love. Another account is that it was a troubadour who got a little to close to the lady, who suffered being hung upside down in a well by the irate Philip.

In 1178/9 Philip followed his father's example by going on crusade. This was at the time when Baldwin IV – the leper king – had just come to the throne in Jerusalem. It was also the time when the king's newly wed sister Sibylle had been widowed from William of Montferrat and was in the first stages of forming a relationship with Guy of Lusignan.

By his father's marriage to a daughter of Fulke V, Philip found himself to be the closest relation to the newly crowned young king. Indeed Baldwin was quite keen to see Philip appointed as Regent – to the intense annoyance of Count Raymond III of Tripoli (the next closest relation) and Baldwin of Ibelin (who was hoping for Sibylle's hand).

Philip had his own agenda however, and eschewing involvement in a planned invasion of Egypt with Byzantine naval assistance, sought to marry two of his vassals to the currently available Sibylle and Isabelle. Another element in all of this, so far unexplained, is that Philip was also ward of two nieces who happened to be direct descendants of the original faery line of Ida of Lorraine. Nothing seems to have come of this however.

When all fell foul of the intense politicking of the time, Philip left to pursue a crusade of his own up in the north, following in his father's footsteps. This unfortunately left the Holy City extremely vulnerable to attack from Egypt, which Saladin duly seized upon, but which ended with the remarkable, almost miraculous, victory of the young leper King at the Battle of Montgisard, allegedly aided by St. George!

Following this, and an unsuccessful siege of Harim, Philip returned home in 1179, just a year before Princess Sibylle married Guy of Lusignan.

Once home, Philip found himself a powerful figure in the politics of France, and on the death of Count Henry the Liberal of Champagne sought to consolidate his position by marriage to Henry's widow, Marie of Champagne, but she elected to devote herself to the religious life. She had until then been the patron of the Arthurian romancer Chrétien de Troyes, who was now, according to Chrétien himself, commissioned by Philip to produce a romance based upon a manuscript with which he provided him – which turned out to be famous and highly fecund, but incomplete, *Le Conte del Graal.*

Given the background of immediate crusading and that of his parents' penchant for it, one is led to wonder what the source of this remarkable manuscript might have been. It is a tale that has deep if unorthodox religious overtones and strong faery elements as well. Of its two heroes, Gawain is clearly in the midst of faeryland with the Castle of Maidens and other events and places, whilst Perceval's paramour Blanchefleur has all the hallmarks of being a faery. What is more, the situation of the Maimed King having a connection with the devastation of the country he rules has a strong resonance with the situation of the stricken Baldwin IV of Jerusalem, and the perilous state of the kingdom. The number of hares that are set running here are many and diverse.

Be this as it may, Philip eventually took the cross again for the 3rd Crusade to take part in Guy of Lusignan's siege of Acre, but on 1st August 1191, died in an epidemic that raged through the appalling conditions of the camp.

We might conclude with some comments of some kind of inner connection between Faery tradition, Avalon, Jerusalem and the Holy Grail. As a well known contemporary Avalonian Ian Rees recently observed on reading my translation of André Lebey's version of the Melusine story, *The Romance of the Faery Melusine* (Skylight Press 2011):

> *Mélusine is a fascinating and intriguing figure, bridging as she does the human and faery worlds and in an odd way the worlds of Avalon and Jerusalem. Both this book and Gareth Knight's two earlier books seem to me to be delineating a current of work that is potentially redemptive in many different directions and centrally tied to the rediscovery of the Grail Hallows, not as external objects but as mystery processes that are held jointly by Human and Faerie.*
>
> *As someone who lives in Glastonbury and who works regularly in Jerusalem I see much potential in what is being offered to us in what can seem like a quaint story of faery ancestry.*
>
> *The juxtaposition of the apparently ethereal world of the Faerie with the blood guts and ancient hatreds and holiness of Jerusalem might seem a trivial thing – a bit like calling on Tinker Bell to save the world, but trust me Faerie can handle it.*
>
> *The encounter with the Christian mystery with Faery is at the heart of the Grail and Arthurian traditions and in these books it seems to me we are seeing a new unveiling of that mystery.*

The earlier works of mine he cites are *The Faery Gates of Avalon* (R.J. Stewart Books 2008), and *Melusine of Lusignan and the Cult of the Faery Woman* (R.J. Stewart Books 2010). Also of note is Wendy Berg's *Red Tree, White Tree* (Skylight Press 2010) and R.J. Stewart's monograph on the remarkable Glastonbury adept Ronald Heaver, *The Hidden Adept & the Inward Vision* (R.J. Stewart Books 2012).

Index

Lightning Source UK Ltd.
Milton Keynes UK
UKOW04f2012120913

217111UK00002B/415/P